C3704   /5

Slow Roads

SLOW ROADS

A Leisurely Journey
Through England, Scotland
and Wales

Anthony Burton

DAVID & CHARLES
Newton Abbot London

To HBL 371W
In spite of age and infirmity you got us there

British Library Cataloguing in Publication Data

Burton, Anthony
 Slow roads.
 I. Title
 914.104
 ISBN 0-7153-9466-5

Printed in Great Britain
by Billing & Son Worcester
for David & Charles plc
Brunel House Newton Abbot Devon

Contents

Introduction

The idea seemed simple enough: to plan a leisurely journey through Britain that would be full of diversity and interest. I had in mind an imaginary request, perhaps from someone who had never visited the country before, or from one of the many who live here, cheerfully trot off each year on a foreign jaunt, but know little of what lies just beyond the back door. The first rules were easily established. Motorways were out on the grounds that they offer neither diversity nor interest. A-roads would be tolerated, and minor roads looked upon with favour, if only because they provide the opportunity for dawdling without the embarrassment of a queue of frustrated motorists forming up at one's rear. In the event, one of the more delightful surprises of the journey was to find just how far one can still travel on comparatively uncluttered roads. I also decided that, although this was primarily to be a journey by car, there should be at least some opportunities to leave it behind and let someone else do the work. It was when it came to deciding on the route that the real problems started.

There were a few locations which it seemed must be included, either because they were strong personal favourites, or because I felt that my fictitious friend would feel cheated if they were not included. Joining up those fixed points was a great struggle, however, as choosing one route automatically precluded the use of another. There was no difficulty in deciding where I would like to go: the agony came in determining what I could bear to miss. It would have been far easier to devise a trip to last for years than one to last for weeks. The route chosen is inevitably a reflection of personal tastes and interests, and even when I had taken what seemed rational decisions when poring over maps at home, I still found myself taking impulsive diversions when out on the road. In the event, there was a good deal of to-ing and fro-ing, trial and error, and my own travels lasted over a long period before the route was finally settled. The journey that emerged should not be thought of as 'the best' route through Britain, but as just one of many possible routes. The one claim that can be made for it is that it is a route which gave me immense pleasure.

Having decided on what seemed to be a manageable route, that could be taken as a single trip, I still felt that there were certain areas which had been unjustly ignored, so four diversions have been added – to Southern England, the South West, North Wales and East Anglia.

To the readers who want to follow this journey a few practical hints may be useful. I found myself covering little more than a hundred miles a day, so that on that basis it will take an average time of three weeks – assuming a few long stopovers. Because a large number of minor roads are used, good maps are essential: a scale of four miles to the inch (1:250,000) is adequate; three miles to the inch better still and the ordnance survey (1:50,000) best of all. Unfortunately, using the latter involves a very high expenditure and carrying a case full of maps, but these are invaluable for any area that you want to explore in detail. In some cases, you will find that the route threads a maze of minor roads and can be difficult to follow. Do not despair at taking wrong turnings as long as you keep going in the right general direction. Who knows, your 'wrong' route may turn out to be more interesting than the 'right' one. Many of my happiest discoveries have come about in just this way. Certain information is deliberately excluded: this is not a where to stay, where to eat guide. Restaurants, cafes, pubs et al. only get a mention if they offer something which seems quite special in relation to that particular place. It would, after all, be unreasonable to mention one restaurant in, say, Newcastle when there are dozens of others that I never tried. The aim of this book is to indicate the pleasures that travel in Britain can offer, rather than lay down any set of strict guidelines.

Finally, I have to thank my wife Pip who did much of the organising, all of the navigating and stopped me from getting sidetracked too often.

1
London to Bridgwater

The journey should begin with a departure from London, simply because so many journeys around Britain do begin in the capital. There is a lot to be said for being in London and a lot to be said for being outside London. There is, however, very little that can be argued in favour of the transition between the two for those forced to drive their own cars. There can be few more depressing starts to what should be a pleasurable trip than a slow crawl through the suburbs or a frenzied exit along one of the atrociously crowded main roads. So, if one does not have to drive out of the city, why do it? Since a lot of people these days use hire cars, the problem is easily solved. Take the train.

There are many advantages to this suggestion, not least that it brings to the start a sense of occasion, since to head west one begins at a truly impressive station, Paddington. The outside gives only a hint of what lies behind, and the concourse, for all its gleaming new-tiled floor, is little better. It seems to have got its priorities wrong: there is nowhere much to sit down, the bar is invariably overcrowded, but there are ample opportunities to buy socks and ties. Does anyone really go to a railway station for their smalls? But all this is instantly forgotten when faced with what is technically known as 'the train shed', a mundane phrase that gives no idea that what one is really going to see is a cathedral built for the glories of the age of travel by steam. The engineer was Isambard Kingdom Brunel, the little man with the big hat and the wrinkled trousers who looks out, rather smugly it seems, over his masterpiece. The architect was Digby Wyatt, who added his own idiosyncratic flourishes. It really is not too fanciful to describe this as a cathedral, for that is clearly its inspiration. The columns and arches that carry the great glass roof march down the platforms forming aisles and naves and, more surprisingly, halfway down one finds transepts. Look up and you see an intricate tracery of iron as satisfying in its structural rhythms as a Norman vault. And

9

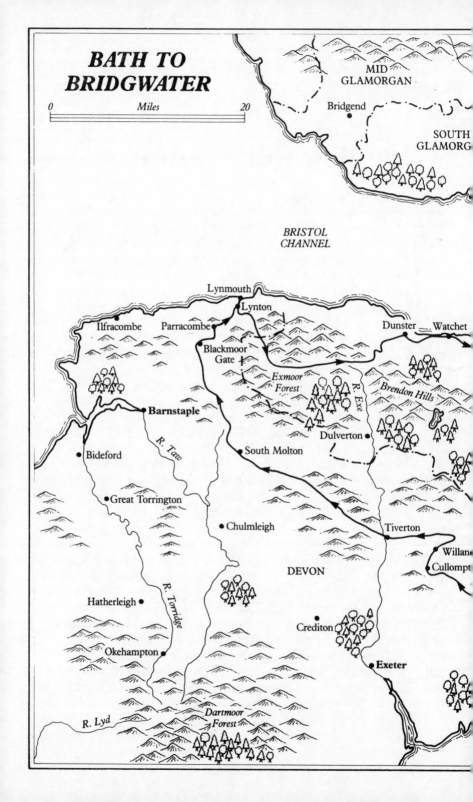

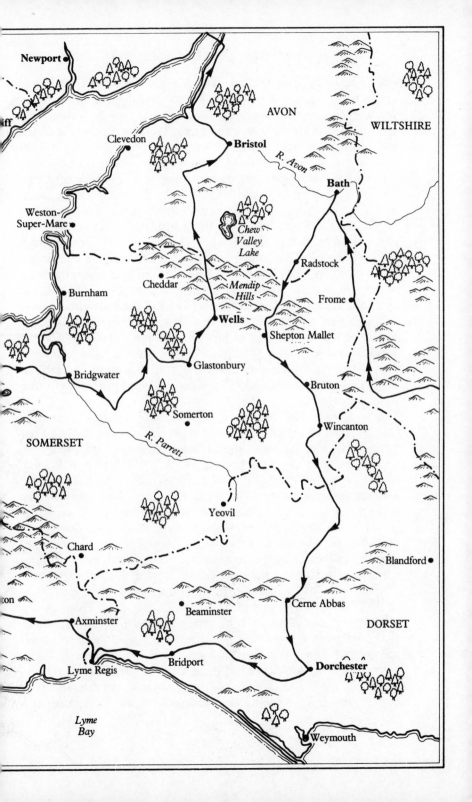

when one looks down the length of this transept towards platform one, a wholly different note is struck, for it ends in an ornate bow window, marking the directors' room. Before nationalisation, the station was the showpiece of the Great Western Railway (GWR) and Great is what it remains.

It is the old Great Western route to the west country that starts us on our way; out past the backs of terraces and gas holders like rows of caged whales; over the viaduct that rides above the roof tops until London is forgotten. On the train goes to Slough, about which the only thing anyone seems to remember is the lines by Betjeman that begin 'Come, friendly bombs, and fall on Slough'. There have been attempts to praise the delights of the place, but they have slipped into the oblivion which the poet wished on the town. I would, however, add a rider – 'but please spare the station'. It was rebuilt in 1879 and the style chosen was that of a French chateau: bulbous roofs covered with fish-scale tiles, elaborate decoration of pilasters and those typically French windows known as *oeil d'boeuf*. Why this should have been appropriate for a frankly dull provincial town is a mystery: perhaps one should just say a thankyou and tip one's hat in respect as the train goes through.

The towns click by almost too quickly. Reading – is that the gaol over there or the biscuit factory? Too late, it has gone. Didcot, and with luck a wisp of steam, a glimpse of shining green locomotive with gleaming brasses at the GWR centre dedicated to the preservation of the giants of the railway past. Dwarfing everything is the power station, which features on a personal list of favourite buildings. There is something immensely satisfying in the contrast between the clean, crisp main building, all severity and strict practicality, and the sinuous curves of the great cooling towers, busily creating their own private weather systems of drifting white clouds. Cooling towers are an ecological absurdity, but can seem as beautiful as great galleons sailing across the fields. Out of the Thames valley and into the Vale of the White Horse, with a distantly glimpsed foretaste of some of the delights to come when the real journey gets under way. Swindon was once the heart of the railway, but the works where the locomotives, which are so lovingly restored and preserved at Didcot, were made, have been flattened. Would Brunel be shocked if he came back and saw the changes? Would he think everything had changed? It was here, after all, that he made the first recorded criticism of railway catering. He had not, he said politely, criticised the coffee because he was not aware there was any. His comments had been reserved for the 'bad roasted corn'. There is no longer a compulsory stop here, so comparisons can be left unmade. Now the route takes a great arc to the south before burrowing underground, vanishing into deep cuttings and finally emerging at the city of Bath. This is where the travellers from London alight to join me on the road.

Bath is a most self-conscious city, constantly on display and very aware of its finery, not unlike the beaux of the Regency who made it the most fashionable place in England. This is one reason for looking up its origins. It began in gloriously unlikely circumstances at some time in the ninth century BC when Bledud, son of King Lear, was tending his pigs, which were grubbing for acorns and thoroughly enjoying a good wallow in the mud. Now these particular pigs were, it is said, infected with leprosy – though quite what a king's son was doing acting as swineherd to these porcine lepers is not clear. However, their splashings about brought about a miraculous cure and the healing springs of Bath were discovered. It is somehow touching to find a reference to this primitive, semi-magical past turning up again in Bath at its most urbane. The Circus is the masterpiece of John Wood the Elder, the architect who began the transformation of Bath in the eighteenth century, and if you look up to the top of the terraces you can see an acorn motif. But we have leapt ahead a long way, and it is time to look back to the first great period in Bath's history.

The Romans came to the magical pigs' wallow and built a spa town which they named Aquae Sulis: Aquae to acknowledge the healing powers of the water; Sulis to honour the Celtic river goddess Sul Minerva. The Great Bath is still one of the glories of the city, speaking eloquently of a civilisation which in its love of formalised luxury seems surprisingly close to the ethos of the Georgian era. The Roman bath is at once intensely practical, lead-lined with a carefully crafted drainage system for the hot springs, aesthetically pleasing with its surrounding colonnades and religious, in a rather empirical manner – the Romans would quite cheerfully add local gods and goddesses to their own pantheon.

Bath decayed and grew again, but by the early eighteenth century it had a somewhat bawdy reputation. Daniel Defoe visited the Cross Bath and described how 'the ladies and gentlemen pretend to keep some distance' but as the bath was rather narrow they 'frequently mingle' and 'converse freely, and talk, rally, make vows, and sometimes love'. Other entertainments on offer included a play, badly designed and worse acted, which no-one minded as the crowds came to see and be seen. It was the arrival of Richard 'Beau' Nash in 1705 which marked the beginning of change. For forty years he was 'Master of Ceremonies', a title which gives no idea of the power he wielded. He introduced exclusivity, and the more people he excluded from his entertainments, the more wished to be included. Bath was well set on the high road to fashionability. This did not, in itself, create the city we see now. Ralph Allen, who made a fortune from the postal service, bought up local stone quarries and brought the architect Wood to Bath. It is the combination of materials and styles that makes the city unique.

It was an extraordinarily fortunate combination of elements all coming together at the right time. Nash made Bath fashionable and created the demand for architecture to match. Allen could supply a stone, a beautiful, rich, honeyed stone, seen at its best on a sunny day, when it seems not so much to reflect the sun as to absorb the rays so that the stone itself glows. It is also a stone well adapted for carving into the swags and garlands, pilasters and balustrades which form the decorative lexicon of Georgian architecture. Wood and his son, also John Wood, have never ranked among the 'great-name' architects, and this too has helped to set the style. The buildings they designed are supremely well-mannered, comfortable buildings. There are great houses which most of us could never even contemplate occupying, yet we can all look at a Wood terrace and at least envisage living there, even if a glance at the price tag might quickly dispel the illusion. These are houses for comfortable living first and showpieces second. Even the grandest of them all, the famous Royal Crescent, for all its monumentality when seen as a whole, still breaks down into individually manageable units. This is the great appeal of Bath. First glance takes in the semi-elliptical Palladian palace, with its dominant row of Ionic columns, but when you turn to the details you find a human scale, and even the parkland in front suddenly shrivels into nothing more than a grander version of a front garden.

And because of the unique combination of formal grandeur and domestic intimacy this great Georgian set piece blends in perfectly with its surroundings, for it is echoed in miniature throughout the city. Bath is not a place for dashing from one famous building to the next but for sauntering, picking up details here and there, enjoying the elaborate townscape of streets and alleys.

There is more to Bath than the town of high fashion. It sits astride what was once a thriving trading river, the Avon. Bath was a terminus, establishing the end of trade and the arrival of the spa with the extraordinary Pulteney Bridge by Robert Adam. The bridge tries its best to ignore the river altogether, for it is topped by buildings and it is possible to walk across without so much as a hint that you are on a bridge at all. But when seen from the river bank it presents a proudly classical face to the world, as grand in its way as the Ponte Vecchio in Florence. But look further downstream and the workaday world appears; warehouses line the banks, as satisfying in their own functional simplicity as the deliberately contrived drama of Pulteney Bridge. It is somehow refreshing to find that Bath is not waiting for a second coming by Beau Nash, that there is life outside the time-stopped world of the Pump Room and the chirpy string trio. There is, however, one little museum where the years have been more firmly arrested than at any other spot in Georgian Bath.

The Bath Industrial Heritage Centre is not quite what its name suggests. This is not a collection of objects but an entire works uprooted and recreated in, of all things, a real tennis court, that is, a court for playing 'real tennis' (a sort of cross between squash and lawn tennis). Here are the works of J.B. Bowler, general engineer, brass founder, manufacturer of fizzy water, plumber and fitter. We live in an age of specialisation: J.B. Bowler was ready for anything and everything. Nothing was ever thrown away. Fittings long since gone out of general use were kept on the principle that they might be needed some day. The machinery was all aged, but as long as it worked it was kept in use. It is a place of rare delights: if Bath is, in general, a city devoted to good order and right proportions, here is a corner where disorder and chaos seem to rule. One has the feeling that there is a desperate need for Bath to cling to its few remaining Bowlers and their like if it is not to degenerate into a place that exists merely to be stared at, admired and photographed.

Heading out of Bath by road is at least easier than coming in and attempting to park. The end of the built-up area seems to come quite quickly. A signpost announces 'Welcome to Wansdyke', which is not a place but a district which derives its name from the dyke which crosses the road beside the sign. It actually runs east to west for some fifty miles and since it crosses over the line of the old Roman road it must have been built at some time in the Dark Ages. A single ditch and bank, it might be defensive or simply a boundary marker, no-one knows. The district name at least makes more sense than the county name. Until 1974 this was very definitely Somerset and to locals it still is, but Whitehall decreed that a new county should be carved out from the old and they christened it Avon. It is named after the river that flows through Bath but quite fails to take into account that there are actually six other Avons in England. Even the name is slightly farcical, for it is an anglicised version of the Celtic Abhain or Afon meaning 'river', so that these seven waterways are called River River, one of which gave its name to the County River. Presumably in the distant past a Saxon pointed to a waterway and asked its name, and a literal-mined Celt answered 'Afon' and the river rivers were born.

The landscape is undeniably that of the old Somerset, a rich landscape of red earth and gently swelling hills, a comfortable landscape where harsh notes are seldom sounded. Even the incursions of the last century or so have been absorbed in good measure and have taken on the same almost cosy aspect. A railway was pushed through the gap in the hills and must have caused quite a stir at the time, but it faded and died and when the last locomotive chuffed along in 1951 it might have been expected to stay dead. The English, however, have a boundless affection for machines as long as they are of no real practical use, and in 1953 the line revived for the benefit of the film cameras. A venerable locomotive was brought back as the hero of the Ealing comedy, *The Titfield Thunderbolt*. It is still remembered in a roadside pub near Dunkerton.

The more distant past makes an even more telling appearance on the outskirts of Radstock. Huge mounds rear up beside the road. They are round barrows, probably dating back to the Bronze Age which began some four thousand years ago. Over the centuries these grassy humps have acquired an aura of mysticism, helped in recent times by the fertile imagination of J.R.R. Tolkien who populated them with evil wraiths. They seem in fact to be simply burial mounds, no more mysterious than a modern cemetery. Some find this disappointing, but it is surely their very ordinariness that is itself remarkable, suggesting that the millennia have not greatly changed a basic desire to inter and honour the dead decently. Philosophical musings on archaeological mysteries are soon interrupted by the sight of even grander mounds on the horizon. No ancient tumuli these, but latter-day spoil heaps, the detritus of mining. For all its idyllic pastoral appearance this was once the heart of the busy and productive Somerset coalfield, the industry that made it worthwhile to build the old railway through such unpromising countryside. One of the joys of travel comes through these historic dislocations: you enter Radstock past the remains of a civilisation we can scarcely comprehend; look out at the remains of modern industry already retreating back into the landscape and leave following the route of Roman Fosse Way. The modern road, however, takes a more circumspect view of the hill. Instead of charging resolutely forward, ignoring all obstacles, it winds its way along the slope to ease the gradients. At least one has time to note the details along the way, such as the charming little rusticated folly of a house on the edge of Oakhill, that could almost serve as a grotto in some formal park.

Some places one can drive through with a nod and a glance, others demand attention. Shepton Mallet is one of the latter. You get your first glimpse framed in the arch of a viaduct. This is a spot where you would be surprised not to find just such a town. Main roads cross here in a countryside whose grassy hills were for centuries cropped by grazing sheep and here, inevitably, the sheep were brought to market. At the heart of this little hilly town sits the market square with its cross alongside the shambles, the old butchers' market, and set back from the commercial centres, but dominating them as it has for centuries, is the parish church.

Philip Larkin wrote a poem, 'Church Going', which all too accurately depicts the slight air of uncertainty and unease most of us feel on visiting a church such as this. In an increasingly secular age its old place of primacy in the community has been lost. It is still useful for the formal celebrations of births and marriages, but unseemly death has been shuffled off to the greater efficiency of the crematorium, so much easier to accept than the finality of

17

burial and the heartbreaking thud of clay on clay. We are no longer quite sure why we come but somehow, like Larkin, we often do. There are good reasons. Its role may have diminished but there was a time when the parish church was the heart of village and town. It is likely to be the oldest building, at least in its origins, still standing. Over the years it will have become both a repository of information and a measure of changing times. It is a building which has probably received more loving care in its construction and development than any other in the area. Shepton Mallet church is no exception. There are still traces of Saxon masonry to be seen; effigies of armoured knights lie on windowsills as though they had just pulled in for a rest before returning to the rigours of the crusades. It has a splendour out of all proportion to the small town it serves, reflecting the prosperity that once went with the wool trade. It also has memories of the darker days of agricultural depression. One answer was to export the poor. Charles King of Syracuse, New York came to live in the town and left a bequest to the rector to assist three 'poor personages of Good Character' – the capital letters firmly emphasised – to emigrate to North America. They were to come from the class of female servants, labourers and mechanics. There is a great richness of material here and yet it is not exceptional. Parish churches up and down the country will provide as much.

Narrow, stone-flagged lanes between high walls lead off enticingly from the churchyard, but sadly the space between the two old centres – church and market – is filled by the New Centre, a formless concrete blob. The good news is that it is unlikely to last; several large pieces appear already to have dropped off.

Different places have their own resonances for different people. Leaving Shepton Mallet on the road to Evercreech, my mind inevitably turned to thoughts of old railways. Evercreech Junction was an important point on the old Somerset and Dorset Railway, one of those lines which in all logic should never have been built. It had to fight its way through the hills, so that even the powerful expresses that once came this way were reduced to crawling along at scarcely more than twenty miles an hour. It should not have been built, but having been built it earned the affection of those who travelled it and is still remembered even as it is steadily obliterated from the countryside. Its effect on Evercreech itself was minimal – little, indeed, seems to have disturbed Evercreech. Even Lloyds Bank, a company noted for some rather grand buildings, makes do here with a country cottage, though one half expects to be able to buy a quarter of humbugs while cashing a cheque.

The road now climbs and winds up Creech Hill and the effort is rewarded by a view that seems to epitomise what one thinks of as the archetypal, unchanging countryside. At the top of the hill are rough, coarse grass and steadily munching cattle. An avenue of trees leads the eye down towards hollows and folds where farmhouses sit snug, surrounded by a jigsaw of fields outlined by trim hedges. It is this swoop of land, the changing shape faithfully followed by the field boundaries, that makes for such a satisfying picture. Yet is not really a timeless landscape at all. In Somerset, the great enclosure movement that took the old common land and carved it up into privately owned fields only really gathered strength towards the end of the eighteenth century. An Elizabethan returning to Creech Hill might well be as surprised by the neat pattern of fields as he would be by the motor car.

As the road dips and sways, new objects keep being thrown up into view. What can one make of that tower on a distant hill – a castle, a folly, what? It turns out to occupy a high point above the village of Bruton and its original use is more surprising than one could guess: the tall, gabled tower is a sixteenth-century dovecot. Somehow, one expects dovecots to be charming little structures, fit for a pretty country garden, not passable imitations of medieval fortresses. This is only because we now think of them as ornamental. When this dovecot was new it was serving much the same function as a modern hen house, providing eggs and birds for the table. The real surprise is that a purely functional building has, in fact, been made into such a picturesque feature in the landscape. Reactions to the next stage of the journey depend on the calendar. Mostly it will be uneventful, but on a few days a year Wincanton comes alive for the races. On other days, the racecourse is simply a wide area of flat grassland, bordered by rather nondescript buildings. There is something sad about an empty racecourse, like a shopping precinct at one in the morning. There is no temptation to linger.

Leaving the B road for the A road beyond Wincanton brings no real sense of difference as far as travel is concerned, though it does have a reminder that the road has been important for some time. It takes a totally logical deviation, keeping close to the edge of the river valley and the names down in the valley tell you why – Marsh Farm, Marshbarn Farm, Marsh Court, Higher Marsh, Lower Marsh and so on, quite sufficient to decide a sensible road builder to avoid the valley even without going to see for himself. There was a road along this line in the eighteenth century, a turnpike on which travellers had to pay for the privilege of use. You can see the old toll house at South Cheriton, jutting out towards the road so that the toll collector could keep an eye open for any would-be evaders. How much you paid depended on who you were, the vehicle you were using, the animals you were driving to market. You can still see the charges listed on a board on the little cottage.

All the time as you travel you become aware of a change in the landscape. The mellow stone has been left behind; the land is flatter and streams and rivers meander seemingly aimlessly, with no obstacles to prevent them twist or spread, branch and rejoin. Patches of woodland dot the land, and here and there an area has been closed off to create the seemingly artless, but actually cunningly contrived landscape of the park. The finest is Stock Gaylard where the scene is dominated by massive chestnut trees. These are such familiar features of great estates, that it seems as if the park was created not by planting trees but simply creating clearings. Yet the chestnut is not a native English tree at all. It was brought over from the Balkans and Asia Minor as recently as the sixteenth century. It has been an undeniable success. The trees here are majestic, so grand in scale that it is all too easy to drive past without noticing the deer resting quietly in their shade: no spread of antlers, no matter how magnificent, can compete with that great spread of branches.

Stock Gaylard comes very close to another division in the land, as up ahead the chalk downland begins to swell. There is a slow rhythm to movement through the Downs. They are seldom dramatic; where in some regions weather will hack away and shatter the foundation of rocks to create crags and precipices, here it is a process of steady erosion, a gentle sanding away of rough edges and sharp corners. Traditionally, the thin soil has provided little incentive for crop growing, and the land has been turned over to grazing. New farming methods are changing that. Fields are steadily nibbling away at the grassland, but in Dorset, at least, it is still the green curve that defines most horizons. The thin soil also provides another characteristic; when deliberately cut into or eroded, it reveals the white chalk underneath. It enables a very special type of landscape art to be created – the hill figure, and none is more striking than the Cerne Abbas giant. He stands 180ft (55m) high, a naked man with a huge club in his hand. Given that the phallus is notably prominent, it has been generally assumed that he was connected with some sort of fertility rite. The club has caused speculation that he might date back to Roman times and be a figure of Hercules, but no-one can be sure. Perhaps the most remarkable thing is that he is still there at all. Left alone, the grass would grow and within a decade the giant would disappear. Assuming the experts are right and that it was cut in the second century AD, the giant has to be cleaned up at least once every seven years. So he has been scoured some 250 times. The giant has survived the Dark Ages, he has been tolerated by the monks who established the abbey in the valley; the Puritans did not trouble him and even the conventionally prim Victorians made no attempt to hide his nakedness. Indeed the only known change to his anatomy came in the eighteenth century, when his penis was actually extended by more than a metre to reach his navel.

It is easy to stop off to see the giant and then move on, but Cerne Abbas itself is well worth exploring, particularly when refreshments seem in order. There were once more than a dozen pubs in the little village and it is still well served. The place presents two contrasting styles of building: the older, jettied buildings are a higgledy-piggledy mixture of odd roof lines with walls patterned by the exposed timber framework. Projecting upper storeys lean forward, giving buildings a slightly drunken appearance. Between them are the formal, carefully proportioned buildings of the eighteenth century. The two styles could not be more different, yet unity is preserved through the old street patterns and the same use of local materials. Of the old abbey which once stood at the heart of the community little remains apart from the gatehouse, wholly domesticated without so much as a hint of a religious past.

Rivers have a hard time finding their way through the chalk and the little Cerne carves the narrowest of valleys which it shares with the road down to Dorchester. On the way it passes the Smith's Arms, which claims to be Britain's smallest pub, and given even a glimpse of the little thatched roadside building it would be difficult to dispute the claim. It was originally a smithy and, according to a popular story, Charles II once stopped and asked for beer. The blacksmith replied that, alas, he had no licence. 'You have now', said the king, proving that royalty has its advantages. This tiny pub shares its character with the road, which may be granted A-road status on the map but scarcely seems to deserve it as it wriggles along between high hedgerows.

The one thing almost everyone knows about this part of Dorset is that it is Hardy's Wessex. Even those who have never read a word the novelist set down have at least the glimmering of a notion of what to expect. It conjures up an unchanging, essentially peasant landscape, in which the provincial towns seem to the locals to have all the eminence of great cities. Dorchester, Hardy's Casterbridge, sits at the heart of this world. Almost the first thing one sees is Hardy's statue, and when walking the streets reminders of the books turn up all the time. The mayor of Casterbridge's house is now Barclays Bank but the facade still keeps its domestic air, even if the sign hung out on an iron bracket makes it look disconcertingly like a pub. Aficionados can have a cheerful time Hardy hunting through the town, but there is a good deal that can just be enjoyed for its own sake. The Dorset County Museum seems at first to be just one more typical municipal museum, so that one feels quite certain that one knows just what will be inside: sombre rooms of glass cases in which are displayed the bibs and bobs of local collections. Instead what you find is a glorious Victorian extravaganza; a cross between market hall and church. The main room has nave-like proportions and the ecclesiastical feel is reinforced by rows of columns and the fact that one end displays a rose window and the other an organ. But the columns do not simply separate nave from aisles; they carry a balcony and the iron used for pillars and arches is given the full decorative treatment. Everywhere is painted, details such as floral motifs being picked out in rich colours. The building is so stunning that one could simply stare at it, walk out again and feel the entrance fee was money well spent. In fact, it is an exemplary local museum with a number of exceptional exhibits, including a reconstruction of Hardy's study.

The one thing which Dorchester and the surrounding area supplies which seems to be of the essence of Hardy is a sense of continuity with the past. There are few regions where one is more conscious of the long toll of years. It scarcely seems surprising here to find that the tree-lined Walks follow the line of the old Roman walls. And history goes back far beyond that. In true Hardy style, it also seems that the more memorable events are uniformly grim. To the south of the centre a grassy bank stands by the main road. Look behind it and you discover it is not a straight bank but a high earthwork with just a single entrance surrounding an oval space. It was first created back in neolithic times, the New Stone Age that began some six thousand years ago. This was a henge. Because Stonehenge is so famous one tends to associate these ancient monuments with standing stones, but it is not the stones that create a henge but the surrounding ditch with one or more entrances. It is assumed that it was used for religious ceremonies, but its shape suggested a new use to the Romans. They adapted it as an amphitheatre and over the centuries it saw many other uses. It was briefly a gun emplacement but the last official act it witnessed was the public strangling and burning in 1766 of a woman who murdered her husband. Small wonder that Hardy chose it as a setting for secret, usually doomed meetings.

The greatest site of all lies to the southwest, reached via an unlikely suburban road where street names designed as a link with the past – Caesar Green and Celtic Crescent – seem only incongruous. There is nothing, however, incongruous about Maiden Castle, a vast Iron-Age hill fort defended by monstrous earth ramparts and defensive ditches like ravines. The entrances are convoluted so that any who came this way ran a crooked path under the eyes of the defending guards. It must have seemed impregnable to the native Celts and probably was. But they could not have known of the technology that was to arrive across the seas from Rome. The fusilade of stones showered down from the ramparts did nothing to deter the advancing legions, marching in close formation, their shields interlocked above their heads like some mythical armoured monster. Maiden Castle fell to the new machines of war, the new age was born.

The country to the south and west is so rich in prehistoric remains that after a while one simply stops registering their presence. The castle may dominate the skyline to the north as you drive past, but the chalk ridge to the south is as humped as a dragon's back with row upon row of round barrows. Even the land itself takes on an almost timeless quality, and the sense of dislocation from the present increases the further you travel westward. It is a convoluted land; the smooth roundness is scrunched up like a squashed bun. It is green, tree-studded in the valleys, open and windblown on the tops. It has a hardness about it, a sense that it has never given itself over easily to man. Roads are lonely; villages sneak away into folds and shut themselves off, so that you are almost on top of them before you realise there is anything there. So many villages these days seem now to be copies of the picturesque views they once inspired. Dorset villages still look lived in. It has become a cliché to speak of unspoiled landscapes, but here the words seem apt. Roads sink down between high banks as though wishing to remain unobtrusive. Even the antiquities spring up as a surprise. Eggardon Hill has another hill fort, not so grand as Maiden Castle, but by way of compensation it has not been taken over as a showpiece. There are no huts to pay your fee, no guide books and none needed, for it is clarity itself. You can stand looking out over the twisting road beneath the ramparts to a scenery that is large but can seem very small – little houses, surrounded by neat little fields and woods. It is the sort of place where you could take a visitor and say: 'If all this means nothing to you, then you can forget about all the Downs that stretch across southern England, for this is the best of them'.

The Downs once formed part of a chalk dome that reached across what is now the English Channel all the way to France, so the chalk remains with you right to the sea's edge. Bridport might be just another of those not-very-big, not-very-small market towns with a sprinkling of Georgian buildings for class and a few cottages for character. But the chalk hills make it. They sit around the town; hummocky outcrops spiked by trees like a circle of Christmas puddings topped with holly. And there is a whiff of the sea here too. Once this was one of the great rope and net-making centres of the country. Now the old crafts are remembered in the museum, but the industry continues, based on modern technology and artificial fibres. Outside the town, the sea is glimpsed occasionally beyond the serrated edge of the cliffs until it is eventually reached at Lyme Regis.

Lyme is an odd place, a curious mixture. Jane Austen wrote early in the last century: 'a very strange stranger it must be, who does not see charms in the immediate environs of Lyme, to make him wish to know it better'. The same is true today. The features that pleased Miss Austen still delight us. The road still rushes downhill to stop at the edge of the sea where the bay opens out with a parade of white cliffs marching on to the Island of Portland. The old houses along the sea front have not changed much since her day and the path still leads on round to the immense curve of the Cobb. Begun in the thirteenth century, it has provided shelter from the sea ever since. It is as full of contrasts as the town: massive blocks set off worn and narrow steps; part is set out in Portland stone as carefully as some great building in London, part is a jumble of rough-hewn rocks; inside its protecting arm the small boats scarcely move, while the swell shifts restlessly against the defences. It is a place to hold the imagination, simply because it has retained its essential character for so long, at once simply practical and visually wholly satisfying. No-one, it seems, can resist the lure of a walk out to sea on the Cobb.

Lyme Regis marks the end of the chalk of Dorset and the start of the sandstones of Devon. Everything changes slightly but it is the change of colour that is the most dramatic. Devon is seen at its very best just after the fields have been turned by the plough, when the green of the countryside is overwhelmed by the red of the earth, not the fiery burnt red of a desert, but a rich, heavy colour that has sunk deep into the land. The first town to be met on the way out of Lyme also has its colourful connections. In 1754, Thomas Whitty, a local weaver, visited London where he saw beautiful, ornate Turkish carpets. A year later he had established a small factory to make carpets with similar patterns, and as a result the name of his home town of Axminster became famous. At first the process was so laborious and the results so exotic that the church bells were rung for every carpet that was completed. The fortunes of the Axminster carpet makers faded and revived and the trade continues still.

Across the valley of the Axe, past the town's cottagey station, is Shute hill and the Shute estate. Shute Barton is one of those typically organic English country houses, growing new bits here, shedding old there as the years go by. It was begun in the fourteenth century and has passed into a comfortable old age and would be pleasing rather than remarkable if it were not for the gatehouse. This is a thoroughly exotic affair of battlements and towers, decked out in full heraldic pomp. This is one of those rare places where the house seems almost insignificant when compared with the majesty

25

of the approach. It is rather like the works of Rossini – everyone knows the overtures, but who knows what comes next?

Journeys are never the same from one day to the next and responses can depend on mere accidents – a trick of light might create that one perfect moment, which an hour or even minutes later will be gone. There will always be drama on the route across Devon, always a feeling of excitement at the first glimpse of the wilds of Dartmoor, but I was fortunate to arrive at one of those magical times. It was early evening. The sun was low in the west so that the distant hills seemed as insubstantial as scenery painted on gauze; layer upon layer of receding silhouettes, greens dissolving to powder blue to grey, each paler than the last, while above them the sky was shredded into narrow ribbons of light. The enchanting view remained until the road dropped down to the valley and Honiton.

Axminster is carpets, Honiton is lace. You come in past another toll house – this time with the toll gates which would once have closed off the road still in place. Unlike Axminster, Honiton's speciality lies in the past, but what a glorious past it was. Lace is on show in the museum, but it is not just the delicate beauty that is so impressive, it is the infinite care of the craft which can turn thread, a few pins and a cushion into, it seems, almost anything from an intricate edge to a handkerchief to an entire tablecloth.

It seems that once you have got started on a theme, it stays for a while whether you like it or not – first carpets, then lace, and now the textile trilogy was to be completed with woollen cloth. The road still kept supplying those tempting glimpses of Dartmoor, but there was another objective to look forward to, a place I have visited many times, and always with pleasure: Coldharbour Mill at Uffculme.

Rather as eyebrows tend to be raised at the notion of coal mines in Somerset, so too the idea of 'dark Satanic mills' in Devon seems a touch bizarre. But the Westcountry was one of the great clothmaking areas of Britain in medieval times. The downland sheep provided the fleeces, the busy streams turned the waterwheels. Uffculme is a classic mill that has been here since the industrial revolution and only stopped manufacturing in 1981. At first the machinery was all powered by water but in time the steam engines were brought in to help carry the work load. It is something of a belt and braces situation, with a water wheel at one end of the building and the steam engine at the other – each capable of taking on the work. And in between is all the machinery you need to go from fleece to cloth. This is a museum now, but a working museum. Textile mills are particularly satisfying. You start with a natural material, wool, and gradually transform it and each step is quite comprehensible – everything is on show, nothing hidden away. The old spinning mules trundle to and fro, pulling out the yarn, twisting it and winding it on to bobbins; backwards and forwards all day like trains going nowhere. Even the Jacquard loom on which patterned cloth is made is not much more than a cross between the simple hand loom and a pianola. Here the punched card determines the movement of the shuttles instead of the banging of the piano keys. For anyone with any interest at all in mechanical ingenuity, a mill such as this is pure bliss.

Another well-known name – well known to me that is – cropped up soon afterwards, Sampford Peverell. I came across it when hunting through old canal archives. The arrival of a canal in this rural area was almost as great a shock as the coming of the mechanical mill. It was not the canal itself that was alarming but the rough, tough, boozy navvies who came to build it. The worst was feared, and in 1811 the worst happened. The navvies were not paid and they went on the rampage. The village had already had its own small-scale scandal, when Mr Chave, a local, had invented a ghost to drive a tenant out of a shop he had bought. The phantom, which included in its repertoire beating out the rhythm of 'Go to Bed Tom', attracted much attention – until the hoax was exposed. It was Chave's misfortune to meet the angry navvies, who pursued him home. He barricaded himself in and, when the navvies stayed outside hurling stones, he fired into the crowd. Two men died. For twenty-four hours Sampford Peverell was in uproar, and all that remains now of those days is a peaceful canal in a quiet village.

Once beyond Tiverton the road leaves the valley to ease its way through the hills. It is a road on which, if nothing else, one can never complain of boredom. Seldom straight, never flat, it presents a constantly changing view. It passes just to the south of Exmoor, but could scarcely offer a greater contrast, for where the latter is dominated by wide expanses of seemingly featureless moorland, this is a wholly intimate landscape of farms and villages, scarcely bigger than hamlets. It is also an area which suggests permanence.

There is nothing fragile here: houses crouching beneath steep slopes are sturdily buttressed, as though defying anything to shift them from their chosen shelter. South Molton, the market town for the area, has the same air of solid prosperity based on a rich land. Yet once you start to look at details, it is a town full not of surprises perhaps – that would be putting it too strongly – but full of slightly offbeat quirkiness. Every town of this sort has its market hotel at the centre. South Molton has the George, highly respectable no doubt, but for some reason the facade has been enlivened by slightly comical masks. Similarly, there is nothing odd about a town's having a chemist's shop, but South Molton has a medical hall, its sign stretched over a balcony that could have strayed over from the French quarter of New Orleans. It announces 'Wine & Spirits Curry Chemist': the order is, no doubt, significant. The Public Market and Assembly Rooms are grander than one might expect and have a statue of Hugh Squier 1625–1710 Our Great Benefactor. Even the century-old post office is highly decorative.

There is one grand exit from the square, under an iron archway through an avenue of trees trained to meet overhead to form a leafy tunnel. It brings one out to the parish church. The path is sunk well below the level of the churchyard and the stone walls on either side are punctuated by gravestones, lovely things of slate carved with crisply elegant lettering. It seems that instead of conventional burials, coffins are slid in like drawers in a filing cabinet. As with so many agricultural areas the movements of population and the march of industrialisation have seen the town slip further and further down the scale of size and importance. The parish church is a measure of what once was. It is a grand church in every sense; grand in size and rich in detail. Some parts, however, are grander than others. The local bigwigs have their own pews, comfortably shaped and supplied with tasselled velvet curtains. There is one true rarity here. A window depicts the three magi at the nativity and one is shown as black. It would be logical to find a black ruler in the Middle East, but I can think of no other church which depicts one. Leaving the church, the slight oddity of the graveyard is continued at the back, where one whole area is covered in inscribed slabs that form a morbid pavement.

The hilly countryside of the approach to South Molton is mirrored on departure. But now as one nears the coast, the rivers, swollen by the streams that drain off Exmoor, seem to gain a new urgency, cutting ever deeper valleys in their rush to the sea. So the route divides, between the airy spaces of the upland and these deep, luxuriant wooded valleys. It dives and loops downhill and struggles back up again. Distant roads appear like green caterpillars, defined by their hedgerows, prominent against the paler coloured fields. Blackmoor Gate is little more than an inn, the Old Station, and sure enough the buildings are still, quite recognisably, railway buildings. Staring round at the hills and valleys you have to ask who on earth could contemplate building a railway line here? And how could it ever prosper? The answers are: the promoters of the Lynton and Barnstaple Narrow Gauge Railway, and it never did prosper. It was an extraordinary line of tight curves and steep gradients, which opened in 1898 and only lasted until 1935. What a delight it must have been – though some passengers complained that they intended to go for a boat trip when they reached the sea, but the lurchings of the little railway had made them trainsick before they even had a chance to get seasick.

A little beyond Blackmoor Gate we took one of those chance decisions which can reap great rewards. The present A-road avoids the steeper slopes by making an extensive detour round Parracombe. We decided to go straight on and see what the local pub could offer by way of lunch. What it had to offer was a bar surrounded by blackboards on which were chalked a whole range of goodies, and the opportunity to chat. The conversation turned to the Lynton and Barnstaple which came this way. The local vicar, the Revd Chanter, used to carry a pocketful of flower seeds whenever he travelled the railway, which he would scatter from the train window to beautify the line. A local then told us that there was still a railway on the line – a miniature railway but a genuine steam railway none the less. We went to look but no-one was around. What we did find was the church in the hamlet of Churchtown. It is no longer used, but is an absolute gem. The Church of St Petrock is named after a sixth-century Welsh monk who founded a number of churches in the south west. This one dates back to the late eleventh century. It is a building of great simplicity, with plain whitewashed walls and the nearest it gets to decoration is the later wooden altar screen. Its appeal lies in its homeliness, in the simple wooden box pews, thoughtfully raked

29

so that the back rows get as good a view as the front. As with almost all English churches there have been changes, but it is the basic simplicity of the old Norman church that is so very impressive.

Back on the road after a memorable detour, there were early glimpses of the hills of Exmoor – very different from the first dramatic views of Dartmoor – before yet another steep wooded valley led downhill to the sea and Lynmouth. There is scarcely room for this village in the tiny bay where the East and West Lyn rivers meet. This is a large part of its appeal: there simply is no space to build anything big enough to destroy the intimate character. This was the goal of the railway and also its downfall. There was no way the lines could be brought down to the sea so the passengers found themselves faced with a long trudge from the station, and an even worse climb back up at the end of the day. Some relief came with the little cliff railway which still runs. It works on a wonderful balance system. There are two tracks and two cars, each car having a tank underneath. The two cars are connected, so that when one is at the top, the other is at the bottom. All that is needed is to pump water into the top tank and its weight will carry it down the slope and pull its partner up – a device familiar to all devotees of the late Gerard Hoffnung and his tale of the buckets. There is as much pleasure in exploring the countryside of Lyn Cleeve, the Valley of the Rocks, as there is in the more familiar delights of the seaside. In season, however, the area inevitably becomes crowded. Those with a taste for solitude can easily satisfy their longings by heading out for Exmoor.

Seen from a distance, Exmoor had presented a very different aspect from Dartmoor: close to, the effect is even more pronounced. Where the latter is characterised by the granite tors that burst aggressively through the earth, the former is a smooth, seemingly almost featureless plateau. Dry reedy grasses rustle and rattle in the wind and you can stand in the middle and look in vain for a landmark to guide you on your way. Even a map is not much help to walkers, but a good compass is an essential. It is only when you drop down into the river valleys that the landscape changes. Trees appear and settlements take advantage of the shelter. As there are more customers for the picturesque than for windblown emptiness, it is only here that anything approaching tourism creeps in. Simonsbath is self-consciously looking for the visitor to appreciate its rather obvious charm. It stands at the edge of the true moorland. Beyond here, the scenery all but disappears from view, blanked out by high beech hedges that occasionally even manage to meet overhead.

The first place of any note to be met along the way is Dunster, one of those tiny places which somehow seem to encompass almost the entire history of the region. It had two great centres of power and patronage. First came the castle on the hill that dominates the valley. There was probably a Saxon fort here and certainly an early motte and bailey, but over the centuries the castle has grown and although still fiercely battlemented is in reality purely domestic. Behind the defences, one is now invited to admire the decorative plasterwork of the ceiling. If the castle has changed, the Benedictine priory has simply disappeared, leaving only the tithe barn and dovecote behind. The attractive tile-hung medieval buildings known as The Nunnery have nothing to do with nuns. But Dunster has always been a place with a living to earn. In medieval times, ships came up river to what was quite a busy port; but as vessels got bigger, fewer and fewer could make the journey and the trade died. The other great west of England trade was practised here, when a special cloth known as 'Dunsters' was being made in the thirteenth century. Cloth finishing included fulling: pounding cloth with great water-powered hammers to felt and shrink it. When the cloth trade also died away, the fulling mill kept on. It was easily converted to a grain mill. Grindstones replaced the fulling stocks. It, in turn, was replaced by a 'modern' watermill in the eighteenth century and that is still at work, turning out wholemeal flour. Dunster was even a market centre in a modest sort of way. The Yarn Market, an intriguing octagonal hall, was built in the seventeenth century and there are further memories of those days when goods were moved on horseback in the medieval packhorse bridge to the south of the village. Add to that a medieval cross near the parish church and Dunster can reasonably claim to be a small place with a great deal to show.

Coming down to the coast at Blue Anchor brings us from the medieval to the Victorian and an old seaside line, The West Somerset Railway. Like so many others it was declared unprofitable and closed down: unlike most of the rest it has been brought back to life as a preserved railway. It runs for twenty miles between Minehead and Bishop's Lydeard on the outskirts of Taunton, and has brought the delights of the steam age back

31

to the seaside. It recreates a time when travel was as much about leisurely enjoyment of the passing scene as a dash from place to place. Even those without the time, or inclination, to travel the line can at least sample the rail delights of Blue Anchor. Here is the old signal box with its rows of levers, connected through a Heath Robinson array of wires and pulleys to signals near and far. The restored station buildings have an air of unpretentious dignity and the waiting room houses a small museum. Many people will say that the railway is the best way to see the Bristol Channel coast, which on close inspection usually turns out to be as much mud as sand.

Watchet is not really a seaside resort: it has none of the glitziness of nearby Minehead. It was a port in Saxon times and still is, so that it retains a working, lived-in air. This is not a place that hibernates until it hears the first tourist of spring; the harbour has yet to be renamed a marina – and with luck it never will be. The neat terraces are for people who, when they cook breakfast, cook it for themselves. Once you get outside, however, a different world smacks you in the eye. Up comes the holiday camp, the caravan park and the wonderfully unlikely Watchet Wild West Society. Do they pull their caravans into a circle each night, just in case?

Once the road heads back inland everything changes again. The Quantocks reach almost to the sea and the road skirts them to arrive at Nether Stowey. The poet Coleridge lived here and the Wordsworths lived nearby. They seemed very strange to the locals, who decided they were up to no good. This was 1797 and Britain was at war with France, so the government sent down a detective to spy on the Romantics. He reported them to be 'a Sett of violent Democrats'. Nothing came of this and now Nether Stowey is happy to welcome visitors to Coleridge's cottage to see the headquarters of the 'Mischievous Gang of Disaffected Englishmen'. It seems comical now, but Coleridge in particular must have seemed thoroughly outlandish in a quiet little Somerset village two centuries ago. As though to confirm that things pastoral are still the norm here, almost the first thing one meets back on the main road is a set of traffic lights – to allow cows to cross. The road leads down to Bridgwater and an area that is as unlike the rest of the southwest as one can imagine.

2

Bridgwater to
Much Wenlock

Bridgwater was built around the lowest crossing point of the navigable river Parrett, and was for a time one of the most successful ports in Somerset. Efforts were made to keep it successful with an extensive harbour complex, and water communication was extended when a canal was dug to Taunton. But a glance at the map and the writhing river is answer enough as to why the port's days would eventually be numbered. It has gone the way of many similar old commercial docklands. The warehouses have been converted to flats; the harbour to a marina. The robust industrial landscape has been softened, but there was really no option. The choices were simple: adapt or decay. But there is something wistfully forlorn about the dock area. It was once so busy, but even the industries of the past are now little more than crumbling reminders of what once was. The brick and tile works which clustered round the water have been taken over; the old kilns no longer send out acrid fumes to drift over the docks, which is at least good news for the neighbours. Bridgwater carries ample evidence of a new, bustling diversification. A postmodernist shopping centre now stands near the old market hall. They form an interesting contrast, for both borrow from the past. But where the old does so with conviction, the new sticks on its motifs as if they were discardable decorations that could be changed as fashion changes. But it is not just as a port that Bridgwater thrived. For centuries it was the main link between the sea-trading routes and that extraordinary area known as the Somerset Levels.

Once this was a region not unlike the Fens, a sunken marshland, where settlements occupied any piece of land that managed to poke its head above water. Rivers such as the Parrett are tidal for long distances, so the whole area was liable to be submerged in a

33

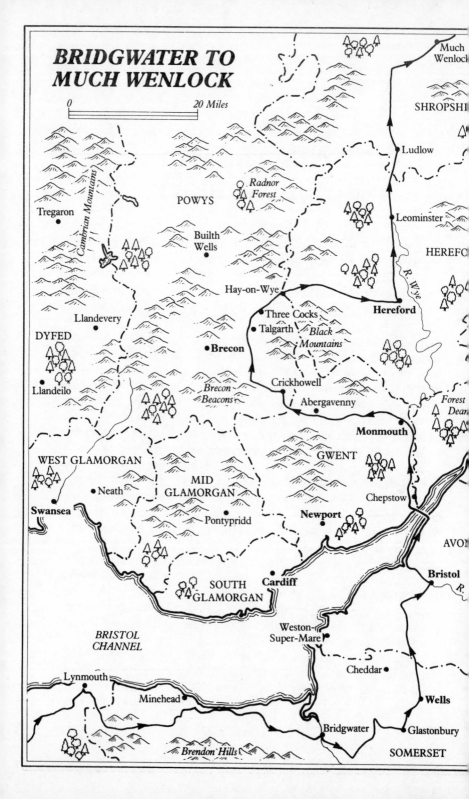

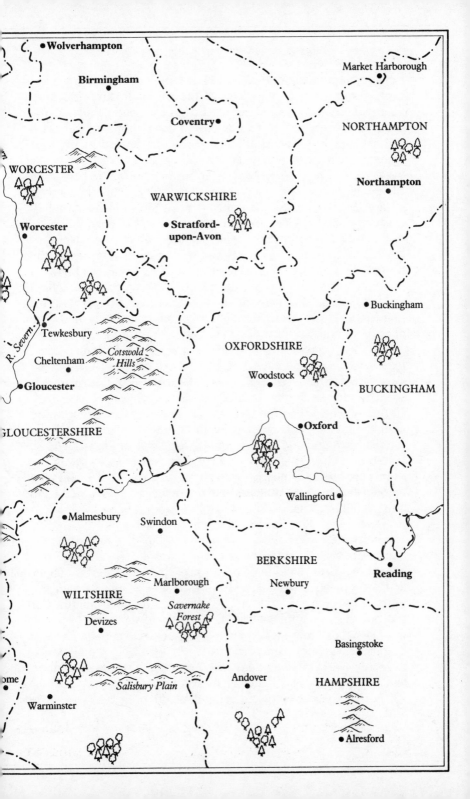

wet season. The long process of reclamation continued for many centuries but the old character of the land still shows through. There is an obvious charm to the green, rolling hills of the southwest; these flat, wet lands have a more subtle appeal. This is a place of wide views, of a chequerboard defined by the long straight ditches with their pollarded willows and the high protective banks that keep the floodwaters at bay. It is a land where each village on its tiny eminence announces itself by church tower or steeple. No need to ask the way to the first stop, for the church of Westonzoyland is a beacon above the fields. It is as grand inside as out with a magnificent angel roof: high above the nave, they look down from the king posts and spread their wings above the congregation. It is now a place of great calm, but it has known a more violent past. In 1685, the Duke of Monmouth's rebellion was crushed on the damp fields of King's Sedge Moor and five hundred prisoners were herded into the church. A few died here of their wounds: twenty-two were taken away and hanged.

The road crosses the moor, with its wide drains laced together by a complex network of ditches, and heads off for the next patch of rising ground. The Polden Hills form a ridge that stretches across the levels, and would scarcely count as hills at all in any other situation. Now the hills seem positively crowded after the expanses of the moor, with little settlements clinging to the rising ground and almost dipping their toes in the water. The land beyond brings us back to the drains and a new usage. Here peat is cut on a commercial basis. It makes for a black landscape, marked out by long trenches with piles of peat alongside. The one prominent – indeed inescapable – landmark on the horizon is Glastonbury Tor, but the first objective is Meare.

The name Meare helps to make sense of this landscape, for once there was a great lake here, which was described in 1537 as being four miles round in winter. It provided fish for Glastonbury and the official in charge had his own house built here in the fourteenth century. It still stands, a plain, rather dour building but a strong one. The official would, after all, scarcely have been the most popular figure locally since his principal occupation was to keep his neighbours away from the fish. All through the Levels, the water has retreated and is still retreating. The day may come when the wetlands of Somerset are wet no longer and all one will see is a flat area of cultivation as dull as the prairie-like fields of

36

parts of East Anglia. So enjoy this unique landscape while you can.

Glastonbury has developed around itself a web of mystery, legend, mysticism and not a little plain dottiness. Avalon and the Celtic underworld, King Arthur and Joseph of Arimathea, ley lines and flying saucers are all said to have powerful associations with Glastonbury. The visitor may select whatever takes the fancy, swallow the lot or chuck them all out and concentrate on what is actually to be seen. There is quite enough of the latter to keep most people content. The abbey is a very ancient foundation, dating back to the beginning of the eighth century, though it has been rebuilt many times. The remains take one from the massive simplicity of the Norman church to the more elaborate styles of Early English and the full-blown decoration of the Gothic. There is something quirkily satisfying, given the exotic stories and legends, that the one building to survive in a good state of preservation should be something as mundane as the kitchen. But what a grand kitchen it is, topped by a fine octagonal roof and lantern. The fifteenth-century abbey courthouse or Tribunal now houses a museum, which among other exhibits includes finds from the Lake Village of Meare, an Iron-Age settlement of houses on stilts. But the best known of all Glastonbury's buildings is St Michael's Tower on the tor. This unlikely lump of earth rising from the flat land was certainly considered a holy, and possibly magical, place in prehistoric times. It is still a centre of pilgrimage for many hoping to find a way back to a mystical past. If the appeal of Glastonbury can seem to rest on something quite intangible, the same cannot be said of neighbouring Wells.

The city centre has its delights, but it is a very strong-minded individual indeed who can delay a visit to its grandest glory, the cathedral. The approach across the green is unforgettable, particularly at sunset when it seems almost alive in the intensity of its glowing stone, or as though it has just been thrown up from the hot centre of the earth. What an extraordinary facade this is, not so much a part of the structure but a great ornate screen thrust up in front of it to dazzle the onlooker. The eye scarcely takes in the main structures of doors and windows, pinnacles and towers, for it is completely overwhelmed by the richness of the carving, of arches, niches, and sculpted figures. And we are seeing the restrained, latter-day Anglicised version of it, for when all this was new it was a riot of bright paintwork.

Stunned by elaboration, you walk inside to be overwhelmed by a simpler, sterner grandeur. The view is dominated by the great double arch in the nave: two pointed arches joined at the apex, one above the other, to form a giant curved cross. It sets up a unique visual rhythm, where in spite of tall straight columns it is the curve that seems to rule. Yet this amazing device came about as a practical solution to a very real problem. For all its many virtues, Norman cathedral architecture had one major fault – it could not always sustain the ambition of the builders. Time and again one reads of a tower crashing down through the roof. It was to prevent this happening that the double arch was built, a solution that far surpasses the simple demands of load bearing. The other great visual delight of Wells is the Chapter House. Stone steps lead up from the nave, then branch, creating a wave-like effect accentuated by the curves worn into the stones by the tread of feet through the centuries. They end at an octagonal room with a fine vaulted ceiling, whose fans of ribs meet and at each meeting are marked by elaborately carved bosses.

One of the dangers of looking at cathedrals is that one sees them as particularly large churches. In those terms they scarcely make visual sense. Everything seems to be clustered round the eastern end, while the vast and undeniably impressive nave seems cut off from this centre of activity. This is no accident. The cathedral of pre-Reformation days was not fulfilling the same function as a parish church. It was not simply a big building for large congregations. Indeed, it could function perfectly well with no congregations. It was built literally for the glorification of God. Masses would be said throughout the day, and special prayers offered up in the many separate chapels. The nave was principally used for formal processions and ceremonials. So distinct were the functions of the east and west end of the cathedral that it was common for the choir to be completely screened off from the nave. The community of the cathedral was not so very different from that of the monasteries and abbeys. Once one grasps this then the whole pattern set by the cathedral becomes much clearer, not only in terms of the building itself but also in terms of its surroundings.

The cathedral was a complex organisation, with the bishop at its head and below him the dean, canons and choral vicars who made up the hierarchy. Around the church there grew up the community of the cathedral close, which is why the surroundings of the great cathedrals are so often a perfect foil to the main building. Nowhere is this more true than at Wells. Beyond the cloisters is the splendid Bishop's Palace, moated and crenellated like a fortress, but softened by the surroundings of trees and gardens. Around the green are the eighteenth-century houses of the canons, and running away from it is a little medieval terrace, Vicars Close. These tiny one-up, one-down houses could be mistaken for workers' cottages, but were home to the forty-two cathedral vicars. And it is the green and the terraces that form the link that joins the cathedral to the rest of the community.

Leaving Wells, one is in no doubt that the Levels are left behind for good. The road climbs steeply and the summit of the hill is marked by a column topped by the figures of Romulus and Remus. Whatever else the founders of Rome may be marking, they are certainly marking the arrival of a very different type of landscape. The Mendips are limestone hills which seem to have more in common with the Pennines than with anything else in southwest England. There are the same straggles of drystone walls tracing out the boundaries of fields but at the same time emphasising the natural contours of the land. At first, however, it seems a gentle country, in spite of the glare of white stone that occasionally breaks the surface. Villages are comfortable places, such as Priddy with its broad green and nothing more dramatic on view than the hurdles stored in a thatched shelter ready for the sheep fair. But there is another aspect to Mendip life which has a quite different character.

As the minor road dips down into the valley near Charterhouse, known as Velvet Bottom, the land takes on a quite extraordinary appearance. It is called 'gruffy ground' – ground which has been bitten into, chewed and spat out again. If you had no notion what had gone on here it could seem quite strange. Deep gullies with rock sides carve into the land; humps and hollows appear everywhere, but there are clues in plenty to be found. At your feet you will see lumps of shiny black material and occasionally you will come across a deep shaft plunging into the earth. This is an area which since Roman times at least has been mined for lead. The chasms are manmade, cut out as the miners followed the veins of ore down from the surface. Close by the stream are remains of areas where the ore and rubbish were separated out, and the black lumps are slag from the furnaces. The old spoil heaps were reworked in Victorian times, and among the more intriguing remains are a set of flues along which gases from the furnace were passed and in which the metal was condensed. The whole region is an industrial archaeologist's paradise, even if the layers of history are now extremely difficult to distinguish. The miniature gorges of the lead rakes may not be as grand as the famous limestone cliffs of the Cheddar gorge a few miles away, but they are certainly a lot more peaceful. Here you can wander and in your imagination people these hills with the men who two thousand years ago were following the precious veins with pickaxe and shovel.

The route down from the Mendips goes through the village of Blagdon to Blagdon Lake, which is not really a lake at all, but a reservoir for Bristol Waterworks. It is also a surprisingly exotic place. The old pumping station has something of the air of a chateau and the ponds and conduits which surround it have pretty little balustraded bridges turning a purely utilitarian site into a miniature Versailles. When it was planned at the end of the last century it was regarded as a work in which the builders could take a proper pride, and that pride still shows. But what the first glance does not reveal are the hidden splendours, for one of the two engine houses still holds a pair of massive steam engines. Perhaps there are some who find such machines of little interest as examples of engineering technology, but they can still be enjoyed as works of art, kinetic sculpture on the grand scale. As one addicted to great pumping engines such as these, it is the combination of basic simplicity – for one must not be misled by sheer size into thinking them bewilderingly complex – with movements that combine mathematical precision with grace. A device may be known by the prosaic name 'Watt's parallel motion', but the actual sliding quadrangle of moving rods is at once both ingenious and aesthetically satisfying. It is good to know that these fine old engines are now going on public display.

From Blagdon the road winds down narrow lanes past the little brewery at Butcombe, home of excellent beers, to arrive rather startlingly at the A38 and Bristol Airport. There is a wonderful preview of the city itself from Bedminster Downs. Bristol is still a city of spires and there is a distant sight of Brunel's famous suspension bridge over the Avon gorge. At this point an author should perhaps, as Parliamentarians do, declare an interest. I made my home in Bristol in 1987 and have fallen in love with the city. My love affair began with the port; there is something wholly enticing about the way in which the old docks bite deep into the centre so that it is always a delight even if no longer a surprise to look out across rooftops and catch a glimpse of masts and spars. There are all kinds of ways of taking to the water. One of the most successful, and certainly the cheapest, is to take the ferry that runs up and down the harbour. Or you can travel in the aged but beautifully restored steam tug *Mayflower* – though this has the disadvantage for those who share this writer's enthusiasms that you may never see anything outside the engine room. But for those who wish to travel in real style and at least begin a proper voyage out from this ancient port down to the sea, there are two ships that offer regular excursions, the *Balmoral* and the *Waverley*. Each is fine in its way but the *Waverley*, the last sea-going paddle steamer in the world, does take one back to the days when whole fleets of paddlers ran down the Avon gorge to the seaside piers of the Bristol Channel, and to steam down that rocky gorge under the Clifton suspension bridge is a truly memorable experience.

The dock area is equally enjoyable explored on land. The city merchants evolved an ornate style for their warehouses that came to be known as Bristol Byzantine. Now many warehouses have lost their old roles but have found new. The Bush warehouse, built in the 1830s to house tea, is now home to the Arnolfini gallery. The grandest of all, however, and quite the best example of the style is Pearce's granary at Welsh Back. This is a real area of delights: a pub with live jazz seven nights a week – just follow your ears – and down the street the Georgian theatre where, it is said, the ghost of Mrs Siddons roams. But the old working port still somehow dominates. It was to serve this port that Brunel built the Great Western Railway on which this journey began back in London, and it was from Bristol that his ships ran to continue the line by water, over the ocean to New York. One at least is still here, the revolutionary *SS Great Britain*: the first iron ship, the ship in which screw propeller took over from paddle wheels, the ship which began the modern age of water transport. The long, laborious and expensive work of restoration continues in the dock from which she was launched in 1843.

41

What else can Bristol offer? A commercial quarter of opulent buildings where a series of pedestals gave a new phrase to the English language. They stand outside the old Exchange and it is here that cash transactions were carried out. They were called The Nails, so you paid on the nail. Round the corner you can find an exotic art nouveau building, once Everard the printers and now a bank, and there is at least one modern office block which shows a lively imagination at work: behind the glass facade of 1 Bridewell Street a white metallic tree climbs up past the floors. The city can boast in St Mary Redcliffe one of the handsomest parish churches in England; this is not just the author's view, for it was Elizabeth I who described it as the 'fairest and goodliest' in her kingdom. Quite the best way to leave Bristol is down the gorge, under the looming cliffs to Avonmouth. This is the new port that has taken over from the old. It is an uncompromisingly industrial landscape that greets you on the edge of the Severn, but a dramatic one. And even more drama lies up ahead. Brunel would surely have enjoyed the view of the Severn bridge which, like his own bridge at Clifton, seems to float effortlessly over the waters. They share the same combination of strength and delicacy, and neither needs embellishment to create its effect. Once across the bridge, you are out of England and into Wales, but there is no great sense of immediate change. This is very much border country and Chepstow is very much a border town.

There are no prizes for spotting the dominant feature of Chepstow. The castle stands high on a promontory guarding the entrance to the river Wye, and the early history of the town can be read in its stones. First came William fitz Osbern's gaunt fortress of 1067, designed to meet the demands of a war lord. The Great Tower looks as welcoming as a prison. With time the town grew, developing as a trading port, and the castle grew with it. New walls were added and new towers, rounded now instead of square. It was still a place prepared for war, but one feels that living in the castle might actually have been more pleasure than penance. Gradually the fortress became almost domesticated. Accommodation was made more comfortable: the new great hall was bright with painted decoration, some of which has survived. Outside, huddled behind its own protective walls, and creeping up to the comforting solidity of the castle, Chepstow too began to prosper and ease itself towards peace. The Wye valley, for centuries a frontier, first between Saxon and Celt, then Norman and Celt, took on a whole new persona in the eighteenth century. It became The Picturesque Wye: Britain's first popular tourist route. It has never lost that role.

It all seems so obvious now: a serpentine river, sometimes wandering between wooded slopes, sometimes overshadowed by crags; a romantic river of ancient ruins and rich historical associations. We are so used to looking at scenery such as this and declaring it to be beautiful that it never occurs to us to doubt that beauty. Yet the whole notion of visiting a place purely to admire the scenery is really quite modern. It was the unpromisingly titled *Observations on the River Wye* by William Gilpin, published in 1770, that set the whole process in motion. Scenery up to then had been largely graded by its usefulness, and if not useful it was regarded as little more than the inconvenient bit between one patch of civilisation and the next. Gilpin taught the British to look, to see scenery as a model for a picture – quite literally to see it as picturesque. His ideal was the classically romantic landscape depicted by the great French artists of the day, Claude, and Gaspard Poussin. Trees were invariably gnarled, buildings preferably ruined, a certain wildness essential. What Gilpin began others continued. The picturesque became the romantic and among the best known of Wordsworth's works are the lines he wrote above Tintern Abbey. When he writes 'The sounding cataract haunted me like a passion' he is expressing the true nature of the picturesque movement, the love of the wild and untamed. But Wordsworth goes beyond the mere scenery as a pretty picture approach, and brings Nature back to a relationship with the 'still, sad music of humanity'. If we can no longer enjoy the excitement of fresh discoveries, we can at least find in the valley areas that have not yet been entirely given over to tourism.

Initially the road from Chepstow abandons the Wye, which is off on one of its more extravagant diversions, and takes a line past the racecourse. So the first real encounter is at one of the favourite spots of the early Wye tourists, Wynd Cliff. The cliff itself is a limestone buttress rising high over the river, and a local landowner decided that the beauty could be improved by making it accessible to ladies and gentlemen. So at the end of the eighteenth century he cut steps from river to top and set out pathways, complete with little grottoes and vantage points. He even created a short tunnel, and it is still there to be enjoyed. From here the road heads down on a rather more gentle descent to the ruins of Tintern Abbey. What changes this area has seen. When the Cistercian monks came here in the twelfth century they chose a spot noted for its beauty and solitude. The essence of the Gothic style was to create a feeling of soaring uplift with walls as little more than frames for huge areas of glass. In its ruins, Tintern comes very close to the ideal, for now the rows of pointed arches have been relieved of their loads and stand proud against the sky, while the windows offer nothing but the remains of tracery to separate the interior of the church from the world outside.

As the monks left in the sixteenth century a new Tintern grew, a Tintern that rang to the sound of hammers and where smoke from furnaces drifted above the valley and wraithed through the crumbling arches of the church. This was for a time one of the great wire-making areas of the country, though you need an expert eye and patience to trace the remains. The pond by the hotel once held water for the waterwheel of the wire mill; the old dock still stands and up in the woods near Llandogo are the remains of a Tudor blast furnace. The industry died, then the tourists came and still come by the coachload. Tintern is a victim of its own popularity. It is an almost insoluble problem. How do you reconcile the enjoyment of a site which should be contemplated with at least a degree of calm with the crowds and the rush of the planned tour? The sad thing is that some people come here not really knowing why, other than a vague idea that it is supposed to be worth seeing. On an earlier visit I was present as one party approaching the abbey met another coming out and the following conversation I swear actually occurred.

'Is it worth going in?'

'No. It's all ruined.'

At which the first party turned round and went back to the coach.

There was a time when tourists mainly came here by train. The railway has gone, but the old Tintern Parva station has been preserved, still advertising such delights as excursions to Chepstow races on trains which, alas, will never run. The main road follows the river, but the road through the woods is by far the pleasanter route, a high level way with river views which seem all the better for appearing quite suddenly at unexpected breaks in the trees.

At Bigsweir the elegant iron road bridge of the 1830s takes you out of Wales and back into England for a while. The river is now a close companion and now that one is above the tideway more pleasant in itself. This is just what one feels the Wye should be, calm and peaceful, but even here one is actually going through what was once an industrial area. There was an iron furnace in Redbrook as early as 1604. The town had a railway before the age of the steam locomotive; horses did the work and trucks were lowered down slopes and hauled up again by cable – which is why just behind the main road in Redbrook you can see a bridge with a steeply sloping roadway over it.

The route returns to Wales at Monmouth, but first a diversion to the Kymin. The hill rises steeply above the river and offers views down the Wye and Monnow valleys. On top is a little white castellated tower built by a dining club who clearly liked good scenery to accompany their food. In 1802, the members built a naval temple crowned by Britannia seated on a rock and the inscription is full of patriotic fervour: 'The painting in front represents the Standard of Great Britain waving triumphant over the fallen and captive flags of France, Spain and Holland.' Why a naval temple on a hill so far from the sea? The answer may be that Nelson and Emma Hamilton visited the Kymin in 1795.

The siting of Monmouth is as logical as that of Chepstow, a fortified town on a border and set at the confluence of two rivers. The castle has, to say the least, seen better days. It suffered the inevitable fate of so many strongholds which had the misfortune to be defended by the losing side in the war between king and parliament. It was, as the old music-hall song had it, knocked about a bit by Cromwell. But by way of compensation there is a splendid fortified bridge over the Monnow, the last of its kind in Britain. It is a pleasant market town with statues to two very different local heroes. Henry V was born here and his statue can be seen in – where else – Agincourt Square, and a pretty awful statue it is too. The other favoured son has fared rather better: C. S. Rolls, who with his partner Royce founded the engineering works which came to epitomise excellency.

Travelling out into Wales the journey begins with a very intimate landscape, having none of the obvious picturesque beauty of the Wye Valley. It is all on quite a small scale – small rivers, small hills, small woods, small settlements. At the same time it offers constant change. You can never quite see what is coming around the corner or over the hill. It is a surprisingly empty landscape as far as actual places are concerned. You keep expecting to meet a village, but few seem to appear. One detour suggested itself, however, which was made more out of curiosity and vague hope than out of any expectation of great discoveries. White Castle seldom features in any list of outstanding tourist attractions, but it was not far out of the way so we went to take a look. As so often seems to be the case, it is when expectations are lowest that the pleasures are greatest. White Castle is exactly what a castle ought to be. It is just like the toy castle of childhood, grown up. It sits on top of a mound surrounded by a deep moat and has a pleasing simple symmetry – just high walls and round towers. You could copy it in Lego in five minutes flat. Abergavenny, the first town to be met after Monmouth, has a much more important castle than this, but it is nowhere near so interesting. The White Castle has a satisfying unity, but why the name? The answer is simple: the walls used to be whitewashed. One thing Abergavenny can provide, however, is knights in armour. The Church of St Mary has a fine array of effigies including one of George de Cantilupe who is shown as a mail-clad warrior, everyone's ideal chivalric hero.

Abergavenny marks the start of the Brecon Beacons National Park. These hills do not have the jagged menace of the more famous northern mountains. They are high but not as high and their shape has been gently moulded, not split and shattered. Yet these comfortably shaped hills can seem wonderfully remote and lonely – and hold their own surprises. A personal favourite spot is Llanfoist just to the south of Abergavenny. If you follow the track uphill past the church you come out by the Brecon and Abergavenny Canal. That in itself is remarkable, as one looks for canals in the valleys, not halfway up a hillside. It is a beautiful waterway and a walk down the towpath is not only a pleasant but also a very easy way to enjoy the hill scenery. But this is only a part of the fascination. A large wharf and warehouse complex indicates that something must have been brought here to justify all the effort and expense. In fact, if you were to follow the track south over the hill Blorenge you would come out at Blaenavon and discover a major iron-making site of the eighteenth century. It is a useful reminder that the valley of the Usk forms a boundary every bit as important as that of the Wye. To the south lie the Valleys, traditional homes of coal and iron and heavy industry; to the north the rough, thinly populated uplands of the sheep farmer.

Our road gives few other hints of the industrial past of South Wales, though the canal is a regular companion. The little towns that snuggle into the folds of the hill are country towns with few pretensions to grandeur and none the worse for that. Houses are built in a simple vernacular style. Crickhowell is the one place of any obvious importance. It is a reminder that even here old conflicts were very real. The name means Hywell's Fort, and though there are Celtic earthworks here the more obvious remains are those of the Norman keep. The town stands on the A40, which was one of the main links between England and Wales long before roads were labelled A, and its position brought it prosperity. The Bear is an old coaching inn which still retains old notions of what an inn should be, a place that not only provides decent food and drink but also allows travellers to relax in comfort. The inn has a rival nearby, a tavern – but a rather special one. It was presented to the town in 1903 on condition that it remained the strictly teetotal Coffee Tavern. What gives Crickhowell its special appeal is the setting between two hills whose names accurately reflect their appearance, Table Mountain and the Sugar Loaf, and the river. The bridge, built in the sixteenth century and later widened, presents an intriguing mystery. Stand at one end and count the arches, then count them again from the other: you get two answers, thirteen and twelve, which gives one something to puzzle over for the next stage of the journey.

Castles seem to pop up at regular intervals and Tretower provides a superb example of how the demands of different times provide quite different answers. Tretower Castle was built by Roger Picard as a typically solid Norman fortress with a gaunt, almost featureless shell keep. Looked at in terms of an age before the use of gunpowder, such castles seem impregnable, yet Tretower fell to Llewellyn the Last in the 1260s. In time the Picards recovered it, and in time peace came to the region. The old fortress was abandoned and Tretower Court built in its place. It is still a solid stone house with immensely thick walls, but now they are pierced by windows and the rather grim exterior is forgotten when one reaches the interior with its attractive galleried courtyard. The new house was built for the pleasures of peace not the necessities of war.

The road skirts the hills of the Black Mountains. Traditionally, in Britain, hills have to top the three thousand feet mark to qualify as mountains. These miss the mark, but only just with a high point of 2906ft. They are still quite high enough to give the towns and villages around them a splendid backcloth, and the steep slopes leave little room for expansion. So villages such as Llangorse seem very huddled, houses elbowing each other to try and find space. And when the hills do come to an end one finds oneself rather to one's surprise back in the Wye valley at Glasbury. The river here has a totally different character from the Wye left behind many miles away. Here it wanders out over a wide plain, often very shallow then gathering itself for a quick dash between rocks. It can be rather more powerful than it appears as I discovered some years ago. My wife and I had decided to take a canoeing holiday, starting at Glasbury. She, very wisely, volunteered to hold our kayak while I got in, negotiated the rapids and joined her at the bottom. I got in, she let go before I was ready, the current then caught the canoe and spun it round. I took my first rapids backwards, attempting to look nonchalant as though it was a favourite party trick. No-one was convinced.

It proved a good deal easier following the road round the hills than it was for a very inexpert pair of paddlers to make their way round them by water. In those days, Hay-on-Wye was simply a stopping place by the river, now it is a town that has been taken over by second-hand bookshops. Hay is a snare into which, as a bookshop addict, I am alas all too willing to fall. I did, however, take the precaution to check the town out in one of the world's best and most idiosyncratic reference books: *Driffs Guide to All the Second-Hand and Antiquarian Bookshops in Britain*. It is not a volume that one necessarily turns to for objective, reasoned discussion. Driff does not like Hay. His view is succinctly expressed in commenting on one establishment: 'bookselling is the exercise of taste, not simply putting everything in neat rows, and hoping that some sucker will bite because they have come a long way'. One sees what he means. There seem to be miles of shelves crammed with the sort of books that are usually left behind at the end of a jumble sale. But the true addict – or sucker – is seldom deterred. This one bit and came away with a rare American book at a bargain price which now occupies a place of honour on the

shelves. But nothing anyone says about Hay will make any difference. The bookworm will never be deterred; others will wonder
what the fuss is about.

The road seems to take its cue from the river, wandering
somewhat aimlessly along through the gently rising ground at
the edge of the valley. The softer landscape seems to demand
a lazier approach. This is a fertile area, the coarse grass of the
upland giving way to lush meadows and orchards. The change
touches everything. The stone buildings that clung together for
comfort in the hills are increasingly replaced by timber-framed
houses as the sources of building stone are left behind. By the
time you reach Hereford the transformation is complete. This
is definitely an English city in a very English landscape. It is the
cathedral that confers the title on what might otherwise seem just
another market town. It is a place that has known great things,
but has seen them gradually slide away. Once it was the capital
of Mercia, but Mercia fell to the invading Danes. It grew again
as a walled town with cathedral and castle, but again drifted back
as the centres of growth switched from the rural areas to the new
industrial regions.

From a distance the cathedral dominates the view, but seems
almost to diminish as you get closer. Attention is diverted to the
old timber-framed buildings, some of which at least now look
uncomfortably out of place. It is perhaps symptomatic of what happens when you start developing an area only to realise somewhat
belatedly that you have lost more than you have gained. So an old
house becomes The Old House. It shows its age, leaning gently
towards the street; standing around for centuries has become an
effort and The Old House looks as if it would like to take a rest.
A shield over the door gives the date 1621 and that does seem
to be the date it was started, for it has all the attributes of the
period. It is jettied, upper floors protruding beyond the lower, and
timber framed with rather more woodwork on show than strictly
necessary on structural grounds. It was a mark of prosperity to
show this no-expense-spared approach, and rich carving adds to
the effect. It is now a museum and parts of other old buildings
have been built in. Murals have been borrowed from elsewhere
but look convincingly at home. They are mainly improving and
moral, scenes from the Old Testament and the classical muses,
but all very vigorous. In spite of the alterations that the years

have brought to the house, it still has a pleasingly domestic feel and the objects on display fit in remarkably well. Look out for a seventeenth-century baby walker which, apart from being in wood rather than plastic, could be put on sale at Mothercare without raising an eyebrow.

Hereford is one of those places which, while it has a definite sense of pride in its own solid respectability, is not much given to ostentation. There are occasional flourishes, such as the magnificent wrought ironwork on the Green Dragon Hotel and an even more ornate porch over what is now the NatWest Bank. But it all comes back to a life tied to that of the surrounding country. Due prominence is given to the Hereford Herd Book Society, where a proud bull stands guard over the doorway and inside the details of the herds are kept with all the solemnity, and much greater accuracy, of an aristocratic family tree. What I enjoy about such places is their ordinariness. Shops are not limited to trendy boutiques and dubious antiques. Even when you get obviously picturesque alleyways and courtyards occupied by craftsmen, they turn out to be real craftsmen, such as watch-makers and shoemakers, not night-school potters with delusions of grandeur. There is room for the occasional flourish; the town hall is an Edwardian confection in liverish terracotta, very turrety, very pinnacly. And one does wonder about the local police view on drink when their headquarters is marked by an old cider press. On the whole, however, this is a modest place – except for its cathedral.

Hereford is a good spot for ecclesiastical browsers, with a number of old churches, but the cathedral demands attention, if not so insistently as it once did. The original Saxon church was destroyed and replaced by the Normans, but it suffered the familiar Norman weakness of an unstable tower. On Easter Monday 1786, the west tower crashed down, bringing the west front and part of the nave with it. The task of restoration was handed to James Wyatt, who set about the job as not so much one of restoration as of rebuilding in the style of his own time. He virtually remodelled the nave, adding a certain Georgian sense of elegant proportion, but sacrificing much of the more robust Norman and Gothic structure in the process. For once it was the Victorians, notably Sir George Gilbert Scott, who can claim to have worked at restoration more sympathetically than their predecessors. The best of the architecture, however, is the least altered. The Lady Chapel is serene and even the Victorian glass in the beautifully ordered lancet windows seem perfectly in place. Hereford's greatest treasure shows the role of the cathedral not just as a place of worship but as a seat of learning. The chained library is a monument to the power of the written word. There are over a thousand volumes of which over two hundred are hand written, dating right back to the eighth century. There are examples of illustrated manuscripts to match the Book of Kells, and appropriately for Hereford a bible in which the warnings of strong drink have been translated as 'he shal not drinke wyn ne sidir' – the cider warning is not notably observed in this part of the world. The volumes are housed in a perfectly restored early Jacobean library.

To the north of Hereford there is an extraordinary estate where the genuine and imitation medieval are mixed with wholehearted enthusiasm. In the twelfth century a chapel was built here, dedicated to St John the Evangelist, patron saint of travellers. It was passed to the Hospitallers who, enthused by the call to arms to drive out the Saracens from Jerusalem, joined the Crusades as The Knights Hospitallers. The order managed to combine, to their own satisfaction, the roles of warriors and priests. Dinmore Manor offered help to travellers and trained young men to arms. The chapel is now all that remains of what must once have been a considerable monastic estate. After dissolution of the monasteries, part at least of the buildings was incorporated into a manor house. It would be a pleasant if unremarkable spot if it had not been bought in the 1920s by Richard Hollins Murray. How appropriate that an estate dedicated to the needs of travellers should have gone to a man whose fortune came from making life safer for the modern traveller. Murray was the inventor of the cats' eyes which wink down the centre of our roads. He wanted a medieval house to match its historic setting. He built cloisters, though the original had none, and a music room in the form of the grandest of medieval great halls. There are stained-glass windows and heraldic devices everywhere, but Murray was not afraid of anachronism. So his medieval music room has an electric organ and his cloisters a grotto like a cave on a tropical island. It should be absurd, but it is done with such conviction that one simply accepts it as unique, a wonder in its own right.

Herefordshire is a county that seems specially designed to create a thirst. If you are not looking at orchards of cider apples you are passing hop fields and oast houses. They certainly add interest to the main-road route, but even so it is still a pleasure to turn off it on to the minor road through Leominster. This countryside seems almost too good to be true, the sort you expect to see shot through misty gauze for a commercial which hopes to convince you that the latest chemical concoction is actually a shining example of natural purity. But it is real. Timber-framed houses were built that way because it was sensible in a country where wood was the cheapest building material. They certainly can be picturesque. One house is so extravagantly jettied that its upper storey juts out like the bow of an aircraft carrier. The road runs between high banks spattered with flowers; woodland, when it appears, is overwhelming, turning the way into a tunnel of oak and beech through which a pale green light filters down. It forms a perfect introduction to one of the most attractive towns in England, Ludlow. It is all too easy to be bowled over by the richness of detail and lose sight of the fact that this is a town developed with impeccable logic.

It all began with the Norman castle set in a bend of the river. Inevitably it attracted settlers around it, drawn by the twin promises of rich patronage and safety. The area grew and prospered, developing as an important market for wool and cloth, and out of that prosperity came a sumptuous church. Seen from a distance, castle battlements and church tower still dominate the scene, and each has its splendours. The oldest part of the castle has nothing to do with defence, but is one of the few circular chapels ever built in Britain. It is a modest affair, quite overwhelmed by the great hall, which retained its grandeur right up to the eighteenth century. It was here that Milton's masque *Comus* was first performed. Later the castle was to become quite domesticated and comfortable, but never lost its outwardly martial appearance. Ludlow church is noble in concept and execution, but its true delight lies in the details. Misericords have become a bit like books with me: an addiction. These little tip-up half seats, which enabled the clergy to survive long hours of standing, are almost always decorated by carvings on the base. These often have little to do with the more po-faced aspects of religious observance. It is here that common humanity finds a place among the stiff effigies of worthies, the gilded angels and the patterns of arches and columns. There are scenes from everyday life, such as the cook in the kitchen preparing to spit roast a pig; the animals of the surrounding countryside are shown in quite natural ways; and there is even room for the fantastical as a sexy mermaid examines herself in a mirror, watched by two fearsome fish sucking their own tails. The tall church tower literally provides an overview of the town, which makes the medieval pattern clear, but Ludlow's fame and popularity rest primarily on its timber-framed buildings with their richly carved facades. None is more exuberant than the Feathers Hotel, and the decorative carving outside is more than matched by the elaborate plasterwork inside. Ludlow went into a period of decline, but revived in the eighteenth century and there was a new burst of building activity which gave the town Georgian houses of quality. If you want an equivalent of the Feathers in terms of over-the-top decoration, take a look at 39 Broad Street which has eight Venetian windows in the facade. Ludlow can at least be said to have something for every taste. The same is true of the surrounding area.

If the route into Ludlow is attractive, the way out is even more so. The minor road to Westhope across Wenlock Edge passes through a deep valley so narrow that the houses have to line up in single file to find space. It is the sort of road that sends all those well-known lines from pastoral poetry spinning in your head, from Marvell's 'green thoughts in a green shade' to Dylan Thomas being 'young and easy under the apple bough'. And the lines scarcely come to mind before the scene to match them appears up ahead: an orchard of old trees bending encrusted branches low over the tall grass where sheep munch among the beehives. If, in many ways, it is a quintessentially English scene of aching purity it also suggests in its pattern of light through the leaves the everlasting summer brilliance of a painting by Monet or Pissarro. Then the road climbs to the narrow knife-blade ridge of Wenlock Edge, which instead of coming as the great climax seems rather the opposite. Trees block the view, giving the briefest of glimpses into the valley, and at the Wenlock end the road seems to disappear into summer snow as clouds of dust drift across from the quarries.

Much Wenlock brings us back to the black-and-white motif of Ludlow, but was a place of importance at a far earlier date.

There was a religious house here in the seventh century, but the present ruins date back only as far as the Normans who established a Cluniac priory. The decoration is pure geometry, a display of architectural fireworks, a facade of interlocking arches like a fizz of rockets hurtling into the sky. In complete contrast are the two carved panels of the twelfth-century lavatorium where the monks washed before meals. One shows two apostles, the other Christ calling Peter from his fishing boat. The figures are robust but confined within arches and niches from which they seem to want to break free. The proportions are all out of scale, almost grotesque, but full of power and energy. It seems impossible that the light tracery and the ponderous, brooding figures could all be part of the same scene, but they are.

The priory marks the end of one phase of the journey through Shropshire. What appears next is a wholly different world with quite different preoccupations.

3

Much Wenlock to
Gretna Green

The first view you get of the Severn valley at once suggests that something different is on the way. The river has cut a deep gorge for itself, which is scenically impressive, yet quite overwhelmed by the cooling towers of the power station. They seem totally out of proportion, as though they were designed for somewhere else and then shoehorned in here with difficulty. This is no whispered suggestion that one is leaving a rural idyll and entering the world of industry; it is a fanfare by the Brigade of Guards.

This area has been called The Birthplace of the Industrial Revolution. This is advertisers' hype, not to be taken too seriously. An historical movement so vast and complex does not happen at one moment in one place. In fact, if you look at the actual event on which the claim rests you have to be a convinced technocrat to feel a sudden surge of hot blood in the veins. It was here that Abraham Darby successfully substituted coke for charcoal in iron smelting. Not, it would seem, exactly earth shattering in itself, but it had immense implications. It made possible a huge increase in the supply of iron on which the machine age was to depend. It brought new demands for coal from deep mines, which in turn created the technology of the steam engine and so the list goes on. Coalbrookdale's claim to uniqueness may be exaggerated but not its historical importance. It is only in recent years that the realisation has dawned that what happened in Britain in the eighteenth century in places such as this changed the world more decisively than all the battles, dynastic squabbles and religious upheavals of the last two thousand years. In the story of the industrial revolution, the Severn valley provided the setting for one of the crucial episodes. What one sees here is the way in which one development spread its effects at first through a confined region, then outwards to the world.

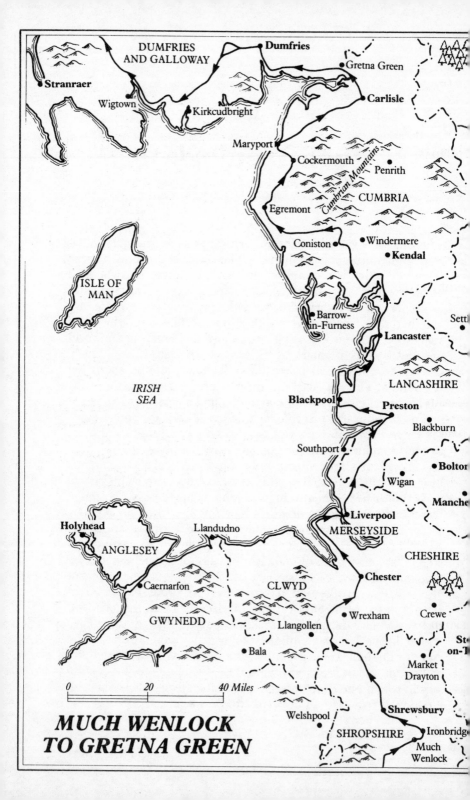

MUCH WENLOCK
TO GRETNA GREEN

The logical place to start is at the old Darby works in Coalbrookdale. Here is the furnace where the new process began, now tricked out with the latest technological gadgetry of optical effects and recorded commentary to 'bring it back to life'. The actual result is to sanitise it, so that it is no longer possible to imagine it ever being part of a real world of dirty, sweating men and molten metal; difficult, indeed, to imagine it having ever been anything except an exhibit. The Iron Museum on the same site is far more successful in showing what resulted from the works of the new iron age. Here is everything from decorative cast-iron work to early rails and steam engine cylinders. It helps to lead you out to the industrial world that crowded in on this section of the Severn valley. Whatever one might think about what has happened to the old furnace, one should be grateful that it and so much else has been preserved. Coming down Coalbrookdale to the river you reach an odd little castellated warehouse, now part of the museum complex, and get a glimpse of the structure that gave its name to a town, the iron bridge of Ironbridge. You would think that anyone contemplating the first iron bridge in the world would begin with a modest experiment. Not a bit of it. This is a triumphal arch, soaring in one high span right across the gorge. Yet it is also an anachronism. Seen from a distance it enshrines the spirit and boldness of a new era; seen close up it is an oddly tentative structure. It is really a wooden bridge built in iron, using the techniques of the carpenter. Sections slot into each other, are joined by mortice and tenon and dovetailed joints, and are secured by wedges. It is also extremely beautiful.

The main attraction for most visitors is the open-air museum at Blists Hill. It is advertised as 'a Victorian town at work'. It is immensely popular and some of the exhibits are closely tied to the industrial history of the area. A small foundry is used to cast decorative ironwork and wrought iron is made by the old techniques of the puddling furnace and the rolling mill, a real spectacular which sends white-hot iron bars whipping to and fro with apparent ease. The site contains a full range of old industries within its boundaries, including an impressive array of blast furnaces, complete with a huge blowing engine that sent air rushing in to raise the temperature, just as the blacksmith's bellows do in a forge. But these now seem subservient to the re-creations – the dentist, the sawdust on the floor of the pub, the chemist's shop and the rest. There is nothing wrong with recreations as such, but somehow the real importance of the site seems to be in danger of being lost beneath the nostalgia. The canal, however, is the real thing. It provides a pleasant walk that ends in a railed incline, which allowed boats to be floated on to wheeled carriages to be lowered down to the next section of canal beside the river. The tub boats used were among the first vessels ever built from iron, yet somehow their significance now seems underplayed. However, the site as a whole maintains a sense of rich diversity, of things left behind from an earlier age, now half forgotten, which makes it almost as enjoyable here as it was before the museum was opened.

The whole valley, it seems, is now a museum. The Coalport Pottery, the tile works, the old furnace down by the riverside road which itself gives you a genuine industrial experience. Mining has created such subsidence that a journey down by the Severn is like a trip on a roller coaster. Eventually it is the total experience of the area that remains in the memory, the accumulation of so much detail in such a setting. You get almost as much sense of the special nature of the area and its industrial past simply by travelling around as you do from the select, preserved sites. If, for me, the approach now seems to have become too sentimentally folksy, the main point is that so much has been preserved. Presentation techniques can always be changed, but once a structure has been allowed to collapse it may never be recovered. What is here is so important that one must be grateful. In the end, quibbles are just that and I have been coming back here for many years, discovering something different every time, and this is still a historical site of the very greatest importance in world terms.

It is amazing how quickly, once you have left the immediate surroundings of the Ironbridge gorge, industry simply fades away. Little Wenlock brings you right back to a very rural, if slightly odd scene. What gives the area its character is the fact that there is building stone here, but it is not very good. It is a soft red sandstone which wears badly. So the church has stone nave and tower but later additions in brick, resulting in an unlikely hybrid. The same theme is carried on elsewhere, sandstone and dark red brick set against each other, while in between are the black and white timber frames of houses whose builders, probably wisely, fancied neither of the alternatives.

The expression 'all around the Wrekin' was already a familiar one, but it was only when coming this way that I really discovered what it meant. The hill itself dominates, changing all the time as the viewpoint changes: sometimes a sugar loaf, sometimes a stranded whale. And round and round you go, twisting through high-hedged lanes until you come back to the flat river valley and Wroxeter.

This was the Roman city of Viroconium. It began as a military base, but what remains has little of the military about it. Viroconium was consciously designed to bring the finest of Roman civilisation to one of the furthest outposts of the empire. Here was a great forum with a colonnaded frontage, market, basilica, shops and that most Roman of all features, baths. It is the sheer size and complexity of the baths that is so impressive. First of all was an exercise area, where the bathers worked up a sweat before passing through a whole series of pools: the frigidarium, just what its name suggests with a cold plunge outside, then a series of rooms which got increasingly warm, starting with the tepidarium. There was also an open-air swimming pool. A surprisingly large amount of building has survived, including the wall of the frigidarium. There are many ancient sites where the past seems remote and impossibly different from anything we can understand, but not here. Take away the trappings of antiquity, repeople the site in imagination and what you have is simply a health club. The Roman administrators from the nearby *civitas* no doubt popped over after work for the equivalent of a game of squash, ending up with a shower or sauna and a swim. They probably nipped off for a quick one at the wine bar in the forum as well.

Only a small part of Viroconium is still recognisably Roman, yet one has the sense of a well-ordered society with standards of hygiene which were not to be found again in Britain for many centuries. An aqueduct brought water to the baths, which not only filled the pools but also flushed the loos. Continuing the journey, one finds different tastes at work. Roman formality meets eighteenth-century contrived informality at Attingham Park. The park occupies part of the old Roman city, but was landscaped by Humphrey Repton to present an idealised picture of an Arcadian countryside. The road that skirts it borrows from its elegance. The bridge over the Tern is as much an ornament as part of the transport system. The

Severn too once had its classical balustraded bridge, but that has been replaced by a newer version which tries to match the style of its older neighbour, but fails. It uses the same motifs, the same architectural language, but handles it clumsily. It is not as easy as it looks to achieve that seemingly artless Georgian elegance.

The road into Shrewsbury is marked by decorative mile-stones, culminating in a fine tall stone at the edge of the city giving distances to other major cities. First impressions are of an old town, full of jettied buildings – jettied houses, a jettied inn, even a jettied gents. It is also a city which clearly does not care for motorists and shoos them off to find their way through a maze-like system of one-way streets. But the city which can be nightmarish for drivers is altogether more pleasant for pedestrians, which is as it should be.

The shape of Shrewsbury is dictated by the river, which almost turns it into an island. Space is so confined at the neck that the station had to be built out to extend over the rail bridge. This is one of the most delightfully mixed-up areas of the city. Here you can stand on the mound by the castle ramparts, built of sandstone of an unlikely brilliance, and look down on the railway station. That was designed in the style of a Jacobean college and looks not unlike the real thing, the nearby Shrewsbury School. Compared with the castle it is positively pallid, but makes up for that with its ornate decoration. For the oddest feature, however, you need to go down to the river to see the platforms striding out over the water.

If the river made life difficult for railway builders, it was no easier for anyone else. Outside the station, two roads meet at an acute angle and a ship-like building sails up between the two, wedge-shaped with salmon-pink brickwork – perhaps not so much a ship as an overgrown slice of sticky cake.

Shrewsbury is also a great place for alley prowlers, for those who love to explore the spaces between the streets. Coming down one of these brings you to St Julian's, with a pavement of old grave slabs. They are now so irregular and cracked that anyone walking this way seems to be in real danger of ending up under one of them. St Julian's itself is now home to a craft centre and health food shop, those two seemingly inseparable companions which cohabit with an air of William Morris worthiness.

61

The road out of Shrewsbury brought yet another landscape change, very humpy and bumpy with little villages and pleasant surprises, such as the old roadside dovecote at Lea Hall. One detour was irresistible, through the village of Myddle. There is little to distinguish it from many another village apart from memories of past importance in the very ruined castle. Yet we know more about this village and its inhabitants at just one time, the end of the seventeenth century, than we do about any other community in the whole country. This is simply because Richard Gough, who was born here in 1635, wrote about it: partly as a straightforward antiquarian's account of the village and partly as a wonderfully gossipy, mischievous account of everyone in the parish who could claim a seat in the church. At the end of the book you feel you know Myddle and its inhabitants intimately, and the visit adds only a confirmation of what was already vivid reality. For those who have not read the book, all one can say is that it still makes an attractive stopping place, and you can pick up a little of the history by asking the landlord about Gough's story of his pub, the house that moved. It would be a shame to spoil the story of the Red Lion by giving it here in advance.

The next stopping point needs no literary associations to recommend it. Ellesmere lies at the edge of what has become known as Shropshire's lake district. This is really rather misleading for there is no grand mountain backdrop here, simply a set of meres, lakes, mostly tree-shaded and tranquil, between which the Llangollen Canal threads its way. Originally this was named the Ellesmere Canal, for Ellesmere itself was then an important market centre. A short arm leads off to a wharf in the town where the Shropshire Union Railways and Canal Company still announce that they will take your goods to Gloucester, Liverpool, Manchester, North and South Staffordshire and North Wales. They won't though, not any more. All the canal takes now is holidaymakers who enjoy superb canal scenery and the greatest canal spectacular Britain can offer – but that comes later. Outside Ellesmere, the road loses the canal for quite a while, for the latter takes a long southward detour to avoid the hills. But problems cannot be avoided altogether and at Chirk Bank the two reunite. The road dips down steeply while the waterway stays up on high on a lofty embankment before striding across the valley of the Ceiriog on a stone aqueduct. It was one of the marvels of the age when it was built, but in 1848 the railways

62

came alongside and took their tracks across the river on an even larger and higher viaduct.

Chirk Castle has been thoroughly domesticated: the last vestiges of a warlike appearance are now no more than set dressing. Inside it appears all gracious living in the approved stately-home manner, but there is another side on show as well. When the castle was aggrandised with its new luxury apartments, the old sixteenth-century dining hall was handed over for use by the servants. Here a sign on the walls reads

'No Noise, No Strife, Nor Swear At All
But all be decent in the Hall'.

Just in case admonitions alone were not enough, a dire punishment was inflicted on offenders: they lost their beer ration. This was clearly drastic for the castle had, and has, its own brewhouse, which was so highly prized that the brewer was one of the highest-paid members of staff. Alas, it is now there only to be seen, not to be used. Also to be seen are the magnificent iron gates made locally by the Davies Brothers of Croes Foel.

The canal visits are not yet over. The waterway is still keeping to its high-level route, but up ahead lies the deep, broad Dee valley and over that it goes on a dizzying aqueduct more than a thousand feet long and over a hundred feet high. You can walk across on the towpath, but for real drama you have to go by boat. The water is held in an iron trough, with low sides so that you literally seem to be flying across, giving the term 'flying boat' a whole new meaning. The canal takes you to a different world. Pleasure boats now turn off on to what was once a branch line, a beautiful hill-hugging route down the Dee valley to Llangollen. But all this effort was not made to provide a picturesque scene and a thrill for tourists. Once you cross the Dee you begin to see the familiar signs of the industrial past, the spoil heaps and slag heaps of mines and furnaces. Yet as soon as you turn off the main road, the scenery changes once again. The mine villages give way to genuine meadows, a sadly rare commodity, bright with wild flowers; trees laze over the road. A brilliant white tower appears ahead like a folly, but turns out to be strictly utilitarian, just a water tower. Then at Minera comes a real curiosity: the little church of St Andrew, with corrugated-iron walls into which Gothic windows have been cut, and the whole thing is topped

by a tiny steeple. Then, on this changeable route, you are back
with the mining landscape again. The area is known as World's
End, and given the dereliction of spoil heaps and crumbling
buildings the name is not inappropriate. The old City Mine has
lent its name to the local pub, which not only sells beer but has
its own brewery attached. Unlike the Chirk brewery, this one is
very much in business and provides a decidedly palatable brew.
The route remains one of startling contrasts. One moment you
are looking over the steel works of Brymbo, the next you are being
presented with a surprise view of distant hills before you dash
down a wooded hillside with a busy stream for accompaniment.
You are never quite certain whether the hill briefly glimpsed up
ahead is going to be a green mount dotted with grazing cattle or
a faintly aromatic spoil heap. Even the more familiar buildings of
the community seem determined to spring their surprises, so that
you pass a Miners' Welfare Institute with a facade that would not
disgrace a gentleman's club in St James's.

That marks the end of the mining region, and rejoining the
main road at Rossett you are once again back to the rural theme,
with watermills by the river on each side of the road. These are
essentially practical things, performing a necessary job in a rural
community, grinding grain to make flour. One of the pair looks
the part, a place with a living to earn. The other, however, could
have been designed especially to be photographed for a colour
calendar. It is dated 1661, but the building itself suggests that
parts at least are older than that. Whatever the date, the style of
black timber framing against white walls will soon become very
familiar, for up ahead lies Chester.

The black and white buildings are probably the most famous
features of the city and none are more famous than The Rows:
shops in two tiers, one pavement and one set of shop fronts down
below, another pavement and another set of shops up above. How
glorious it all seems, what a wealth of ancient, ornate woodwork
and decoration. Then you look a little closer. Hidden in among
the curlicues you may well find a date not sixteenth but nineteenth
century. A surprisingly large number of the quaint old buildings
may be quaint but they are not old. They are fakes, but exuberant
full-blooded fakes that work surprisingly well. The real thing, like
the Bear and Billet built as a town house in the seventeenth century,
is unmistakable when you see it, but that need not detract from

the Victorian pastiche. One old house carries the pious message 'God's Providence is Mine Inheritance'. This is the one house untouched by the Black Death. Nearby, another timbered building bears a similar message 'The Fear of the Lord is a fountain of life', but this one is the work of Victorian architect W. H. Kelly. One of the more entertaining games to play in Chester is 'spot the phoney', so long as it is not taken too seriously – there is nothing wrong in admiring the Victorian efforts any more than there is in enjoying the elaborate jubilee clock over Eastgate. Chester has gone the other way as well, taking the old and renewing it. The arched facade of the former Westminster Coach and Motor Works has been preserved and reused, most successfully, as the front for a new public library.

The best way to see Chester is to walk round the walls, for this is the one medieval city where it is still possible to make a complete circuit and view the changes of the centuries. You peer down on the remains of the Roman amphitheatre and even for a while walk above the last of the original Roman wall itself. This is a city of renewals: battered by wars, the old has been left to stand, the ruins cleared and replaced by the new. We can thank the Georgians for the pleasures of the walk, for they turned the battlements which, as recently as the Civil War, had still been vital defensive works, into a promenade. They also gave the city some of their own stylish buildings, notably round Lower Bridge Street. The walk also helps you understand the city's pre-eminence. As with so many English cities it first came to prominence as a port, and just when those days seemed ended along came the canals of the industrial revolution and it was a port again. The Chester Canal could be mistaken for a moat as it runs beside the walls, but it brought new, vigorous life to the old city. This is perhaps the overwhelming impression of Chester; through the centuries of change it has retained its vitality.

After Chester, the journey down the Wirral is frankly a little dull. It has become a sort of suburbia by the sea but the nearer you get to the end of the peninsula the better it appears. The road itself becomes more varied and includes a dip into a sandstone cutting that looks as though it was designed for a railway. Houses are not so much grand as grandiloquent. West Kirby comes as a shock, not so much redbrick as vermilion brick with row upon row of turreted villas. Pastiche rules here. A house appears as a sub-Wedgwood concoction with a blue and white plaster version of the Elgin marbles across the front. A mock Tudor mansion all gables and chimneys turns out to be a thirties roadhouse, which looks as if it was designed for one of the farces of the period. The gaudy red is all pervasive and not even the churches have escaped. It all seems a world, not a ferry ride, away from the city across the Mersey.

Liverpool is an ancient settlement. It was granted borough status in 1207 by King John, but where Chester wears its old age with pride, Liverpool has lost it. The little settlement on the windy shore of the Mersey was thrust into prominence by the industrial revolution and trade, particularly with America. For a time it seemed as though the port would keep on growing forever. It got its first enclosed dock in the late eighteenth century, but it was the nineteenth century that saw the great period of expansion. Docks multiplied: on and on they went, mile after mile of them. Ocean liners called on regular runs to North America. Cargo vessels from around the world brought goods in and out. Liverpool is still a port, but now the working docks have moved further out, nearer to the river's mouth. The old docks, ignored and forlorn for so long, are becoming the showpieces of the city centre. Trade may have gone but the magnificence remains. The monumental offices of the shipping companies and harbour authorities give the waterfront its famous skyline, typified by the liver birds. But it is the transformation of the old docks that marks an attempt to rejuvenate the city. The maritime museum tells the story of the past and the restored Albert Dock has transformed the whole area. Some have criticised the scheme as yuppification, an irrelevance that comes nowhere near tackling the city's real problem. But no-one can deny that the dock represents the high point of Victorian maritime architecture, a scheme realised as a whole, carefully planned and executed with panache.

Albert Dock is a closed dock ringed by warehouses that stand out boldly on sturdy pillars above the wharf. It is a model of ordered regularity, visually satisfying yet intensely practical – and it has its surprises. Rap the pillars of the dock-office portico and there is a ring of metal instead of the expected clunk of stone. The one pity about the new development is that visitors cannot see the roof, for that was designed as an undulating sea of iron plates. Now the docks have the maritime museum, the northern branch of the Tate Gallery and a row of shops with flats above. The shops are very gift orientated, but that scarcely matters. Use can change, but if the devastation had been allowed to continue there would have been nothing left to change. Not many years ago, when the dock was simply a sea of mud, there were proposals to drain it out and use it as a car park. Visit Albert Dock now, with boats riding at their moorings, and give thanks.

Albert Dock is the centre of one of Liverpool's grand set pieces; the other is based on the buildings to the east of St John's Gardens. There, exuding civic dignity, is one of the best groupings of neo-classical buildings in the country, dominated by St George's Hall. This magnificent Corinthian temple is wholly convincing, a building of impeccable proportions and solid worth. Inside is a visually stunning concert hall, with granite columns, opulent tiling, dazzling chandeliers and classical details, which at the same time is both practical and comfortable. It was built with an efficient central heating system and, remarkably for the 1840s, air conditioning. Air was drawn in, cooled by fountains and circulated by steam-powered fans. St George's Hall may draw its architectural inspiration from the ancient worlds but its mechanics are pure Victorian. Across the road are its classical fellows, which include the Museum of Labour History. It is somehow typical of Liverpool that it should want to tell the story of its ordinary people and should choose the old County Sessions House as the setting. The wealth so obviously on display in the structure of the building had its origins in poor immigrants and hard work. Liverpool has never been ashamed of that aspect of the past, and even the name 'scouse' comes from a cheap workhouse stew.

Anyone who looks at this city only in terms of its grander buildings and public displays is going to miss a lot. It has some great pubs, not just the astonishingly ornate Philharmonic with its extravagent art nouveau entrance, but spread through the city and out into the suburbs. There are surprisingly attractive old buildings down in the city, such as the Bluecoat School of 1717, now a lively arts centre. But when it comes to visual excitement, you still cannot beat the journey down the docks road towards Bootle. It gives you the measure of what Liverpool was in its heyday, and the local pubs all seem to carry memories of sailors and voyages and emigrants hoping for a better life across the seas. Liverpool is a place touched by sadness. It was the place from which the poor set out, from necessity not choice, leaving everything they knew behind them.

The countryside beyond Liverpool is generally flat but has, at least, metaphorical high points. Ormskirk boasts a parish church endowed by two sisters. One favoured a tower, the other a spire, and unable to agree they gave it both, one beside the other. But quite the finest place along the way is Rufford Old Hall. Built in the early fifteenth century, it has inevitably seen many changes but through them all has retained a lively charm. There is a special quality to big, timber-framed houses. However overlaid with decoration they become, the solid framework can always be understood. Outside, the house 'reads' as a series of boxes, elaborately decorated boxes perhaps, but boxes none the less. Inside, the hammer-beam roof of the Great Hall owes its effect as much to the practical solutions of the problem of spanning a wide space as to the carvings that embellish it. The same is not quite true of the 'moveable' screen that stands just inside the hall, in front of the main doorway. It is almost grotesquely monumental, heavily carved, topped by high finials – and one would imagine that an army of strong men would be needed to shift it. But this dark monster is offset by a noble bay of beautiful proportions, as light as a summer house. Much of the hall's character derives from the fact that from the time it was built until it was taken over by the National Trust it remained in the Hesketh family. It was home first and stately second – a building for use, not for display, though there have been great events here. Tradition, and tradition for once has more than hearsay evidence to support it, declares that Shakespeare acted here in St Thomas Hesketh's company of players. Even that notion seems to sit easily with the house, and imagination conjures up not a colourful pageant but a meeting of friends come to enjoy the entertainment.

You do not get long for this sort of musing on the journey for you have scarcely moved on before industry is back again – Leyland with its motor works, Preston of the mill chimneys. Time was when the cotton lords of Preston wielded far greater power in the world than any lords of Rufford. For me, the visit was not altogether joyous. We drove past the *Manxman*, the very last steam-powered ship to run between Liverpool and the Isle of Man. I was on her for her final voyage out of Liverpool and up the Ribble, accompanied by a flotilla of little craft, planes overhead and bands playing. She will probably never move again and has no future other than to provide a colourful background for a leisure complex. The new owners may well have done a splendid job on the old steam packet, but somehow I could not quite bring myself to go and look, so drove on to something a good deal cheerier.

If you come to Blackpool you have to take Blackpool on its own terms. It is no good groaning about vulgarity and noise; Blackpool has taken vulgarity and noise to its heart. Take away the fairgrounds, the cheap boarding houses, the bingo and the candy floss and you have lost Blackpool. The town seems stuck at a moment of time, in a seaside world of McGill postcards, and sees no reason to change the fundamentals. Trams still run because people like trams and they are ideal for travelling the long, straight sea-front track. The fairgrounds are the ultimate in brash noisiness because who wants a sedate fairground? The front echoes to alternating amplified music – all thump and no tune – and the clickety-clicks and Kelly's eyes of the bingo caller. The boarding houses are cheap because they are in a cut-throat business and no-one dares charge a penny more than the neighbours. They are unsophisticated, matey, assuredly not designed for the calorie conscious or the gourmet and they survive by giving the customers exactly what they want. There really is only one thing to do with Blackpool: give in. Chuck yourself into the place wholeheartedly and if you don't like it get out quickly, for there are few things in life more depressing than being unhappy in Blackpool. Everywhere around you are crowds totally determined on enjoyment, dedicated to excess: too much food, too much drink, too much noise, too much everything. It is simply no use admiring the architecture of the piers and deploring the amusements on them. Blackpool piers are doing what they were built to do. Did I enjoy it? Well, a day is fine – but a week would send me round the bend. It was pleasant to renew acquaintance with Blackpool, but it was even better when I went there as a child. Then it seemed one of the best places in the world to be; many years later the sheer barefaced effrontery of the place was still enjoyable. All those Gypsy Petulengros and Gypsy Roses who are not so much consulters of the stars as consulted by the stars. At least that is what the photographs outside are supposed to make you believe – but notice none of them actually says that superstar

X came here, just leaves you to draw your own conclusions. Does Blackpool have a Golden Mile or a Tawdry Mile? Both really.

Rather surprisingly, Blackpool also has its subdued aspects as you travel out along the north shore. The trams have their own little stations out among the grassy dunes. There are grand hotels, one of which boasts impressive castellations – a fortress with chips – but even that is outshone by the Miners' Convalescent Home. Blackpool seems likely to stagger on for ever, but the coming of the Wyre estuary calls a halt, bringing marshes and waders and harsh bird calls on the wind. The road to Lancaster appears to cross an entirely flat landscape, yet perversely advances through a series of right-angled bends. So, since it is impossible to go straight to one's destination, one might as well make a virtue of necessity and take a diversion beside the Lancaster Canal to Glasson Dock, a place of good honest values. There are more pleasure boats than working boats, but enough trade to keep this as a plain no-nonsense dock. The visual pleasures are provided by lock gate and paddle gear, bollard and anchor and the waving reedlike fringe of distant masts. It is not a bad introduction to Lancaster, where the pleasures also come from the almost accidental patterns created in a working environment.

Lancaster was a major port when Liverpool was a hamlet. It made a valiant attempt to keep up trade in the late eighteenth century by improving the river and extending communications through the canal. But Lancaster still held to the old pattern of an open riverside wharf lined with warehouses. It could not compete with the closed, mechanised state-of-the-art port of Liverpool. You can see Lancaster's hopes in the customs house on St George's Quay with its Palladian portico, and read its failure in the fact that now it is just a museum telling of the maritime past. But the best exhibits are not inside, but all around it: the warehouses that still line the quay. Everyone wanted to be down here, so the warehouses are squeezed together, pushed upwards, so that the facades form a rhythmic pattern of loading bays and hoists. There is a wonderful solidity about these old buildings, with their beautifully dressed stone blocks contrasting with the worn timbers of hoists and cranes. No wonder they are finding new uses as offices and houses. St George's Quay is, or should be, what Albert Dock is to Liverpool.

The quay is always my first stop in Lancaster, not that there is

not a great deal more to enjoy. It has its own curiosities including a northern version of the Taj Mahal, a monument to a dead
wife almost as grand as the famous Indian temple. The Ashton
memorial is the most prominent landmark for miles around. On
looking at it in more detail, however, it begins to look less like a
monument to a mourned wife and more like a celebration of the
wealth that made such a gesture possible. Where other memorials
might have grieving cherubs, this one has puffing locomotives.
Lancaster's other grandiose building is the hospital, which could
easily pass as an Italian Renaissance town hall. But these are
exceptions: Lancaster's true style is much more restrained. Dark
stone gives everything a slightly sombre appearance, suggesting
a place that knows its own values and has no need of fripperies.
Which is probably about right for Lancaster. Even the canal,
which has its moment of triumph here, does so with real dignity.
The Lancaster canal's engineer, John Rennie, was notable for his
architectural accomplishments. On the Kennet and Avon Canal
he designed an aqueduct that is all classical lightness; here, the
far greater aqueduct across the Lune is also given a classical
treatment, but with much more gravity. If one carries the spirit
of Greece, its northern counterpart is more soberly Roman.

Lancaster marks another transition in the landscape; a move
away from the plain towards the mountains of Cumbria. It is
almost impossible not to want to rush along, knowing what lies
ahead. All the elements begin to gather together. Stone walls
border the road and spread out to the fields, while the same dark
stone dominates villages and towns. But there is the particular to
note as well as the general. The road is comparatively traffic-free
thanks to the M6 and, where the latter announces everything on
signs the size of snooker tables, the old road still has memories
of more leisurely travel, when you could still read distances off
wayside milestones. The stones tell you more than just distances:
a change of design indicated a change of ownership of the road, and
you can see those changes varying from plain stones to cast-iron
plates. They carry the history of the road itself.

There are also attractions to tempt you to stop. At Carnforth
there is Steamtown, home to such famous locomotives as Flying
Scotsman, though the residents do spend a lot of time out on
the tracks hauling special trains. Milnthorpe has the lure of its
river, running deep and strong. Then comes Levens Hall, an

Elizabethan house which marks the transition from fortress to home. The first building on the site was a pele tower which was quite simply a gaunt, featureless fortress, a place to retreat to when the border raiders came down from the north. There you could sit it out until the raiders had gone and you could emerge to find out how many belongings you had left. On to this was tacked a conventional house. Stately home addicts never need any encouragement to call in and wander round inspecting the ornamental plasterwork, the portraits of former owners and the fine furnishings. Levens Hall, however, does have two different attractions to offer. First is the topiary garden, laid out in 1692 and planted to the same design ever since. It has a sense of strict formality. Flowerbeds form patches of uniform colour among the trim bushes. The effect has to be one of perfect regularity throughout; one weed would destroy the whole as totally as an errant blob of paint splashed on a Mondrian would wreck it forever. The garden is brilliant but scarcely surprising. What one might not expect to find at a stately home is a Steam Collection. In the courtyard among the outbuildings and stables, the order of the Elizabethan and Jacobean world gives way to the gruff rumblings of heavy engines. Showman's engine and steam tractor, tipping wagon and even a steam car are regularly put through their paces. The latter is a reminder that there was a time when it was at least a possibility that steam rather than the internal combustion engine would rule the highway as it did the railway. Steam cars reached a peak of development in the 1920s with the Doble sports car, which could get up steam in less than a minute and accelerated silently to a top speed of over a hundred miles an hour. There are still people around who talk wistfully of a comeback of the steam car to replace the infernal combustion engine. The collection also shows the development of steam power through a range of nodding and bobbing small engines.

It comes as a bit of a shock after Levens Hall to find one-self turning on to a dual carriageway which speeds you through pleasant but unremarkable scenery. Then the dual carriageway ends and the character of the journey changes on the instant, as you are confronted by a high limestone escarpment. The sense of approaching the lakeland grows stronger. The mountains appear on the horizon as faded cut-outs. Nearer at hand, the land is carved into small fields divided by stone walls. Slatey farmhouses seem as natural as the rocks forcing their way up through the crests of the hills. The first actual lake to appear is Windermere. The main road up the eastern shore is generally nightmarish, nose to tail stuff, for this is the most popular of all the lakes. The route up the western side is narrow, twisting but comparatively deserted. It may be a little busy at first as you run along beside the wholly delightful Lakeside and Haverthwaite Railway, a line which I have travelled many times and of which I never tire. You keep it company to the river at Lakeside, where the steamers run – except that they are not steamers, having long since been converted to diesel. They are, however, still attractive vessels and it is far pleasanter to see Windermere from their decks than from the A592. But I was saving up lake excursions for later. For the moment I had a quite different objective in view.

It might seem perverse, when the one thing the Lake District is famous for is its natural scenery, to head straight for an industrial museum, but Stott Park Bobbin Mill really is splendid. What it did is easy enough to explain. It took lengths of timber, cut them to size and shaped them to make bobbins for the textile industry, from big bobbins for the mills to the familiar cotton reels for the sewing basket. What you find is antique machinery, up to a hundred years old, all run by a bewildering array of belts whizzed round by overhead shafts. It looks terrifyingly unsafe and was. The guides take special delight not so much in demonstrating the machines, though they do that with great flair, but in curdling your blood. My favourite story, if that is the word, was of the young lady whose hair was caught and was literally scalped. Like all early industries the bobbin mill contains wonderful examples of man's ingenuity in designing machinery, and less wonderful examples of the callousness that put profits first and safety a long way last.

From the mill the little road winds up through the wooded hills, with occasional glimpses of the sparkling lake. In late spring it blazes with rhodedendra and in all seasons is a delight. The best is saved for the last as you turn across the head of the Grizedale Forest to cross the hills for the next valley and the next lake. As you come over the top you can enjoy one of the most glorious views in all Cumbria. Those who have felt cheated by only getting glimpses of Windermere now get Coniston laid out before them, the star player in an amphitheatre of hills. Windermere now seems the overture to this, the main work. At Coniston itself there is

73

an opportunity to travel the water in real style. The steam yacht *Gondola* was launched in 1859 as an attraction to lure passengers to use the new railway that had just been opened. The railway has gone, but the yacht has been restored in all its plush opulence. Its name is not inappropriate, for the highly decorated, steeply raked bow would look very much at home on a Venetian canal. Steam on the water has the advantage of being smoothly silent, with little more than a whisper of steam to disturb the tranquillity.

There may be some who find it a little tame being transported across the lake and look for a closer involvement with the mountain scenery. The next stage should more than satisfy such yearnings.

North of Coniston is a signpost pointing to the Langdales and Wrynose Pass. It warns of 1 in 3 hills, sharp bends and narrow roads – and delivers them. It is not a road for nervous drivers, motorists whose hill starts are a trifle dodgy or anyone with doubts about their brakes. The chance of negotiating the hairpin bends of the two high passes Wrynose and Hardknott without coming to a halt on a sharp bend halfway up a 1 in 3 slope is virtually nil. The probability of not spending a good deal of time travelling backwards to the last passing place is likewise slender. If all that makes it sound slightly scary, then in a way that is just what it is. But the rewards are immense. This is the nearest you can get to enjoying the true essence of the lakeland hills without actually leaving the car, getting on your boots and walking off to a distant summit. It cannot match the exhilaration of standing on the summit of Helvellyn or reaching the top of Bow Fell, nothing involving a car could, but it comes a reasonable second. And at least the effort of driving over Hardknott is rewarded not just by grand scenery but also by a great archaeological site, the Roman fort.

Wroxeter seems even now to be a comfortable, civilised sort of place. This lonely fort in the Cumbrian hills must always have been a rugged spot, even if the inmates did enjoy one essential Roman luxury, a bath house. It was occupied by troops from what is now Jugoslavia, who at least would have been used to the mountains even if not accustomed to lakeland weather. It remains immensely impressive. The big parade ground has been levelled out of the hillside, and the fort looks out on one side to the road over Hardknott and on the other down into the green

74

valley of Eskdale. It was not occupied for long: built in the first century AD it was disused by the end of the second, but it was built to last, it seems, for ever. The stone walls still stand to a considerable height, even in little outlying buildings such as the circular guard tower. In the remoteness and grandeur of its setting it is as impressive as Hadrian's Wall.

After that almost anything must be a bit of an anticlimax as you leave the high hills behind you. For some of us at least there is compensation in the air as a steam whistle blasts out its echoing message. Dalegarth is the terminus of the Ravenglass and Eskdale Railway, universally known as 'the Ratty'. This tiny railway with its miniature versions of mighty main line expresses is no toy. In its time it served the local quarries, even if now it is entirely devoted to tourists. It is a demanding line of steep gradients and the little engines that pant their way up and down have to work hard for their living. It provides passengers with fine lakeland scenery which seems all the more impressive when seen from a scaled-down railway. The traveller by road, however, finds the scenery changing. The openness of the fells gives way to a closed road bounded by stone walls, from some of which boulders jut out in a decidedly alarming manner. Then even these give way to flowered banks and hedgerows, while the hills soften and the jagged, rocky edges are left behind.

The coast road takes you on past the nuclear power station of Sellafield where the prominent towers look from a distance like a Disneyland castle. But who is at home: the good fairy or the wicked witch? This is an area of sharp contrasts. Egremont is in many ways a typical small market town that developed under the protection of its Norman castle, but it also sits at the edge of an area which enjoyed a great burst of prosperity in late Victorian times. From the castle walls you can look down on a landscape of mines and spoil heaps. Cumbria turned out to have the perfect iron ore for the new Bessemer process for manufacturing steel. Suddenly it was boom-town time in Cumbria. Not that it shows that many signs of prosperity. Villages appear as terraces staggering up hillsides, rows of four-square houses, solid but dour, and even liberal use of colour washes cannot remove the sober monotony of a place such as Cleator Moor. The newer mining world rubs shoulders with the older world of country market towns such as Cockermouth. They still hold street markets and cattle markets here and the town would probably have remained unremarked, quite content to go its own way if the estate and law agent for the wealthy Lowther family had not lived here and if his son had not shown a genius for poetry. Cockermouth does not seem to have been too keen on celebrities, nor presumably the tourists they attract, for they wanted to knock down the house where the poet was born to build a bus shelter. But the National Trust stepped in, bought it up and Wordsworth House is now a place of pilgrimage for admirers of lakeland's best known poet, though it never attracts the numbers who flock to his cottage in Grasmere. Wordsworth had no enthusiasm for the world of industry that was coming to dominate England in his lifetime, nor for its philosophy. In 'The Excursion' he wrote of coming upon a mill and seeing the men, women and children going to work. It was, he felt, a temple

> where is offer'd up
> To gain – the master idol of the realm,
> Perpetual sacrifice.

The changes were felt throughout West Cumberland as an industrial area grew up in the narrow band between mountains and sea. New towns developed to match the old, though for some the prosperity never lasted beyond the brief period during which the mines prospered. Maryport was such a place. It was built by Humphrey Senhouse and named after his wife. It has fallen on hard times and now has a somewhat seedy air, nothing to suggest the busy days of ore movement and shipbuilding. Yet once you get down to the docks you see that the basic elements are still there. Dockside buildings have largely been demolished but the place actually works: fishing boats come and go and you can even arrange to be ferried across to the Isle of Man. It still fulfils something of its old function. But change is on the way. Already, there is a small but delightful maritime museum and work is going on in the harbour where craft, including a steam tug, are being restored. Inevitably there are plans for a marina. It would be sad if the well-meant desire for improvement and revitalisation ruined the essential character of the unpretentious working port. One benefit should be the provision of a decent home for the Senhouse Collection, for the Senhouses not only gave the area a new port but also put together a magnificent

collection of Roman remains. These include a whole set of al-
tars from the garrison at which troops swore their allegiance. It
is hoped to display these in an appropriately military setting, the
nineteenth-century Battery on the bluff above the town.

Driving north you are not so much going to Scotland as past
it, for it stretches a long southerly finger across the Solway Firth.
Villages tend to be elongated, some with extensive greens, and
even if the names can be both intriguing and exotic – Aspatria
sounds as if it had drifted over from Tuscany – the appearance
is slightly dour. In Wigton, the general effect is not helped by the
aromas drifting across from the chemical works. The town does,
however, have an unusual war memorial. The subject matter is
conventional enough but it is heavily gilded and literally shines
out in the centre of town.

Carlisle shows itself at once for what it is, with the castle
overlooking the river crossing and the citadel in the town centre.
This is a frontier town. It was once in Scotland, but William
II marched up in 1092 and claimed it. That did not settle the
matter and arguments, often bloody, continued for a few more
centuries. But it was during the English Civil War that Carlisle
took its greatest battering and lost many of its noblest buildings.
The cathedral was largely dismantled by the Parliamentary forces,
who carted off the stone to rebuild the defences. It was restored by
the Victorians, but their efforts can hardly be called a great success.
The original red sandstone has been restored using paler stones
to create a patchwork quilt of a building. Inside there is only a
hint of what it was like: two of the twelve bays of the nave are
all that survived the onslaught but they are big enough to make
one yearn to see the original. The truly massive round pillars
with rough squat capitals are almost brutal in their effect, and
when there was a whole row of them the effect must have been
dramatic; dark, brooding and charged with an almost menacing
strength. Now the nave is rich in ornament from star-spangled
ceiling to elaborate organ. There are, however, survivors from
the days when this was an Augustinian monastery. The Augustine
Screen consists of a series of scenes from his life painted on wooden
panels in the late fifteenth century. There are twenty-two pictures,
all crude but executed with immense vigour. In one Augustine
looks only mildly apprehensive when confronted by a horned
devil who not only has an evilly contorted face conventionally set

77

on the front of his head, but also has another equally ferocious visage on his backside.

The city seems now to have shrugged off the memories of war. It has its municipal museum, a product of one of the glummer Victorian schools of architecture, all dark panels and moody tiles. The exhibits, however, are good and it does have a Roman road running right through the grounds. The Guildhall, dating from around 1400, has Punch-like figures squinting down at you from under the eaves. The nineteenth century did give the city a superb station. It was designed by Sir William Tite in a Tudor-collegiate style which is still impressively convincing, even though the station was greatly extended later in the century. The twentieth century has been less kind. British Rail has to have its 'corporate image' and seems to believe that covering carefully thought-out and well-worked facades in bits of plastic makes the place look more modern and therefore more efficient. What it actually looks like is just what it is – a well-designed building with a ludicrous addition. Carlisle and the station deserve better.

There is not much choice about the way north unless one fancies a long and somewhat meaningless diversion to find a different crossing of the Esk. So one is faced with the dull dual carriageway and the pounding trucks that obliterate the view. It seemed wisest to avoid the tourist honeypot of Gretna Green and the blacksmith and to turn off as soon as possible to enjoy the delights of Scotland.

4

Gretna Green to Fort William

It comes, paradoxically perhaps, as a surprise to discover that there really is a difference when you cross that short stretch of water that separates England from Scotland. There are few changes, at first, in the scenery. This is not the Scotland of heather on the hills but a rather benign, gentle landscape. It is also mercifully free of the traffic that thunders continuously between north and south. The first change you notice is in the buildings. There is a sudden preponderance of single-storey houses or houses with low upper storeys marked by dormer windows in the roof. Many are whitewashed with the big stones that form the quoins picked out in black. They are very distinctive, and it is decidedly satisfying to find that, having crossed a border, you really are in another country.

You will not find Annan, the first town of any size you meet in Scotland, featuring very prominently in any tourist guide, yet it is well worth a second glance and has some of the features that one comes to think of as typical of the region. The buildings are very much of the area, built using local materials, which in this case is bright red sandstone. They are rarely outstanding, but have dignity. The church is eighteenth century with a stepped steeple and little Venetian window; the town hall is Scottish baronial with typical round turrets. Streets are broad, houses plain. One is just beginning to grow accustomed to Scottish vernacular, when Cummertrees appears. Here houses are three storeys with timber decorations, which would be mock Tudor if the architect had not added an array of balconies and little turrets creating a curiously Germanic effect. But it is only a brief interruption and one is soon back with low, stone cottages.

Dumfries and Galloway has a character all its own. Here, near the shores of the Firth it is largely agricultural land, with the distinctive Galloway cattle munching in the fields. Roads are

79

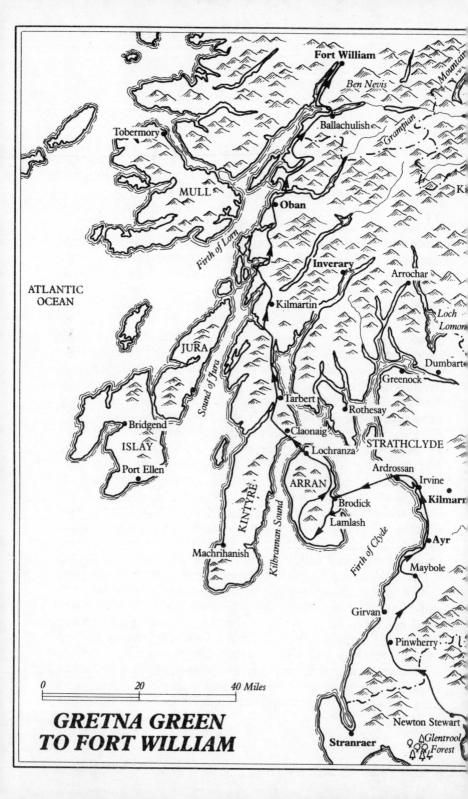

GRETNA GREEN
TO FORT WILLIAM

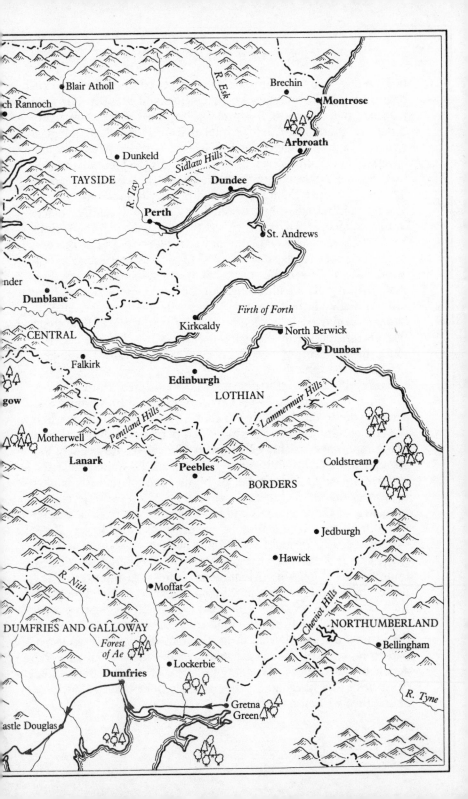

bordered by hedges, many of them composed of thickset broom, providing a brilliant yellow border. It looks like nature's own no parking zone. Then at Ruthwell, you get a choice of two very different attractions. A left turn takes you to the village, a typical street of simple cottages, one of which, outwardly just like the others, is the birthplace not of a famous individual, but of a world-wide financial movement. It was the world's first Savings Bank. A local man, Henry Duncan, appalled by the miserable poverty of the agricultural labourers, decided to set up a Friendly Society in this cottage. In 1810 he opened the first ledger of the savings bank. This impoverished community responded and at the end of the first year funds stood at £151. This was more than a local effort. He publicised the success and savings banks modelled on that at Ruthwell spread throughout the world. Now this is a little museum, and all the more touching for its modesty. It is also, as befits a former friendly society, a very friendly place. One thing that visitors notice in this part of Scotland is that life seems a touch more leisurely; people seem to want to talk to strangers and make the time to do so.

Ruthwell's other attraction is to be found in a church across the main road, the Ruthwell Cross. This was a preaching cross set up in the seventh century as a centre for worship at a time when the community was too poor to build a permanent church. It is a noble monument, richly carved with biblical scenes crudely but strongly modelled. Oddly, these holy scenes are quite outclassed in terms of sophisticated design by the natural representations on two of the sides. Intricate patterns of leaves and intertwined branches surround animals and birds. Across the cross is a runic inscription, part of Caedmon's poem 'The Holy Rood'. This extraordinary monument should not be here at all, for in 1640 the General Assembly of the Scottish Kirk ordered the demolition of this 'Idolatrous Monument'. The local minister of the day obeyed the letter but not the spirit of the order. The cross was taken down, broken – with great care – and then stored away until the day when attitudes would change. Now it is the glory of the little church; a church, in fact, too small to take it, so it has had to be sunk into a special recess in the floor. Ironically, the action of the General Assembly preserved the cross from three centuries of weathering. So they actually helped keep intact the object they wished to destroy.

The coastline beyond Ruthwell is an area of salt marshes, now a nature reserve, which has its finest moment in winter when the entire Spitzbergen population of barnacle geese arrives here. There is also a special enclosure set aside for the natterjack toad. It must be a problem raising funds for a scheme such as this. The public responds to cuddly animals and it is not too difficult to cash in on the 'aah' factor. Produce a baby badger and you get enough 'aahs' to blow out a large candle. Toad protection is not quite so easily promoted. So it is really charming to find this creature, who even Shakespeare described unfairly as 'ugly and venomous', being given a home of its own. But those who have little enthusiasm for toads, or even geese, can enjoy one of the area's great romantic ruins, Caerlaverock Castle. It really does have everything. There is not one moat, but two, the inner lapping round the walls so that the fortress is itself an island. It is unusual in that it is triangular in plan, with round towers at each corner and double towers covering the entrance, reached by a bridge over the moat. This is a true border fortress fought over time and again, sometimes held by the Scots, sometimes by the English. All this appears in the rugged face it shows to the out-side world, but walk inside and there is an instant transformation. The castle has been tamed, but in a quite astonishing manner. A whole new block was popped down in the middle, described in a contemporary account of 1640 as a 'dainty fabrick'. I am not sure that dainty is the word that comes to mind. What you see is a great sandstone wall, adorned with windows topped by decorated pediments. It is difficult to say why it looks so incongruous: it is, after all, not unusual for castles to become domesticated. It is possibly the nature of the stone, for the new wall looks like a cliff face with unusually sophisticated carved openings, a sort of Scottish Petra.

Non-Scottish visitors are more likely to feel like strangers in a foreign land in Dumfries than almost anywhere else, not because it is in any way outlandish, but because everywhere you turn you are greeted by the name of Robert Burns. There is Burns House, where the poet lived for the last years of his life, and the Burns Centre. When you visit the little eighteenth-century house on the bridge, which one would have thought attractive enough in itself, you find a Burns exhibit. This is a diorama of the view from the house as Burns would have seen it had he been here and looked out of the window. There is no evidence that Burns ever did visit the house, but he might have done, and that is justification enough. The Burns phenomenon is remarkable. There is simply no English equivalent. Everyone it seems can quote lines from Burns and lots of people can manage quite sizeable chunks. Try and think of another English language poet for whom the same could be said. Try and imagine any other poet who is honoured by his own Night with elaborate dinners, not just dinners held for cognoscenti, but dinners attended by people of all sorts throughout the land. Burns has a hold on the national imagination which no other British poet has ever achieved. Perhaps part of the appeal is expressed in his own epithet on William Muir:

> Some rhyme a neebor's name to lash;
> Some rhyme (vain thought!) for needfu' cash;
> Some rhyme to court the country clash,
> An' raise a din;
> For me, an ain I never fash;
> I rhyme for fun.

He also rhymed out of an obvious joy in the exuberant variety of plain, ordinary humanity. If a country has to have a hero, then it could do far worse than Robert Burns. But Dumfries has more than just Burns to offer. One of the great delights can be found near the Burns Centre. The Dumfries museum has – how could it escape it – a Burns collection, but it also has a centrepiece, an old windmill tower at the top of which is a camera obscura. At least no-one can say you are following Burns here; the camera was not installed until after his death.

The scenery of this corner of Scotland is very much its own. It is neither massively rugged like the Highlands, nor neatly manicured like the English Downs. It is neither blatantly picturesque nor overly pretty. It is a lumpy land, where the structure shows through. Rocks poke out at odd angles to break the symmetry of distant hills, spiky shrubs and coarse grasses break up the surface near at hand. It is a busy landscape and it has its surprises. If you turn off the B-road on to the even-less-used minor road to Glenkiln reservoir, then keep your eyes open as you travel, for scattered around the landscape are sculptures, four by Henry Moore, an Epstein and a Rodin. There is a pair of figures by Moore, King and Queen, in the middle of a field looking out over the reservoir.

Actually, they look more like a pair of pensioners who have settled down on a bench to enjoy the view and take the weight off their feet for a while. They do, however, look comfortably at home in the landscape. Rodin's John the Baptist, however, looks just as he should – a wild, naked man defying the elements. Most successful are the abstracts by Moore, which echo without copying the shapes of the landscape. His Standing Figure looks like a prototype for a natural form. The special qualities of these sculptures come from the sense of discovery: they are not signposted, there are no admission charges, they are not even easy to find when you know they are there. It is almost as if they had been abandoned and forgotten. One hesitates to tell people about them, just on the offchance that someone might possibly have found themselves at some time driving this road or walking these hills and then come upon the statues purely by chance. What a wonderful surprise it would be. And even if you dislike all sculpture, the detour gives you some fine scenery. There is a beautiful section through a wooded valley, its floor hazed with bluebells.

Castle Douglas was once a town of considerable importance and still has an air of showing off its finery, its carved shopfronts and an ornamental clock tower that manages to stop just short of out and out vulgarity, but only just. Towns in this part of the world seem to favour clock towers, but this is the most extravagant. Rather calmer pleasures are to be found on the edge of town – a pretty loch with boats, Threeve Castle on an island in the Dee and Threeve Gardens, which experts say should be seen in spring when two hundred varieties of daffodil are in bloom. As one who had always thought a daffodil was just a daffodil, I found the information quite impressive but am still uncertain whether two hundred varieties of daffodil look any better than two hundred daffodils of the same variety.

With the next stop I at least felt myself on surer ground. Gatehouse of Fleet was familiar for two totally different reasons. Firstly it is the setting for one of Dorothy L. Sayers' Peter Wimsey stories, *Five Red Herrings*. This is actually the dullest of the tales since the entire plot depends on the mechanisms of clocks, train timetables and the like and has all the emotional content of a crossword puzzle. What it does have, however, are vivid descriptions of Gatehouse and its surrounding scenery. When the book was published in 1931 the place was, it seems, almost infested with landscape painters, so that the reader is left in no doubt that the area is wholly picturesque. And so indeed it is. But there is another side to Gatehouse of Fleet which is not quite so obvious. Look at Birtwhistle Street and two thoughts may well strike you: Birtwhistle is scarcely a local Scots name and the houses have an English look to them. In fact, Birtwhistle came up here at the end of the eighteenth century, attracted by an area of low wages, to establish a cotton mill. A second mill was soon added, and by the beginning of the nineteenth century they were employing three hundred people, of whom two hundred were children. Gatehouse had joined the industrial revolution. Now the mills down by the river are simply romantic runs and the life of the labouring children scarcely a memory.

The road through Galloway starts by offering you a view of a ruin which most people would regard as perhaps more enticing than an old cotton mill. But Carsluith Castle is really rather incongruous. For a start, it is not a castle at all but a tower house, stern and gaunt enough for a castle admittedly but only dating back to the sixteenth century. It rises up unexpectedly in the middle of a farmyard on the edge of the shore. The road itself now winds gently between the network of small creeks of the estuary and the distant soft plumpness of the hills. For accompaniment at first it has fields and hedges, but as the road climbs higher up the Cree valley its character changes. Now on the one side you have the busy river while on the other is woodland that leans over to give a permanent shade. This is the edge of the Glentrool Forest, but as road and river separate so too the woodland also begins to change. Native pine and broad leaf trees give way to the glum, sterile darkness of the new conifer plantations. Where you do emerge into the light it is to a land cleared, scraped clean and furrowed for more conifers. It may be economically sound and practical but it is unlovely. It is a pleasure to be clear of it.

Pinwherry brings relief from the march of progress. Views open to hills, blotch faced with gorse, while older woodland strides along with the road. Even the railway that arrives to keep you company produces a fine effect with a lattice-girder viaduct. It looks a good line to travel, but the road is also offering its own enticements. You zoom up the steep hill from the river valley to a hillside of tussocky grass and steadily lawn-mowering sheep. The road now runs along the rim of a valley, offering wide views across the river to where the route continues snaking up the opposite hillside. You cross the river again and head towards Dailly on a narrow, winding moorland road. Not many cars seem to come this way, judging by the behaviour of the local cattle. Hearing a car in the distance, they wander down from the hillside, munching, to stand in the middle of the road, blinking at you with mild, brown-eyed interest. They wait while you toot your horn and only when you have edged forward until you are face to face do they decide that curiosity has been satisfied and they shamble slowly out of the way. It is very tempting just to stop and join the cattle in quiet enjoyment of this delectable countryside. It is certainly not surprising to find some grand establishments round here – there must be many a worse place for a country estate. The monks of Crossraguel Abbey certainly knew how to select a good site.

The abbey was established as a Cluniac monastery in 1244 and was used by the Benedictines until the end of the sixteenth century. It is a place of contrasts. At first sight you would take it for a castle, with a tall tower rising up beside the main gatehouse. The tower now houses a collection of stones: Celtic crosses and floriated capitals show how highly decorated the buildings once were. Now the rooms are bare, yet with a hint of domesticity in the stone window seats. The restored chapter house is altogether grander, with an ogee-arched alcove where the abbot sat to preside over meetings. But it is in the more intimate details that the life of the monastery seems to survive. There is a little barrel-vaulted passageway with stone benches on either side, where the monks were freed from the silence imposed in the cloisters. It is easy to imagine them popping in for a natter and a giggle; it must have been hard work remaining pious all the time. There is also one building which might cause a little puzzlement. It stands at the corner of the walls and looks like a pottery kiln or even an exceptionally large bread oven. It is, in fact, a dovecot or, this being Scotland, a doocot.

The approach to the coast is dramatic – a bend in the road and there is the sea and across it the peaks of Arran, while in between is the perfect symmetry of little Ailsa Craig. Tiny as it is and isolated as it is Ailsa Craig still has its castle and lighthouse. Its symmetry declares its origins as a volcanic plug. Arran, even from a distance, conveys a sense of wildness, but this section of the mainland coast is altogether gentler, even urbane. Here one can find one of the great works by one of the key architects of the eighteenth century, Robert Adam, the Father of the Classical Revival. But Culzean Castle owes nothing to the influence of Greece and Rome. It looks instead to its antecedents in a fourteenth-century fortified tower, and Adam's great battlemented house clearly picks up the theme. Yet at the same time no-one could possibly mistake it for a genuine medieval fortress. In between the arrow slits are round-headed windows in relieving arches and even pilasters put in an appearance. It ought to be an impossible amalgam, but it works simply because the rhythms of the building are consistent, with tall windows echoing the upward thrust of the towers. This is mock medievalism with a light touch, set among formal gardens. Inside, the pretence of Scottish baronialism disappears. Just look at the beautiful swirl of the oval staircase, the round drawing room and the delicacy of the plaster ceilings. Whatever message the outside may be giving, the interior makes it clear that this is very much a grand house of the eighteenth century. The other major buildings on the site are those of the home farm, and here Adam felt no inhibitions about building in his own favourite style. Everything is serene, clean and crisp with a prominent archway leading into a courtyard beyond which is the sea. It is almost impossible to imagine it ever being used in earnest. One feels that the cows would have to wipe their feet on a mat before coming in for milking.

The road from Culzean goes along an extraordinary stretch with an equally odd name, Electric Brae. Look at the road and when you think you are going downhill you are actually going uphill and vice versa; it is a perfect and perfectly bewildering optical illusion. It leads down – or should it be up – to Dunure, a good place to pause for beyond it is the built-up coastline. There is not a lot here: a crumbling castle on the headland, a tiny harbour with one or two idling fishing boats, a pleasant pub on the quay and grass to sit on with a view of Arran. Not much – but what more could you ask for? The towns that are soon to follow, however, do turn out to have their own charms and interest. Ayr has a busy harbour, approached through what can only be described as a gateway, and a remarkably handsome bridge actually built in the 1870s but looking as if it could be a century older. The pride of the coast is Irvine. Once this was the seaport that served Glasgow. The Vennel was then the main street, cobbled to give

88

a good grip for the horses that trundled an endless procession of carts to and from the harbour. Now restored, it is a street of great charm and contains the home and workplace of – who else? – Robert Burns. But the much greater restoration scheme is the one that is creating the Scottish Maritime Museum. The obvious prize exhibits are the old vessels in the harbour, notably *Spartan*, a Clyde puffer built for the Admiralty in 1942.

Those whose notions of what a puffer should be, based on the glorious Para Handy stories, may be a mite disappointed. *Spartan*, which began as plain Victualling Inshore Craft Number Eighteen (*VIC 18*), was not only renamed but completely modernised in 1961. Out went the steam engine and in came the diesel. She got a smart new wheelhouse and what is for puffers positively luxurious accommodation. Para Handy used to boast of his clapped out old coaster the *Vital Spark*: 'oh man! she wass the beauty! She was chust sublime! She should be carryin' nothing but gentry for passengers, or nice genteel luggage for the shooting lodges.' *Spartan* comes close to answering the description, though her cargoes were seldom more romantic than bricks and coal. Around her are a variety of other vessels but these are only a part of the story. There are indoor exhibits, examples of industrial machinery from the shipyards, a restored shipyard worker's tenement and a forge. The most important building, however, is the Denny tank. Opened in 1883 it was one of the very first tanks ever built for the testing of ship models. Vessels of all kinds from transatlantic liners to submarines, aircraft carriers to yachts have been put through their paces in miniature before being built for the real high seas. It is not just the tank that is preserved, but also the modelmaking workshop. The Scottish Maritime Museum is still in its infancy, but is already well set for a lusty maturity. After Irvine, Ardrossan is a horrible anticlimax about which the best one can say is that it is a splendid place to leave behind, for it is here that you board the ferry for Arran.

If one is lucky and the weather is kind, then the approach to the island is a magical experience. We travelled in the early evening, when the sun was behind the mountains, obliterating every detail but laying down a carpet of light at their feet. Arran is like Scotland in miniature, with something for everyone. There is jolly holidaying Brodick, which is the destination for the many visitors who leave their cars behind on the mainland, and, at the

other extreme, the rocky peaks of Goat Fell: rough, rugged and
with a real sense of lonely wildness. In between are all kinds of
variations. We chose a leisurely route that seemed to take in a
little of everything, and at the end only wished that there had
been time for a great deal more. It began with as lonely a road
as you will ever hope to find. It runs out through the forest to
a valley of beautiful simplicity. Sliddery Water glides down the
bottom between rounded hills and halfway down you come to
a solitary farm. The lambs in the field walked up to the wall
and cheerfully nibbled at fingers rather more it seemed in hope
than expectation.

The west-coast road confirms the island status, for the leap-
ing, curling road keeps popping up with views across to the long,
fingering peninsula of Kintyre. Drumadoon Bay backed by gently
rounded hills almost demands that you stop careering round in
the car and take pause – or better still take to your feet. The tiny
harbour at Blackwaterfoot curls sheltering arms around a clutch
of little boats and is a pleasant place just to sit and watch nothing
in particular. Equally pleasant is a stroll along the coast, up past
the Iron-Age fort whose ramparts run round to the edge of the
dark cliffs that offer all the protection anyone could ask for. From
here a path wanders down to the shore and brings you to King's
Cave. This dank and gloomy hole is said to be the spot where
Robert the Bruce sat and watched the spider whose persevering
web-building efforts inspired him to continue the struggle against
the English. It is certainly a habitable cave, if not very comfortable,
but romance has to be tempered with the knowledge that almost
every cave in western Scotland seems to claim to be the one true
spot where the Bruce received his inspiration. But you do not
need to worry about historical associations to enjoy a situation
where the birds far outnumber humanity. Gulls screamed in
raucous argument above the cliffs while a cuckoo added its own
impolite commentary on their proceedings. The oyster catchers
down on the shore ignored all this and simply got on with the
serious business of probing for lunch. Back on the clifftop, history nudges your elbow again, for the moorland is pitted with the
circular remains of stone huts which were once home to people
of the Bronze Age. One short walk has taken us from Bronze
Age to Iron Age and medieval legend and, somewhat reluctantly,
back to the present and the road.

The other road across the middle of the island brings you back to busy Brodick but also takes you to the craggy mountains. It is surprisingly easy to leave the car and set out on foot to get, if not the full flavour, at least a taste of the hills. Like all wild upland regions, these hills demand to be treated with respect and only fools attempt long cross-country routes without proper equipment and decent maps. Glen Sannox, however, does offer the possibility of a gentle stroll, albeit with a certain amount of boulder hopping across the mountain stream. The further you go up the valley the grander it becomes until you reach a natural amphitheatre ringed by jagged peaks. The ground rises steeply before you, leading to The Saddle which sits at the centre of the rock ridges that spread in all directions. This is Highland scenery at its best. It was near here on a separate occasion that I was brought by a friend with the promise of seeing golden eagles. We walked up the glen and I kept scanning the crags through binoculars. Was that dark moving spot a distant eagle? Then the real thing appeared with startling suddenness. The bird filled the field of vision as if it might fly straight down the glass towards me. This was, unmistakeably, an eagle. There were, as it turned out, two of them, a pair hunting together covering two flanks of the mountain – wonderful, majestic creatures which sent a thrill right down me. Nothing else seemed to move on the mountainside except one lonely browsing stag. I cannot promise every visitor that they will enjoy such a sight, but Arran will always have something special on offer – even if it is only rain of a heaviness that one thought was limited to the monsoon areas of Asia.

Lochranza seems almost urban after the glens, with its neat villa guest houses. It does, however, have that commodity so rarely met in Scotland, good drinkable real ale, which is a great compensation for some of us. It is a place that has seen better times. The old steamer pier has collapsed, and now the ferry simply runs up to a dull, concrete ramp. But there is compensation in the short trip to the mainland, for the view back to Arran is even better than the view coming over. A practical word of warning to travellers: the ferry only runs in summer, has no reserved places and only takes twelve cars.

Back on the mainland the road nips across the narrow neck of land to West Loch Tarbert and on to Tarbert. This is a spot I fell in love with years ago and have returned to many times since. It may be picturesque but it is still very much a genuine working port – though by no means the easiest to get into by sea. The approach from Loch Fyne is through a slalom course of buoys, and berthing a large vessel is not made any easier by the presence of a little island in the middle of the harbour. Once inside, however, Tarbert is snug as can be, closed round by comfortable hills. It is also a decidedly good-humoured spot. No doubt the local bars do close occasionally but I have yet to visit Tarbert and find them empty. My only regret on this visit was that I was coming by land and not by water.

Ardrishaig, the next port up Loch Fyne, marks the entrance to the Crinan Canal, a short waterway that saves vessels the long voyage round the Mull of Kintyre. Here, if you are in luck, or if not here then somewhere out in nearby waters, you may well see another Clyde puffer. This like the Irvine museum ship is a VIC, the *VIC 32*. She has never been given a more glamorous name, nor has she had her old steam engine replaced. The only way to get the *VIC 32* going is to light the boiler and start shovelling coal. She has seen some changes for she has been converted from cargo carrying to holiday-making, but in every other respect she is a thoroughgoing, geninue coal-fired steamer. It was the *VIC 32* that first brought me to Tarbert and a day spent in the wheel-house is still the second-best way of spending a day in Scotland; the best day is, of course, spent in the engine room, shovelling coal, crawling around the thumping pistons with an oil can and getting gloriously schoolboyishly mucky. But even for those not fortunate enough to be on board, the sight of the puffer trailing streamers of black smoke remains one of the memorable sights of the West Highland coast. This also marks the point where one leaves Loch Fyne and it offers the last chance, not to be missed, to sample the famous local kippers.

The road now runs along by the side of the canal which climbs up to a summit through a succession of locks, and having got there, like the Grand Old Duke of York, it marches down again on the other side. It may save a long trip, but boat crews have to work hard all the same. Cairnbaan provides one last puffer, steaming across the inn sign. The road away from the canal is certainly unusual for this part of the world – dead straight and flat across the estuary, past statue-playing herons. The scenery lacks the obvious Highland grandeur, but these low hills were very attractive to settlers and they are rich in ancient remains. The whole area is spattered with them and it would take a few days to visit them all: the extraordinary and enigmatic rock carvings of Achnabrek, the Iron-Age fortress, the Bronze-Age standing stone. There are a number of sites in the area of Kilmartin and the church itself is home to some famous monuments. There is not much on the outside to suggest anything special. It is a rather plain church with a squat tower and a stepped gable, but inside are richly carved early crosses and out in the graveyard are even more remarkable carved grave slabs. Unfortunately most are displayed in an unremarkable little hut, propped up against the wall as if waiting for collection. The carving itself is lively, with intricate Celtic patterns and recumbent knights, but somehow putting them so obviously on display diminishes rather than enhances them. It is worthwhile, however, wandering around the crowded churchyard to hunt out other slabs, which, if not so grand, do at least have a wholly appropriate setting.

Those without the time for prolonged antiquity hunts can be reassured by the fact that the road passes conveniently close to more than one standing stone. In any case one is easily seduced from ancient sites by the constantly changing and ever more dramatic scenery. Sea lochs bite deep into the land and the road twists and turns, dives downhill and crawls back up again. One moment you are staring west over a rippling loch to the open sea, the next you are looking down a narrow valley to the hills. Along the way are grand establishments such as Barbreck House and scattered settlements. Near Arduaine, a little harbour gets protection from the islands sprinkled over the bay. Kilmelford offers a leafy diversion, a hamlet almost lost in the trees, before a sharp climb over the Pass of Melford brings you down into Oban.

Oban is the area's principal town: part port, part shopping centre, part holiday resort. It developed because it sits at the edge of a splendid natural harbour, where almost anything might be at anchor from a ferry to a barque. The town wanders out along the shore and clambers up the hill behind to its most famous monument, McCaig's folly. This is Scotland's answer to the Colosseum, a huge circular building pierced by Gothic arches, which, if it does nothing else, provides a superb viewpoint. McCaig had it in mind for greater things, part monument, part museum, but he died and no-one else wanted the expense of creating a Roman theatre on a hilltop. So it was never completed and it just sits there, a great classical edifice containing nothing grander than a rather ordinary municipal garden.

The road up Loch Linnhe offers similar scenery to that south of Oban – a castle on an island, water glimpsed through trees, diversions round the lochs that continually thrust into the land. The road bridge across the head of Loch Etive seems an unlikely affair, a mixture of castellated masonry arches and cantilevered steel. It actually works very well visually and was originally used by road and rail, though the rails have now gone. Its stylishness was supplied by its engineer – Henry Brunel, Isambard's son, suggesting that heredity does work sometimes. All the time one is getting nearer to the highest of Scotland's mountains. There is a brief glimpse of the hills of Glencoe as you cross the bridge over Loch Leven, then you see the squat bulk of Ben Nevis and here, you say to yourself, must be the true heart of the Highlands. What you get, however, is a suburban crawl to Fort William and a depressingly large quantity of tourist trash. It does, however, offer an opportunity to leave the car for an excursion which includes a visit to the Isle of Skye and two of the best rail journeys in the country.

5

The Rail Excursion

The railway line from Fort William to Mallaig is altogether splendid, with not a false note struck anywhere along the way. 'Wonderful engineers, the Victorians', a passenger remarked with a touch of awe as the train rounded yet another sweeping curve, crossed a tall viaduct and rushed headlong and headstrong straight at a craggy mountain. So they were, but they can only just claim credit for this line as it was not completed until 1901, the year of the queen's death. It has, in fact, more of the twentieth century about it than the nineteenth, for if you look closely at the grand structures such as the 21-span Glenfinnan viaduct you will find that it is not stone at all but concrete. Yet the planning, the daring, the exuberance and confidence that pushed a railway through such a region is purely Victorian in spirit. And there is no better way to enjoy the line than to travel it as the first passengers did, behind a steam locomotive.

Some people contend that it is simply misty-eyed nostalgia to want to travel by steam, when a far more efficient diesel is available to do the job instead. In strictly practical terms this is quite true, but as this journey is being undertaken purely for pleasure, then steam wins the argument every time. A steam engine is quite unlike a diesel; it talks to you as it goes along. Travelling uphill – and there is plenty of uphill travel on this route – it pants like a middle-aged commuter running for a bus. Reaching a summit it sighs with relief and the harsh pant of the exhaust gives way to more regular breathing. It is easy to sit in the train and simply watch the scenery go by but the steam engine gives you a running commentary on the route you are travelling. Everything about it adds to the pleasure: the heady mixture of coal smoke and hot oil seeps its aroma through the window, there is a smoothness to the sounds in contrast to the harsh clatter of internal combustion. Of course nostalgia comes into it – and why not? But there are still special qualities possessed by a steam locomotive that you will find

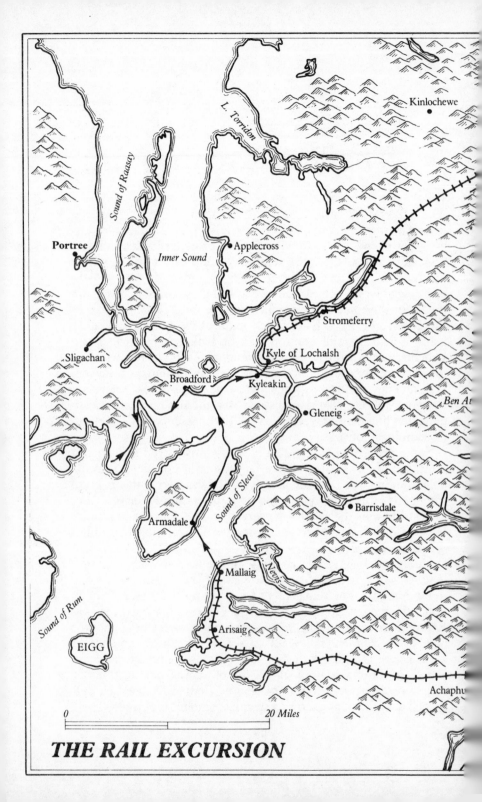

THE RAIL EXCURSION

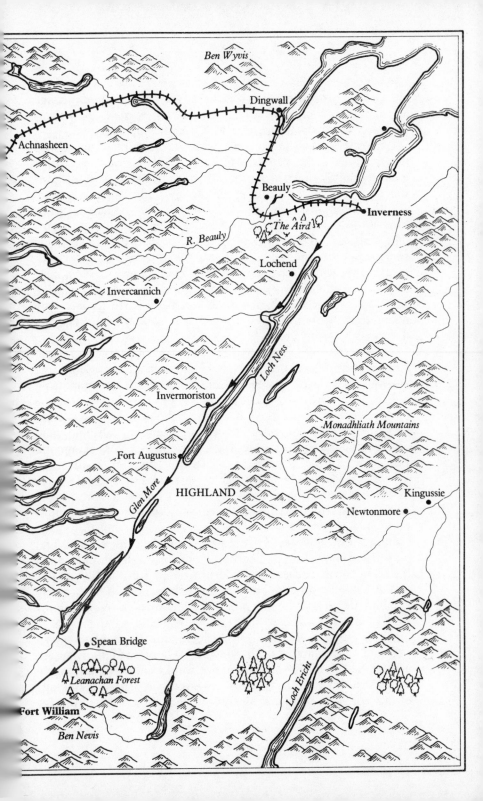

nowhere else. And it not only gives pleasure to the passengers, it is enjoyed by those who watch it go by. On this trip, we were chased all the way to Mallaig by a taxi, sticking out of the back window of which was a small Japanese with a large video camera.

There is a ritual to the start of the journey that begins with the walk down the platform to admire the engine. The driver looks haughtily down from his cab like a character from a pre-war poster, and we look up at him in envy. Then it is time to go and the locomotive slips smoothly out over the flat land between Fort William and Corpach and crosses the Caledonian Canal. The canal was the wonder of its age, designed to take seagoing ships across the middle of Scotland, and it begins here in spectacular style with a series of immense locks, known as Neptune's Staircase. Yet already, when it was opened in 1822, down in the coalfields of northeast England the first locomotives were rattling uncertainly on their way, starting a process that would consign the canal-building age to history.

Once clear of Corpach, the railway builders had little choice over where the line should go. It squeezes into the narrow level strip between Loch Eil and the steeply rising hillside. Stations along the way are rather charming, not unlike overgrown cricket pavilions or summer houses, but once again they are built of concrete. No wonder Robert McAlpine, who was the engineer responsible, was given the nickname 'Concrete Bob'. Each station also seems to mark a change of mood. Loch Eilside has scarcely been left behind by the last wraiths of smoke before the train is heading for the hills, slicing through in rocky cuttings and disappearing briefly into the first of the tunnels. It eventually emerges at one of the best-known and most dramatic sections of the journey. Glenfinnan is a place of disaster. It was here that Bonny Prince Charlie set up his standard and rallied the clans to his cause. The enterprise ended in the bloody defeat at Culloden in 1746, an event which marked the end of the Jacobite dream and the beginning of many years of repression for the Highlanders. The monument is a splendid affair in a magnificent setting at the head of the loch, and the events are now well and truly wrapped up in romance. There was little romance in the realities of those years, and it would not be unreasonable to say that the Highlands never quite recovered from the effects of the Young Pretender's adventure. The one real triumph here is an engineering triumph, the great Glenfinnan viaduct, built on a curve, which has the advantage that passengers can see the locomotive on the bridge from the carriage windows – and a hundred clicking shutters acknowledge the fact.

Beyond Glenfinnan, the line breasts a hill and descends to what is perhaps the loveliest section of all. Loch Eilt, with its background of hills given double value in reflection, and its dotted, tree-clad islands, is everyone's ideal Highland scene. The line, however, leads on providing a new alternation. The hills are as much a part of the scene as ever, but now the sea provides a watery accompaniment. It is a landscape full of delights, of hillside streams which in wet weather foam down the hillside as if a load of cream had been spilt on the summits. There are smaller incidental pleasures – a little whitewashed chapel at Arisaig forming a perfect focal point. And the railway continues to supply its own interest. It marches over the sea at Loch nan Uanh on a 8-arched viaduct and leaps the Borrodale Burn with a central arch over a hundred feet across.

It is not a long journey: just an hour and a half after leaving Fort William the train is pulling into Mallaig. At least there is no sense of anticlimax that this wonderful journey is over. Mallaig itself was developed as a fishing port by the railway company with a new harbour built, inevitably, in concrete. It is still a fishing port, but the days when eighteen special trains a day were needed to take the fish into Glasgow are no more. The ferry, too, has lost something of its old importance. Most drivers prefer the short, cheap, regular service to Skye from the Kyle of Lochalsh. But Mallaig has the great advantage that it really does create a sense of adventuring over the sea to Skye. If you want some easy money find someone who will take a bet on whether or not anyone will start whistling or singing the song: someone always does. There are other advantages to this route when you get across. Kyleakin has developed as holiday Skye, very bungalowed. At Armadale, you are scarcely off the boat before Skye's special qualities are thrust upon you.

Skye, even more than Arran, is an island of many faces and many moods. Fortunately for those who arrive on foot, local bus services cover a great deal of the island and open it up for those who want to continue on foot. Skye offers superb walks and even better climbs. The highest range, the Cuillins, is not really

99

for the walker, for many of the peaks on its narrow, rocky ridge are genuine rock climbs – not difficult but to be taken with due seriousness. That still leaves a vast amount to be enjoyed. The bus route from Armadale takes you to Sligachan near the northern tip of the mountains. This is Scottish mountain scenery at its very best – on the days that you can see it. It is all too easy to spend even quite a long holiday on Skye without having so much as a glimpse of the peaks lurking behind drawn curtains of cloud. Better still is the view from Elgol at the end of the peninsula that looks across Loch Scavaig to the Cuillins. From here you can get a small boat which will take you to one of the wildest spots in Britain, Loch Coruisk. It is possible to get there on foot but not easy, involving an exciting little scramble known, very accurately, as The Bad Step. Coruisk itself seems surrounded by the dark mountains with their spiky, frayed edges. A close acquaintance with the rock reveals it to be gabbro and its appeal to climbers is at once obvious, for it is one of the roughest, coarsest rocks to be found; you stick to it like a fly to flypaper. Many of the British hills are dismissed as minor affairs by those who have known the peaks of the Alps or Dolomites, but not the Cuillins. They may not be as high as their continental counterparts, but here they rise straight from the sea, comfortably passing the mountain qualifying mark of three thousand feet. But it is not just a matter of measurement that makes a mountain; it is the rough grandeur, the challenge thrown down to those who would stand on the summit. The Cuillins more than qualify.

This is Skye at its mountainous best, but it is not the whole of Skye. There is even a quite different, mountainous Skye to be seen, an area of shattered rocks and isolated pinnacles, formed through the centuries by the harshness of wind, rain, ice and snow. It is a fantastical land with its own special appeal. There are other things to enjoy, castles and towns to visit, gentler hills and valleys to walk, but for me the appeal will always lie with its wilder areas where you can walk in solitude. Skye has become a stop off on the tourist route, but there is still space enough to find one's own way and even the most popular spots can hold their surprises. Dunvegan Castle is high on the list of attractions, an ancient fortress with rich historical memories, yet, in spite of its banners and trophies on the walls, now rather cosy. But take a boat trip round the bay and you can go and visit the seal colonies.

With seals, one is never altogether certain who is watching whom. Bewhiskered faces pop up from the waves and you find yourself scrutinised by dark, liquid unblinking eyes. They seem, on the whole, unimpressed.

Skye is a place to linger, but the leaving is made easier by the knowledge that there is another rail journey, which is one of the few that could offer a serious challenge to the claims of the Fort William–Mallaig line to be the most scenic route in Britain. It begins in style, with a station that suggests that the engines really wanted to go all the way to the island, but abandoned the idea at the last moment, for it extends out on a pier. From the very first the line announces itself as a scenic special, as it skirts over the edge of the headland with a succession of little bridges over creeks and a last view of the mountains over the sea. Halts seem to come at the unlikeliest places. Diurnish qualifies as a station, but its lonely platform and single track hurrying away through a seemingly empty land remind one of the sort of station where the sheriff waits for the bad men who are coming to town. Plockton though is quite different, a pleasant little seaside town which it is far easier to reach by train than it is by road. It stands at the mouth of the sea-water Loch Carron. The cliff hugging engaged in by the Mallaig line is nothing compared with that of the route round the loch. It follows every bend and curve of the hillside, then drops right down to the shoreline to wriggle its way around the foot of the cliff. It is joined by the road and when the cliff finally shoulders its way down to the water's edge, road and rail dive through it, each in its own tunnel. Space is found for one station beneath the tall cliffs, but otherwise there is nothing to interrupt this fjord-like passage.

The end of the loch at Strathcarron is marked by what one might call a proper station, with two tracks for passing, two platforms joined by a pretty lattice-girder bridge, built in 1900 by an Inverness foundry and presumably brought here as an early cargo for the new railway. The main buildings are attractive – rather more so than many of the scattered houses the station serves. For a time the railway engineers could relax, for the line runs comfortably on the broad floor of the glen, but as the land dips away towards Loch Dughaill the line keeps its level, seems indeed to climb as it vanishes into the woodland. At one point there is a flash of a view: a bridge over a river, rushing and cascading

101

through a lush vegetation of rhodedendra and azaleas. This detour was caused by the owner of the lodge who refused to sell his land and banished the trains to an outer edge and a switchback ride, which produced one bizarre accident. A mixed train was being made up. Passengers were settled in their carriages, which were being coupled up to trucks of timber. Unfortunately, the job was bungled and the trucks began to roll away down the slope. It was then that the driver determinedly set off in pursuit of his errant waggons. The latter gathered speed until they reached the bottom of the slope and then they rattled on up the slope on the other side of the dip until their momentum was lost. The driver charging towards them then saw to his horror that his trucks were on their way back again, dashing towards him. He decided on discretion and leapt from his cab. The passengers were not given the option, and there were a good many sore heads that night.

Diversion over, the route begins to fall into a pattern – forced on to a narrow ledge beside the lochs it emerges into the broader glen where the river winds and twists under low bridges. Then there is a panting little dash up the hillside and a gentle coast down to the next loch and the next glen. The immediate view is of gentle slopes of bracken and heather dotted by boulders, beyond which the more distant mountains stand aloof, even in summer flecked with unmelted snow in the darker corries. Then at Contin it all changes. The Highlands give way to the gentler hills of the east coast. The land no longer stretches away to distant horizons, but is broken and divided by walls and hedgerows. The green of fields is interrupted by the startling yellow of rape, far more glaring and obtrusive than the gorse in the moorland.

At Dingwall the line from Kyle of Lochalsh comes to an end at a junction with the east-coast main line. The station has a suitably important air. A canopy is carried over the platforms on decorative iron pillars, and the footbridge is a close relation to the one at Strathcarron. The style of the main building is difficult to describe: Scottish baronial cottage would seem to be the nearest. It is red sandstone with granite dressings and embellished with arrow slits and stepped gables, but the effect is definitely lessened by the very domestic chimneys. It is now home to two unlikely bedfellows: the Christian bookshop and the Shunters Bar. Theoretically I was to travel on by train to Inverness but in the spring of 1989 a great flood came down the river Ness, sweeping away

the rail bridge, so that passengers had to complete the next part
of the journey by bus.

It was interesting to catch glimpses of what we had missed.
Paradoxically, having left the Highlands for the coastal plain the
engineers found the task of railway building to be, if anything,
even harder. The glaciers of the ice age had scraped out long
valleys in the west, but here the land is all humps and hollows.
A railway would either have to meander on a hopelessly serpentine course or simply tackle the lumps as they come. It does the
latter: constantly vanishing from sight down deep cuttings. The
line curves round the end of the bay, while the road now takes
a more direct route via the new bridge across the Moray Firth.

A later trip revealed some of the things I had been unable
to see previously. Here was a swing bridge over the Caledonian
Canal, not unlike the one back at the other end of Fort William.
Where the western end has Neptune's Staircase to admire, here
the great canal is built out into deep water, carried in a vast artificial
embankment. The chief engineer was Thomas Telford, and there
are verses in his honour carved on a plaque outside the company
offices. The lines by Southey are very complimentary, but not,
alas, very good. The other sight I wanted to see was the bridge.
It seems incredible to think that this shallow, gurgling river could
ever have exerted such force. It splashes along as placid as can
be, but the evidence of its fury was there. The old stone viaduct
had stood for 137 years but now it was simply torn apart. One
span strode boldly from the shore and after that there was just
a serrated edge and a few stones stuck up from the river bed. It
was a salutary reminder of the power of natural forces. The latest
information at the time of writing is that rail traffic should have
returned during 1990.

What does Inverness itself have to offer? Two very Scottish
treats, a whisky distillery and a prize haggis maker, the perfect
combination. The river is still at the heart of the town and has an
attractive suspension bridge for pedestrians, but otherwise this is
an unpretentious spot, not ugly but not possessing any outstanding
buildings either.

The circuit has to be completed by road. The bus skirts interminable Loch Ness. It is not, by any means, the most beautiful of
the Scottish lakes – too long, and too monotonous. But, of course,
it has the monster. One would not like to suggest that monster

spotting has been one of the great PR exercises of the age, but it is doubtful if there would have been the same rush of tourists without the lure of Nessie. They are certainly fully catered for. It is hard to find a layby on the main road which does not have its kilted bagpiper ready to pose for the camera and play 'Amazing Grace' at the drop of a bonnet. It sometimes seems that you cannot see the scenery for pipers and Nessie souvenirs – Nessie eggs, Nessie teatowels and even, Heaven help us, Nessie burgers. It actually comes as a relief when Loch Ness ends, for the rest of the journey has far more variety and interest.

Fort Augustus is always a popular spot, for the Caledonian Canal again goes through one of its periodic leaps up the hillside through five interconnected locks. Nowadays they are mainly used by pleasure boats, yachts and cruisers and the occasional fishing boat. It is a slow business going up and down these locks, and there was a suggestion once that boats would be taken on specially adapted rail trucks over the Kyle of Lochalsh–Inverness line, but nothing ever came of it. But though it may all be frustratingly slow for the boaters it provides endless fascination for the spectators. The road continues to follow the canal and the scenery is pleasantly varied, dominated by the steadily increasing bulk of Ben Nevis, announcing the fact that Fort William lies just ahead. Then it is time to resume the journey and start to head back towards England.

6

Fort William to the Borders

At first the route south simply retraces the path taken up to Fort William, but now instead of crossing the head of Glencoe, it turns east for the pass. By far the best approach is on the minor road through the village. It does not plunge you straight into the darker aspects of this sadly notorious valley. In fact, the first thought is what a charming spot this is, with the little folk museum telling stories not of bloody massacre but of the everyday life of hard working people. The road wanders through woodland, so that the mountains are no more than suggestions, hinted at by the rock that insistently pokes out between the trees. Just before the Clachaig Inn, a path leads through the woods. You walk softly on a way carpeted with pine needles, which sneaks you in past high jutting rocks into a silent conifer forest, dark and, it seems, slightly melancholy. Is this just suggestability, the knowledge of what lies ahead and its place in history? Maybe so, but there is a curious lifelessness and stillness about the wood. The end of the walk comes at Signal Rock. It was here, it is said, that on a dark winter morning in 1692 a fire was lit to set the massacre of Glencoe on its way.

The massacre is remembered not so much for the numbers killed as for the treachery and the breaking of all the rules that govern Highland life. The Macdonalds and Campbells had feuded for years and no doubt each was to blame. Cattle raiding was simply an accepted part of the life of the region. It was the Jacobite rebellion that brought a new element to the equation. The Macdonalds' chief was late in swearing his allegiance to the king in England, William of Orange. He had prevaricated, left it to the last moment and in the end was held up by bad weather and swore his oath a few days late. It was all the excuse his enemies needed. And it was here that the bitterness entered the story. Captain Robert Campbell brought his troops to Glencoe, asked for and received hospitality, but carried with him orders

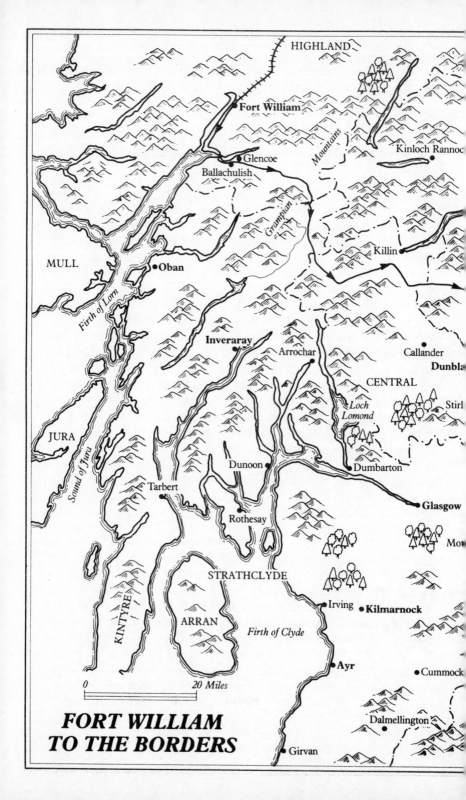

FORT WILLIAM
TO THE BORDERS

HIGHLAND

Fort William

Glencoe

Ballachulish

Grampian

Mountains

Kinloch Rannoc

MULL

Oban

Killin

Callander

Dunbla

Inveraray

Arrochar

CENTRAL

Loch Lomond

Stirl

Firth of Lorn

JURA

Dunoon

Dumbarton

Glasgow

Tarbert

Sound of Jura

Rothesay

Mo

STRATHCLYDE

Irving

Kilmarnock

KINTYRE

ARRAN

Firth of Clyde

Ayr

Cummock

0   20 Miles

Dalmellington

Girvan

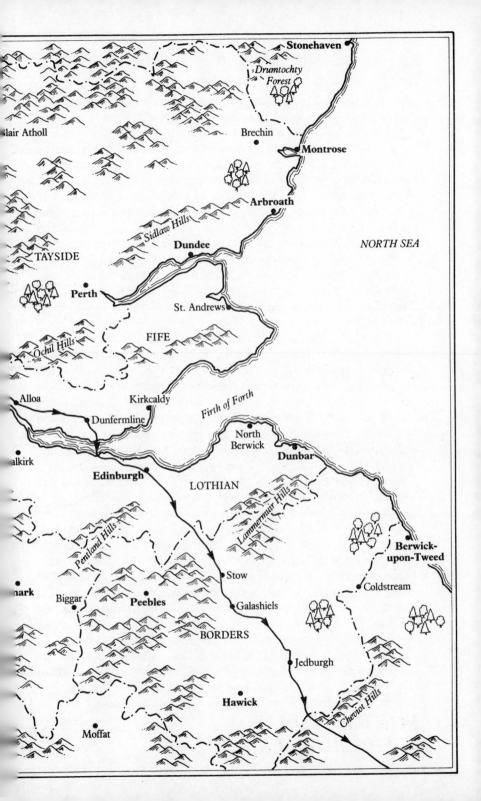

'to fall upon the Rebells, the McDonalds of Glenco, and putt all to the Sword under seventy'. Immoral, amoral, the Highland clans might have been but one law was sacrosanct: hospitality must never be abused. Yet the soldiers under Campbell were to rise early in the morning and begin the butchery. In the end, it was a miserable botched affair. Some said the soldiers had little stomach for what they had to do; others, less charitably, put it down to incompetence. Less than fifty were killed – hundreds escaped. But even now if you stand on Signal Rock and look across at the cold, inhospitable mountains it is impossible not to feel not only for those who died by the sword, but for the others who fled, half naked, to the snow-covered mountains. Many places have been the scene of dark deeds, but there is something in the still woods and the high mountains that bear down on the narrow pass that gives Glencoe its unforgettable atmosphere. The memory of 1692 will, it seems, never go away.

The road through the pass itself is as dramatic as any in the country, and it makes little difference what the weather does. Sunshine lightens the gloom and reveals the tall crags that rise up on either side in impressive array; clouds that come down low convert the pass into a claustrophobic tunnel, dark and menacing. Glencoe can be almost unbearably oppressive, yet if you walk in the hills, perhaps following the zigzag route known as the Devil's Staircase, all this doomladen course of history seems to slide away in the clear air of the peaks. But, for true desolation, for a complete sense of being in a barren wasteland, then nothing can match Rannoch Moor. The mountains drop to foothills, then to humps rising above a dank, watery landscape, treeless apart from a few struggling shrubs bent by the wind like wizened old men. Once it was forest and the petrified remains of giant trees still litter the bogs, but now Rannoch Moor simply seems as cheerless a place as one could find. The road mostly skirts its edge and most people are content to leave it at that. But in a country whose empty spaces are steadily being filled, the moor does offer an interlude of genuine wildness.

Bridge of Orchy appears without much sign of a bridge. It is there, tucked away behind the hotel, and once carried the military road built by General Wade to ease troop movements in the years following the Jacobite rebellion of 1745. You can still follow the old road from here, past the Inveroran Hotel and out over the hills back towards Glencoe. Much of it still has traces of its old cobbled surface and it remains a clear feature on the ground. Long after the military lost interest in it, the road was used by drovers bringing their cattle to market. Now it forms part of a long-distance footpath, the West Highland Way. It makes a pleasant diversion to wander the old route, though trees and rivers are to be avoided, particularly as evening settles in, for then it becomes the haunt of some of the most ferocious midges it could be one's misfortune to meet.

An overnight stop at Inveroran brought a perfect illustration of how suddenly the weather can change, and how the mood of the area changes with it. The previous day had been bright and clear, and the overhead parade of towering clouds seemed to shrink the mountains, reducing their stature. The next day, rain clouds hung tattered curtains of grey over the tops. The hills seemed literally to reach the heavens. Days such as this also have their splendours. There is a reminder as you come down over the hill to Tyndrum that bad weather is not unknown in these parts. There is a gate at the bottom ready to be swung across the road, with the notice 'Road Closed. Snow'. A sign also informs you that you are leaving Highland and entering Central. Fortunately, whatever administrators may decree, the scenery pays no attention. There are changes, however, and they are not all welcome. Roads have been improved to make journeys easier. The result is that drivers can now dash at speed through this wonderful scenery, and because they speed the authorities then need to put up crash barriers that might look at home on the M25 but are a hideous eyesore in the Scottish mountains. Near Crianlarich one can look wistfully at the old road with its border of mellow stone walls but not use it. By way of compensation, the nearby farm provides you with a sight of its herd of Highland cattle: hearthrugs with horns.

Gradually, almost imperceptibly, the landscape has begun to change. The hills are a little further apart, the glens that bit wider. Outlines become smoother; fewer rock ridges mark the horizon. Farms are still dependent on livestock, but one begins to see signs of the infield-outfield system. It was once universal: sheep and cattle grazed free on the uplands through the summer while the farmer tended the meadows that would provide the winter feed. Down in the valley you can see the patchwork of fields with their stone-wall boundaries. Just when you are beginning to think that the wilder Highlands have been left behind, you come to Glen Ogle.

When the Caledonian Railway came to build a line up the glen, the navvies christened it 'the Khyber Pass'. One sees what they mean, for it must have presented an extraordinarily difficult task. The line runs high up the western side of the valley, crossing the numerous gullies on a series of bridges and viaducts. Now it is only used by walkers, and reading some accounts of train journeys it is perhaps as well. On one memorable occasion in the winter of 1881, the night mail left Stirling on Friday and reached Oban on Tuesday. But even when seen from the road, it is still an impressive undertaking. It is the last glimpse of the true mountain scenery, for after passing along the edge of Loch Earn, you come upon something quite unknown in the Highlands, hedgerows.

Now you are at a genuine division between Highland and Lowland, not a line drawn by administrators on a map, but one caused by natural forces deep below the ground. You are about to pass over the fault line, which if not on the scale of the San Andreas fault in California still continues to give the area the occasional very minor shake. As you come into the town of Comrie you see an attractive high arched bridge over the river. If you cross the bridge, the road will bring you to a little building, like a gazebo on a hillside – the Comrie Earthquake House. In 1839 the local postmaster, Peter Macfarlane, devised scales to measure earth tremors and his friend the shoemaker, James Drummond, kept the records. They sent a paper to the British Association and as a result a committee was set up to investigate Scottish earth-quakes and the Earthquake House was built. Originally tremors were measured using a pendulum, but that has been superseded by more modern equipment, still in place in the gazebo on the hill. Comrie itself is a surprisingly delightful and friendly spot. Everyone says 'good morning' as you pass in the street. And somewhere there must be a persuasive sign painter, for there are few places with as many signs hung up as this, and so many are witty and original. The chippy has fish and chips in newspaper on one side and a contentedly munching customer on the other. The toy shop has a doll's house, closed on one side, open on the other to show the rooms, all occupied by dolls, including a kilted dad. Perhaps it is a polite nod up the road to the Tartan Museum where visitors are invited to trace their clans and, of course, buy their tartan. Even the church has its painted sign of loaves and fishes.

Scenic changes become ever more pronounced as you come away from Comrie. Hills are grassy and divided into fields; woodland appears with silver birch, hawthorn and oak. Even when you climb up to the moorland with its pale tufts of reedy grass giving way to heather on the higher slopes, you are still aware of the farmsteads with their surroundings of brilliant green, the lush grasslands being nurtured ready for winter. The scenery is a Neapolitan icecream arrangement of browns and purples at the top, pallid moorland grasses in the centre and bright green in the valleys. The further south you go, the more the changes become apparent. The scale reduces, a road is hemmed in by an avenue of chestnuts, ploughed fields show a rich red earth. You are even beginning to approach something suspiciously like an urban area, as the intervals between towns get shorter and shorter.

Dunblane is chiefly notable for its cathedral, which has not had a happy history. The only remains of the original Norman church are the lower stages of the tower. The main structure was built between the thirteenth and fifteenth centuries, but in the sixteenth century the nave roof collapsed and remained in a state of ruin until reconstruction work began in 1886. It was not completed until 1917 and the result is a curious *fin de siècle* mixture that is strongly expressed in the windows. Like them or not, they are an inescapably dominating presence. It is like a meeting between some of the wilder excesses of art nouveau and the dreamiest sentimentalism of the pre Raphaelites. Adam and Eve look so soppy that you really cannot blame the angel for bundling them out of the garden. The animals going into the ark on the other hand are full of vigour and movement, created by strong, sweeping lines and swirls of brilliant colour – reds and blues and purples. All in all, Dunblane cathedral is quite a curiosity. The town itself could never be called that. It is sturdy, even perhaps a little stolid. Its virtues are typified by the Chapter House of 1624 with its rough-cast walls set off by massive stone quoins and surrounds. One begins to realise that if the scenery is not perhaps what it was, the towns and their architecture are going to offer adequate compensation. Even better can be expected when scenery and buildings combine to produce something quite extraordinary.

To the south of Dunblane, two piles of volcanic rock rear up from the plain, each capped with buildings. The first appears a fantasy, a conical hill with a rotten-tooth top, reminiscent of Mervyn Peake's Gormengast, but before you can reach it you have to go through Bridge of Allan, the very opposite of fantasy. This is the town of sedate, well-mannered Victorian villas, with prosperity discreetly on show. Then you climb the hill – literally, for the car park is at the bottom – to the tower which turns out to be a fantasy indeed. The Wallace memorial is as unmistakably Victorian as the villas, an outrageous piece of mock medievalism full of the strangest motifs, including a stone rope that winds itself in and out of the building as though mooring it to the ground. From the top of the 220ft tower you can look over to the Trossachs and to Stirling, the other castle on the hill which, though genuine, cannot begin to compete with this splendid imitation. The monument celebrates Sir William Wallace, who in 1297 led his troops to victory over the English at the Battle of Stirling Bridge. This is not perhaps the ideal spot for an English visitor, not because of its decidedly enthusiastic praise of all things Scottish, but because one is left in no doubt that, in the quarrels between England and Scotland, right and virtue lay entirely with one side. There are no prizes offered for guessing which side that is.

The monument is a romantic building in a romantic setting. It is interesting to leave it and head for a genuine medieval building in a setting as unromantic as one can imagine. Cambuskenneth Abbey lies at the end of a suburban street off Alloa Road. It seems to have few visitors, yet is a place of rich historical associations. It was founded in 1147 as a house of Augustinian canons and the Scottish Parliament met here in 1326. James III was buried here and his tomb was restored at the order of Queen Victoria. Of the abbey itself, however, all that remains above ground is the tower with an attractive vaulted room at the base. It looks at first to be plain to the point of dullness, but then you see the gargoyles: knights' heads, grimacing faces, a really evil little demon by the staircase turret and, inexplicably, one pig. It makes a pleasant overture to the main work that lies ahead, Stirling.

One of the sadnesses of modern travel is the ease with which you miss places altogether. I have often come this way, but always it seems en route to somewhere else, dashing down the motorway. Now I discovered one of the most rewarding places in Scotland. It is like old Edinburgh with a fraction of the crowds and an even smaller fraction of the tourist trappings. Everything is there, squashed together on a tiny hilltop site. It is, in fact, this very shortage of space that gives Stirling much of its character. The temptation is to charge straight up the hill towards the castle, but it is worth pausing to look at the two bridges. The New Bridge was actually built in 1831 to the design of Robert Stevenson, not one of the best known of engineers, but it provides another link with Edinburgh for he was also responsible for that city's Regent Bridge. Alongside is the Auld Brig, some four centuries or so older, yet what strikes one is not the differences but the similarities, the sense of continuity that comes not so much from conscious decisions as from the limits imposed by the use of stone. Structural necessities as much as aesthetic choices determine the shape of arches and the width of spans. Even when you get up the hill, it is still no bad thing to advance slowly on the castle, to enjoy the wealth of fine buildings that surround it.

Bruce of Auchenhowie's house demonstrates perfectly how you can make the best of a narrow site. No need to waste space inside on a staircase; put it in a turret that can project out on to the pavement. There is a wonderful solidity about houses such as this which comes largely from the way they are built. Technically the walls are random rubble, which simply means that they are built of unevenly sized stones which have been assembled in a complex jigsaw pattern and have been left to show their rough faces to the world. So although the house may be as well proportioned as a Georgian terrace, the effect is altogether homelier. It is a grand house certainly but looks and is lived in, part of a living community, just as it was in the days when the Flesh Market was held outside the front door. 'Homely' is not, however, a description that could be applied to every building on the hill.

Just around the corner is the Guildhall, looking out over a bowling green which has been there since 1712. Members of the guild who fell on hard times could be cared for at Cowane's Hospital, built in the mid-seventeenth century. Mr Cowane was not a gentleman who believed in doing good by stealth. A plaque informs you that he built it, his statue stands over the entrance and his initials are to be found all over the building. As you get nearer to the castle so the pattern of development becomes clearer, and the nearer you get to the outer walls the grander the houses become: an aristocratic pecking order. Mars Wark is not, as it might appear, a city gate but a private house built by the Earl of Mar around 1570 when he was governor of the castle. It is all very ornate and high on dignity: coats of arms are as widespread as Cowane's initials on the hospital and serve much the same function, to remind you who paid for such splendour. The house opposite looks more like a French chateau than a Scottish house, but it was built for William, Earl of Stirling in the seventeenth century, a time when there were close ties between the Stuarts and the French. Its sophisticated finery hides thwarted ambitions. It was hoped that with the restoration of the Stuarts to the throne Stirling would once more enjoy the splendour and importance it had once known. It never did. Now the house, Argyle's Lodgings, is the most unlikely and grandest youth hostel one can imagine.

The castle does not suffer from comparisons with the splendours around it, unless one comes expecting some great fortress. The defences are there, but inside are the comfortable domestic apartments of the Stuart kings. Even the walls, when seen from inside, are not so very stern. They are richly decorated, and somehow their defensive role cannot be taken too seriously when you find the first things they are protecting are a pretty little garden and bowling green. Some of the buildings have elaborate exteriors with rich carvings; others reserve their best effects for the interiors. In later years, the castle suffered from being used as a barracks and the wonder is that so much survived. A notable feature of the King's Own Hall was the array of ceiling bosses, the Stirling Heads. Mercifully they were saved and put on display. These were not just any old heads, carved and put up for decoration, but portraits of real people, full of vigour and personality. Everyone was represented from the haughtiest courtier to the court jester. Equally remarkable is the Chapel Royal of James VI, which is not quite so grand as it appears at first glance. At the top of the walls are *trompe l'oeil* windows – much cheaper than the real thing. Brocade covers the otherwise rather plain walls. Furnishings were kept to a minimum: a pulpit for the preacher, a chair for the king and a great deal of standing room for everyone else. The Great Hall suffered more than most of the building, when it was sub-divided to create barrack rooms. Now masons are at work restoring the ashlar front and the whole building is slowly returning to its former glory.

114

The castle is more than just an appendage to Stirling, it is the very heart of the place. In its rise and decline you can chart the rise and decline of the city; in its renewal you can see a growing realisation that Stirling is a place of special qualities. The town that spreads out below the castle is full of character, with the occasional outstanding building. There has been a prison at the Tollbooth since the fifteenth century, though the present one is a comparative newcomer of 1705. They were still holding public hangings on the gallows outside as late as 1843. But as with the aristocratic houses on the crest of the hill, the houses here have a solid worth. Broad Street is just that, and is unmistakably Scottish, not just in the details such as dormers and stepped gables, but in the stern rigour of the facades. But what makes it so appealing is that this is not an area given over to tourism. The houses are homes to families; the shops sell real goods, not just souvenirs. If I had to take a visitor to see a town which somehow epitomised the best of Scottish values and history and had to choose between Stirling and Edinburgh, the temptation to come to Stirling would be strong. Though if the same visitor announced that they were enthusiasts for shopping, I might have to change my mind. There is no Princes Street here.

The road from Stirling to Alloa runs between hills; natural on one side, manmade on the other, the Ochil Hills to the north, colliery spoil heaps to the south. Alloa announces itself first to the nostrils, with the sweetly pungent smell of the brewery. Beyond the town the country is gently rural with the occasional colliery. It is admittedly somewhat alarming to find oneself back at Comrie, but be reassured that this is not the same Comrie. It cannot quite match the charm of the first, but it does have a little prospect tower on the hill. Dunfermline soon appears as an exciting spot – once you have found a way in. For some reason, the local authorities seem to want to keep that a secret. It is worth the effort for Dunfermline does have something for everyone. There is, at one end of the scale, a model and moral story of self help. Edward Carnegie was born here in a modest weaver's cottage, went to America, made a fortune and then gave away literally hundreds of millions of dollars in charity. This should be a genuine 'rich man in his castle, poor man at the gate' story, for the cottage does lie almost within the shadow of the old royal palace. You may draw whatever moral you wish from the fact that the ancient palace of kings is a ruin, albeit a romantic one, perched high over a deep glen, and the cottage was the birthplace of a man who was to become one of the richest in the world. Perhaps the line will have to be rewritten: 'the poor man in his castle, the rich man at his gate'.

Next to the palace are scant monastic remains. Part of the abbey was in fact converted to create the palace, but the church still stands. Nothing in the approach prepares you for Dunfermline abbey. The impact of the place is extraordinary, but it is very important to approach in the right way, entering at the west end. The nave is almost literally stunning. It stops you dead in your tracks, overwhelmed by sheer brute power. Massive pillars march down the nave, the last pair incised with a typical Norman chevron pattern. It is an architectural expression of a simple faith in a spiritual power that is just that, a power – as real a power as that of a feudal lord. The eye is drawn towards the last two columns, with their insistent rhythmical pattern focussing attention on the altar. There are great churches which compel you to hunt out the telling detail. You can do that here, and discover an almost perfect Norman doorway, but that is not the real message the church is sending out. Everything, inside and out, has the same monumentality: even the buttresses have no truck with Gothic frippery. Simple solemnity is all.

Just when you think that you have got the measure of the abbey, you find it is not one church but two. The other end of the building is the parish church of the nineteenth century. It is full-blooded Gothic revival. During its building, the tomb of Robert the Bruce was discovered and he was reburied here in style. His name is spelt out in stone in the parapet of the tower, a truly horrible device which could only be improved by the use of a large sledgehammer. It is the one wholly false note in the entire building. What can the rest of the town do to compete? It has city chambers in full-blown Scottish baronial style, but it is a walk in the park that reveals the surprises. Why is there a steam locomotive outside the cafe? Who built the gloomy brothers Grimm staircase to the ruined tower?

The approach to Edinburgh is a mixture of excitement aroused and disappointment. First, you have to make quite sure that when you come to cross the Firth of Forth you stay in the outside lane, otherwise fate will certainly decree that you will cross with a truck on the inside depriving you of a sight of the famous railway bridge. Its outline is as famous as Sydney harbour bridge, though scarcely as graceful as it humps its way across the water. If it had been built as originally planned it would have been a very beautiful structure: a pair of suspension bridges meeting at a central tower on the island of Inch Garvie. Whether it would still be there is a different matter. It was the Tay railway bridge disaster that sent the engineers scuttling back to their drawingboards. The decision was taken, very wisely, to abandon elegance in favour of safety. So we have the present solution, very impressive, a great piece of engineering, but no beauty.

Once across the Forth there is a long run in through the suburbs to the centre of Edinburgh, with almost nothing of real interest to catch the attention. There was a momentary hope of better things as a fine martial gateway appeared with bold castellations, but behind it was nothing more romantic than a bus station. Edinburgh itself is not one city but two, as different as can be. Logic suggests that you should start with the old and, if you are a motorist, necessity may well make the choice for you, since parking in the new is a virtual impossibility.

The old city sits up high on the rock and looks its age. Wheel-chattering cobbled streets intertwine with little closes and wynds. You can see how it all started out quite sensibly with the castle and the road leading up to it providing an obvious axis for development. But everyone wanted to cram in, and shopkeepers above all wanted to face out on to the main street. Squeezed on to a narrow frontage, there was nowhere to go but up. The builders of Edinburgh beat the builders of Manhattan to that solution by a good few centuries. You can see it all work in the building known as Gladstone's Land. In the early seventeenth century there was a tavern in the basement and a couple of small booths opening on to the street with five floors of living accommodation above that. It is, if you like, an early-seventeenth-century block of flats with a shop on the ground floor. The squeezing process had its limits, but the efforts to fit everyone in gave Edinburgh its unique character – of steps hustling up and down the hill, of little openings and secluded courts, of narrow passages and surprise views. Today, this is largely tourist Edinburgh, with the castle and the tartan souvenirs, but it is still a good area for the wanderer who enjoys hunting out the secret places.

Once the old town was full, there was nothing to do but start again. If Gladstone's Land typifies the old, Charlotte Square characterises the new. A second city was created, a planned city on a formal grid, enlivened by squares and circuses. The north side of Charlotte Square is New Edinburgh at its most sophisticated. This is Robert Adam as one expects to find him, strictly formal, severely classical. No need here to worry about space for there was ample room to spread. The emphasis is all on the horizontal, with gables at the ends of the terraces echoing, without imitating, the central pediment. You could hardly find a greater contrast than that between medieval and Georgian Edinburgh. If anyone only has time to see two buildings in the entire city, then Gladstone's Land and Number 7 Charlotte Square, refurbished as The Georgian House, are the two that will give you the nearest thing to an overall survey. Most people, however, will not be content with just two buildings. It is a capital city with the range of buildings one would expect, including a full set of museums. Many have the advantage of offering a great deal, but on a manageable scale. The National Gallery of Scotland, for example, provides a whistle-stop tour of world art. Masterpieces in plenty for you to gaze upon, from Rubens' Salome with the ample, quivering flesh of a Turkish belly dancer, to Impressionist views of the Thames. There are the occasional quirks thrown in, such as the famous skating clergyman, blissfully aloof and unaware of his incongruity. There are exotic botanic gardens, all very luxuriant, and a Royal Museum which is itself a Victorian masterpiece. But this cannot be a guide to every attraction in Edinburgh. The best advice is to roam, preferably without the benefit of maps, following your own instincts in the old city. It is made for mooching. Decide what you want to see and go straight there in the New. The wide spaces may give the place a gracious charm, but they are hard on the feet. Then when you have had your fill of the crowds, move on, when you will discover a remarkably empty landscape waiting for you.

The Moorfoot Hills to the south of the city seem totally uninhabited, smooth and green they roll onwards like a heaving sea with grazing sheep as the flecks of foam. Villages are scarcely more than hamlets, but there are reminders of packhorse days in the bridge at Stow with its three tall, unevenly matched arches. The local economy depended – and to an extent still depends –

on the wool from the sheep of the hills. Galashiels is very much a wool town, with an interesting history. The undyed wool from black and white sheep was mixed to create plaid. With the advent of the Romantic movement things Highland came very much into fashion. Plaid benefitted, helped by the needs of those taking outside seats on stage coaches to wear something that would prevent them freezing to death. This is no hyperbole, passengers really did die from cold on winter journeys. The local form of cloth was known as 'tweel' but a local clerk from nearby Hawick, whose writing was not as it should have been, despatched a load to London in 1832. The recipients misread the word as tweed and the name stuck. Tweel was, after all, only a variation of the common twill: tweed was distinctive and unique. Manufacture moved from cottage to mill and the mills are still dominant buildings in the town. Peter Anderson's is a typical small weaving mill, originally powered by water turbine. It is still at work but has also added a very good little museum and offers factory tours which end inevitably at the mill shop. Tweed and tartan rule Galashiels as they have since the first mill was built nearly two centuries ago.

The man who did more than anyone to promote the romantic view of the Highlands, and indeed the romantic view of much else, was Sir Walter Scott. His medievalism may have had more to do with historical wishful thinking than any recognisable reality but no-one could doubt its popularity. There is a splendid opportunity to see the past repackaged at Melrose. Here is the medieval abbey church and the house Scott based on its themes and motifs. One thing at least can be said: Scott could hardly have chosen a better model. Melrose Abbey is the perfect foil to Dunfermline. Where the one has all the solemn purity of Norman architecture at its best, here one is faced with Gothic, often at its most fantastical. Just look at the delicately decorated ogee arches that cover the simple stone seats of the cloisters, the beautifully carved foliage of the capitals and the exquisite vaulting. Even the mutilated statue of the Virgin remains startlingly fresh. The sway of the body which balances the weight of the child held on the hip is clearly conveyed under the sculpted folds of the drapery. Richer still are the figures that decorate the niches that surround the south doorway. You can see how it must have appealed to Scott and what he did with it. Abbotsford House was built between 1817 and 1822 and it is pure romance, with all the trimmings of armour

119

and trophies. It is an idealised recreation of the medieval past, minus the discomfort. It is one of those places which accepts no halfhearted response: one either succumbs totally to its panache or rejects the whole thing as phoney.

Abbeys are certainly a feature of the main lowland towns. Jedburgh is one of the four founded by David I at the beginning of the twelfth century. It has a wonderfully unfussy simplicity which creates effects from a sense of rightness rather than by elaboration of detail. Arches gradually diminish as you look up from the aisle to the triforium and the clerestory: first single arches, then double, and finally a regular arcade. The elements are nearly all pure Romanesque in the main body of the church, but others have also been at work. The west end was Gothicised with pointed arches and a fine rose window. Then in 1681 the Earls of Lothian acquired the north transept for themselves and proceeded to get buried there, not perhaps in style, but certainly in pomp. Even more elaborate is the west processional doorway 'restored' to what it never was. It is a courtesan in a nunnery.

The old abbey buildings have been excavated and what a pleasure to find the effort has been made to make the remains comprehensible. Everyone knows the feeling of wandering around such a site to be confronted by a 6in high square of stone walls and a little plaque saying 'frater' or 'lavatorium'. One stares for a moment trying to look intelligent and then moves on to something a little more comprehensible. Here they have provided very full notices and added pictures to show how the buildings probably looked. So, to one's surprise, one discovers that 'the west range' probably appeared very like a nineteenth-century textile mill.

Those who, by now, are sated with old abbeys may be relieved to learn that there is a great deal more to the town than this. At the lower end is the Newgate Tower or Old Bridewell Gaol, inscribed with the date 1755. Then you go round the other side and find the date 1720 – very odd. The main street is reminiscent in a way of Edinburgh. Everyone here also wanted to be at the heart of things. So the spaces behind the main facade were built on to create closes. Some are really secretive: one close is approached through an archway so low that it is necessary to stoop to get through it. It makes for a very satisfactory relationship between town and home. You can live literally a couple of paces from the main street yet enjoy a secluded intimacy.

120

The town runs uphill between stone terraces to the castle. There was a medieval castle here, but it was pulled down and in its place stands The Castle, which is not a castle at all but a gaol built in 1820. It certainly manages to look more castle-like than many a genuine citadel. It is a facade that hides a spot of a certain grimness, but one where the social niceties were still preserved. If you were poor, you got a small, bleak windowless cell; a little wealth bought you a window and if you really had cash to spare you could have a window, a fireplace and arrange to have your meals brought in. There was a definite pecking order in the prison, thieves and other criminals at the bottom, women next and debtors doing quite nicely. But no-one had the benefit of a prison hospital or sanitation of any kind.

The best-known house in Jedburgh is Mary Queen of Scots' House. Actually, it is not her house at all, though she did stay there once: or, at any rate, it is quite likely she stopped off when she came to preside over the Circuit Court. The house itself does not really need royal justification. It is a handsome place in salmon-pink sandstone, but the royal connections cannot be avoided. It is a museum of relics, though not everyone necessarily feels a thrill at the sight of a portion of the dress that unhappy lady wore at her execution.

The road from Jedburgh runs out through a deep river valley, overlooked by high sandstone cliffs, past the sixteenth-century Border fortress of Ferniehirst Castle. For those not yet saturated with antiquities it is an interesting place. You have here an excellent example of the turreted style that forms the basis of Scottish baronial. But this is the real thing, not one of the many Victorian copies. It is, in any case, almost the last stop in Scotland. The scenery too is changing. At first it is hilly, but well covered in trees, then it opens out to a strange moorland. You would see the same effect if you gave a little child a flat board and asked for a lot of hills. These are the same: little lumpy mini mountains stuck around haphazardly. They seem to be trying to be proper mountains but somehow they have not quite made it. Then a bigger hill appears. The road zigzags up and there on the summit a stone, faintly inscribed England – and one solitary piper. Goodbye Scotland.

7

The Borders to Hull

It is easy to see why the border between England and Scotland was so hotly disputed; why border raids in both directions were so much a part of everyday life. There is simply nothing but the one single stone on a hill crest and a wavering line on a map to diferentiate one side from the other. The Cheviots spread across the border, which keeps to the high land, while the road follows the valley of the Rede down to the Redesdale Forest. This is very much a taste of things to come. The roadside may be planted with deciduous trees but beyond this decorative fringe lie acres of close packed conifers. The road does its best to compensate for the dull uniformity by marking off each mile with attractively carved milestones, as though encouraging you to believe that change will come – if not in the next mile then perhaps in the one after that. And so it does. The claustrophobic woodland comes to an abrupt conclusion and you are freed for a switchback ride over the moors. It gets even lonelier when you turn off the main road, just miles of grass, a few sheep and the occasional farmhouse in a huddle of outbuildings. This must the ideal place to live for anyone who does not get on with their neighbours. It is only when you get down to the sheltered comfort of the valley that you find the focal point for the area, the little market town of Bellingham. Places such as this have an irresistible logic. Houses are built strong and close together for protection; around them you put the sheep pens and in the centre you hold a market. This is a different sort of border town, a town which stands between the more comfortable land to the south and the wind-scoured moors.

You notice the change when you leave. The moorland is out of sight and almost forgotten. The road follows the twists of a river valley and you come into Wark in triumph, down an avenue of tall trees, to be greeted by the finest tree of all, a giant chestnut that almost roofs the village green. How quickly it seems the mood changes. This is altogether richer farmland of fields, hedges and trees and the richness supports far more families, so that farms appear at ever shortening intervals. It no longer seems like border country yet just ahead lies the most famous ancient border in Britain, Hadrian's Wall. It was Julius Agricola in AD 84 who conquered the Brigantes of Northern Britain and established forts at Corbridge on Tyne and Carlisle on the Solway Firth. The two were joined by a road, but it was only when Hadrian arrived in AD 122 that the line of the road became a permanent frontier, marked by the vallum, a great ditch flanked by high banks and the wall. Everyone knows the name, Hadrian's Wall, but for much of its length, the vallum is all that one sees.

The first encounter with the wall is at one of the more interesting Roman sites, even if the wall itself is not especially prominent. Chesters was one of the larger forts that sat astride the wall, an imposing headquarters with a colonnaded courtyard and a strong room for the regimental cash. It was also a river-crossing point and part of the original bridge still stands, largely because the river itself changed course leaving the eastern abutments of the bridge stranded on dry land. As always with such sites, what is most impressive is the degree of civilisation that the Romans brought in terms of engineering and hygiene. There was a waterwheel by the bridge and a bath house.

The B6318 is very much the road of the wall, running alongside it, occasionally crossing it but rarely losing sight of it. Not all the sites are of interest to the non-expert: many of the mile castles, small fortlets set, as the name suggests, at mile intervals, appear as no more than hummocks on the ground. Even quite a large fort such as Brocolitia is nothing more than a grassy platform, looking slightly less impressive than the parking lot alongside. But just below the road is the Mithraeum. How very odd it seems in this very British setting of moorland and fields to find a temple to a Persian sun god. Mithras himself is shown in a crudely carved figure, crowned by the sun's rays. The temple is now open to the sky and the sense of mystery which once pervaded the building has been blown away by fresh northern winds. It is hard to imagine the effect of entering the narrow, darkened building, passing through the annexe and then being confronted by the sun god. How alien it seems under dark Northumbrian skies.

The most important preserved site on the wall is at Housesteads, and wallhoppers will no doubt call in here as the next stop, but

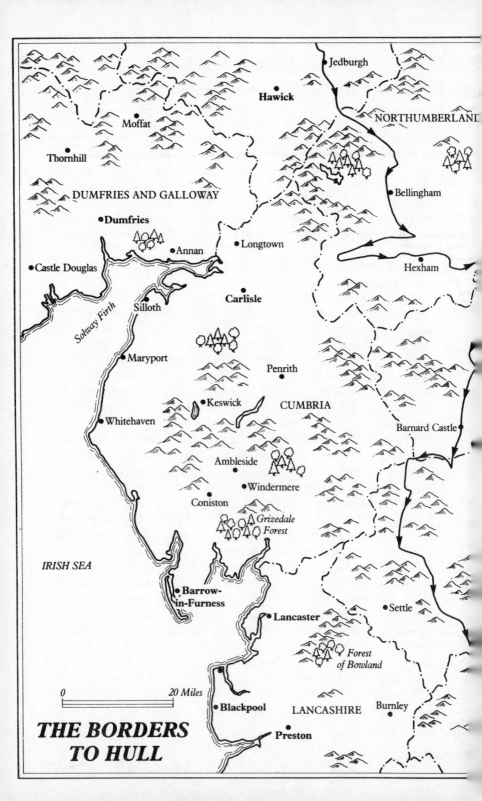

THE BORDERS
TO HULL

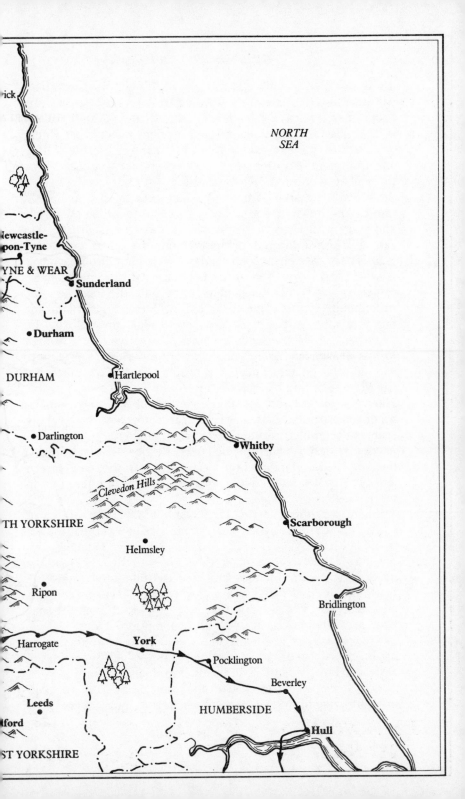

those who plan to walk part of the wall, if only for the exercise, will probably find it more rewarding to drive on past and walk back. Then it forms a splendid climax to what is, in any case, one of the most exciting walks through ancient history that Britain can offer. A minor road leads up to a car park at Steel Riggs and from here it is over two miles back to Housesteads. This is the wall at its most impressive and the border at its wildest. It is the relentless march of the wall which creates such an intense impression, downhill and uphill it goes, striding high above lake and crags with views across an almost deserted landscape. You can walk beside the wall or march along the top as the Roman guards once did. There is no need to worry about historical details of which fort is which, how it was built, what were the technical problems – it is the atmosphere of the wall, the loneliness, the inexorability of this stone snake curling across a giant land that one remembers. It is when you have walked the wall that the importance of Housesteads becomes clear. If you were brought to this distant land from continental Europe, to a wild country with an inhospitable climate and hostile tribes to the north, you would hope to find a base offering as many comforts as possible. Here was your reassuringly solid stone barrack block, with running water and proper latrines. The latter feature for some reason always seems to be modern visitors' favourite. It might not be Rome – or in the case of the cohorts billeted here, Belgium – but it brought a touch of civilisation. It was a place to relax, with shops and taverns and temples where, no doubt, many prayers were offered up for more congenial postings.

There are other sites to visit, notably Vindolanda with its re-construction, but one could turn south here content that one has seen Hadrian's Wall at its very best. An alternative route takes you down to Haltwhistle – a quick up and over to the main road that heads back towards Newcastle. There are still more Roman sites. Corbridge is particularly well preserved, but inevitably comes as an anticlimax. The sensible thing seems to be to admit the fact and carry straight on, ignoring all tempting diversions. But one diversion really is worth making, to cross the river so that the approach to Newcastle is from the south. There is no city in Britain that offers a more dramatic introduction than this.

You arrive at the steep-banked Tyne, crossed by an extra-ordinary array of bridges, beyond which the city clambers up the hill. It is the combination of elements which makes it unique. Just look at a few of the bridges. There is Stephenson's high-level bridge, a double decker, one layer for road, one for rail; the New Tyne Bridge throwing its great arc of steel over the water, and in between the little swing bridge with its gazebo-like house in the middle. Anyone who gets the chance to see the workings of the latter should grab it: the hydraulic machinery that moves the whole thing with seemingly effortless smoothness is the same machinery that did the job when the bridge was opened in 1876. Perhaps this is no surprise. Newcastle is, after all, noted for its engineering history, from the works of such famous men as George and Robert Stephenson, the railway pioneers, to the great ships, such as the *Mauretania*, that were launched on the Tyne. So, one tends to arrive with an image of an industrial city, a product of the industrial revolution. But Newcastle is no such upstart, and a good correction to that view is to start an exploration at the quay under the shadow of the bridges. Two buildings at once take you back far beyond the industrial revolution. The seventeenth-century guildhall has fallen on rather hard times, but its interior at least is still magnificent. More impressive by far is the Surtees House, one of those timber-framed jettied buildings which seem to have developed almost by accident – a layer of windows here, a filling of carved wood there, like a cake that kept growing. From here, there are two ways to go. The first is down the quay to discover maritime Newcastle. The little Maritime Centre has its own story to tell in the building itself, constructed from Flemish bricks brought over as disposable ballast – waste not, want not. Just round the corner is Trinity House, established here by Henry VIII. It is a delight. Behind a deceptively plain facade is a banqueting hall full of rich detail, with mermaids swimming around the fireplace and ships sailing across the ceiling. The chapel carries an air of even greater antiquity. The alternative to the quayside walk is to head straight up the steps to the New Castle itself with wonderful views over a tumble of roof tops along the way. But the nineteenth century thrusts itself forward, the viaduct literally overshadowing the medieval Black Gate. It is an indication that the city above the river will not be the same as that of the quay.

If forced to choose, my favourite building in Newcastle would have to be the station. The purity of the form has been slightly muddled by twentieth-century additions, but nothing can really detract from the effect of the sweeping curves of the rails matched by the triple arched roof up above. This is an engineer's station, but the classical facade that looks out over the city is a purely architectural contribution. The two men responsible were Robert Stephenson – though it is father George who has the place of honour on a pedestal outside – and John Dobson, who did as much as anyone in creating modern Newcastle. The city was largely redeveloped in the nineteenth century, and what that has done is to provide a formal unity. It has also given the city one of the best streets in England. Grey Street runs in a sleek curve, in which the proportions of each individual building have been calculated to a nicety, following the rules of the classic golden mean. It might all have been too perfect but it has a genuine focal point in a monument at the end and the line is broken by a fanfare of columns that proclaim the presence of the Theatre Royal. To balance this strict formality you can turn to one of the other developments of the period. Grainger Market is at first sight all higgledy-piggledy hustle and bustle, which is as a market should be. But the framework which contains it has an iron and glass roof almost as grand as that of the station. There is one survivor from the past here as well, a genuine Marks & Spencer Penny Bazaar, though not alas with the old penny prices. So the new city brought pattern and purpose to Newcastle whilst still keeping vitality at every level.

There is much to see here, but it is not just the past that demands attention. Newcastle is home to one of the most important housing developments of modern times: Byker. People think of it in terms of the wall, which suggests a grim Berlinian theme. But the wall is not just a tower block laid down on its side. It is a protection from the noise and rush of traffic outside. Behind it there is a vast housing development which manages to retain an astonishing intimacy. As a visitor, one cannot put it to the real test of living in it, but everything suggests it is a success. There were no obvious signs of vandalism, few graffiti, and a carefree feel to the whole place. It looks good and feels good: how sad that it has had few imitators. There are worse memories to take away from Newcastle than this.

Getting out of Newcastle on the right road can prove decidedly tricky. Signposts seem not to cater for those individuals who perversely refuse to use the motorway to head south. But once clear of the built-up area of Gateshead, it is possible to relax and begin to enjoy yourself. Railway enthusiasts can, no doubt, easily be tempted into making a short diversion to see the bridge known as the Causey Arch near Tanfield. This was built for a tramway, a precursor of the more familiar railway, on which horses not steam locomotives hauled the trucks. What gives it a special significance is the date it was built, 1727, which makes it the oldest surviving railway bridge in the world. Being the oldest is not in itself any guarantee that the thing will actually be interesting but this is a majestic structure, a single stone arch soaring high over a wooded gorge.

The North East was among the first areas in Britain to have tramways and it was here, more than anywhere, that the crucial early development of the locomotive took place. Engines ran elsewhere earlier, but it was in serving the collieries of the region that they proved their worth as practical machines. This is one of the themes developed at the North of England Open Air Museum at Beamish. In many ways it is similar to Ironbridge: a large site which makes use of existing features to tell its story. But because everything has been brought together on to the one site, it has more coherence. There are three principal elements: the colliery and colliery village, the town and the farm, and these are linked by a transport system of road, tram and railway. I first visited the area in the early seventies. Then there was no museum, just the colliery engine house with a rather dilapidated rusting steam engine inside. The engine house was taken to pieces and reassembled at the museum and its occupant revived as the centrepiece of a pithead complex. The colliery village has also been uprooted and restored: the old cottages were built by the Hetton Coal Company in the 1860s. Everything has been preserved, right down to the netty at the bottom of the garden. Colliery and cottages are linked by a railway along which chuffs a working replica of Stephenson's Locomotion, built for the Stockton and Darlington Railway in 1825. In action, it looks like a sewing machine on wheels.

The town at Beamish actually has the air of being a real place and it is being developed all the time. The next phase is to take the road round the corner to a new street. It has vitality and life, helped by the clanking tram and hoof clops of the brewer's dray. It is a fantasy town, but a convincing fantasy. The farm, however, is real, one of the groups of buildings that were here before the museum started. It was a model farm, all carefully planned in the 1790s and mechanised over the years with such important additions as a steam thresher. Probably the main appeal for most visitors is the animals, but the farm does represent an important part of the history of the area. The industrial revolution depended on the success of the agricultural revolution: you cannot create towns unless the countryside can feed them. An older farm is also being developed. Beamish never, it seems, stands still; every visit brings something new and enjoyable. On this occasion my good opinion was only slightly coloured by the fact that I was invited on to the footplate of one of their nineteenth-century locomotives for a little amateur train driving. The *Coffee Pot* is about as basic as you get: forward gear, off with the brakes, open the regulator and off you go.

Beamish gives you the flavour of the old industrial north and you still see plenty of remnants from the past. Brick terraces, pigeon lofts and men in flat caps do exist outside television programmes; growing champion leeks is still a matter of intense pride. But all that is changing, and changing rapidly. What the popular image of the North East always seems to leave out is the magnificent scenery. It is as if the world stopped at the end of the terrace, or at best was hidden from sight behind a slag heap. It may not always be spectacular or very obviously picturesque. It is a comfortable landscape, of sturdy farms set down among their fields, well-ordered places, not so very dissimilar to the model farm displayed to the admiring crowds at Beamish. Signposts even produce some surprising names – Quebec, for example. There are touches of a more extravagant stylishness. Hollingside Hall boasts a Gothicised estate village, but such places stand out simply because they are exceptions. Wolsingham is altogether more typical. The road comes down the hill to Weardale, where it is joined by the Waskerley Beck. It makes for a sheltered site protected by the hills. There is not much space to spare, so you get a little market square with everything crowded round it. Houses are solid stone with little in the way of showiness, but they look as if they could last for ever. There is nothing perhaps very special about Wolsingham. Its appeal lies in its very ordinariness, its clear sense of particularity, of belonging in just that one spot.

You are hardly into Weardale before you are out again, climbing smartly uphill towards the Hamsterley Forest. This is not one of

the more modern plantations: old firs and silver birch mix in with
the more modern spruce. Once the road has reached its summit
it runs along a ridge above the trees. You look out across them
at the moors beyond, while the immediate surroundings have
an openness and brightness that you would never get from a
journey through the heart of the forest itself. From here it is
only a short drive to Barnard Castle, the last town you will meet
before reaching the Yorkshire Dales. You could scarcely ask for
a better introduction.

There is a castle here, Bernard's castle, in fact Bernard
de Baliol, whose father fought with the conqueror at Hastings,
but the castle no longer seems a major feature in the town. It
is geography that gives Barnard Castle its appeal. Perched high
on the river bank, its main street almost tumbles down the hill
to the Tees. It is a market town, a town of some prosperity, of
handsome inns where the better-off farmers meet to exchange
views and clinch deals, and of equally handsome town houses.
Everything about the place proclaims it to be a prosperity based
on solid values. Barnard Castle depends on land, sheep and wool.
You know what to expect in a place like this, which is what makes
the Bowes Museum not just remarkable but somehow slightly
shocking. What is a French chateau doing in a Teeside town? The
answer is that George Bowes married a French actress and when,
in the last century, he decided to create a museum he brought in
a French architect. One can imagine several northern eyebrows
shooting up towards northern caps at this foreign frippery. The
result is a sumptuous building with one of the best art collections
in the north of England, but nothing will ever make it look other
than alien in this setting. Once across the Tees and you used
to be in Yorkshire, but not any more. The seventies boundary
changes moved a large chunk over to Durham, but one august
body at least has never accepted the change. Yorkshire County
Cricket Club at once reassured all those families removed from
the county, informing them that whatever Whitehall might say their
sons would still be eligible to play for Yorkshire. Yorkshiremen
could thus rest content that no really important changes had been
made after all. Another old division also still applies. One is now
very definitely entering the Dales.

The trouble with driving through the Dales is that one simply
wants to stop doing it, leave the car and walk. The road crosses

the Greta and one longs to get out and stroll down the riverside woodland of Brignall Banks. It gets worse as one goes on. You go through The Stang, forestry at its darkest, but come out to the full glory of open moorland at the hilltop start of the National Park. People up here are easily outnumbered by sheep, and even the road itself seems no more than a minor interruption in the scenery. It brings you down to one of the loveliest, most remote and most peaceful of all the dales.

Arkengarthdale has all the elements that make the Dales unique. The area as a whole has become popular with tourists, but its character has been formed by use. Almost the first thing you see as you drop down to the dale is the tongues of spoil licking down the hillside from old lead mine workings, but by far the most prominent features are the patterns made by fields and barns. Agriculture here means cattle and sheep. In summer they graze the uplands, and in winter they need to be brought to the valley and fed. There is scarcely a village that warrants the name village to be met on this part of the journey, just a steady regular procession of farms. Around each are the fields, spaced out by drystone walls that clamber up the hill side. In the fields are the barns of rough-hewn stone. It is an ancient system that we now, belatedly, recognise as ecologically sound. The meadows are harvested to fill the barns with winter feed; the cattle in the byres provide the natural manure that will prepare the ground for the next season's crop. It is a beautifully designed system, but one which depends on human labour, and that is the problem. It is the system that created this landscape, and if the system dies who knows how long the Dales themselves will survive. Without the voracious animals trees would soon re-establish themselves in the uplands. Without the need for many small fields and many barns, the appealing contrast between patchwork valley and open moor will be lost. But for the present at least it is there to be enjoyed by those of us who come here for pleasure – and do not have the hard labour of preserving this landscape.

At the head of the valley, the road climbs up to Tan Hill and the highest, and certainly one of the loneliest pubs in England, the Tan Hill Inn. Built to slake the thirst of miners and packhorse drivers it now fulfils the same function for the steady stream of walkers, stomping along the Pennine Way. Road and long-distance path keep each other company down West Stonesdale, an altogether apt description for this narrow valley which ends at Keld and another of those places where the temptation to get out and walk is irresistible. So why resist? You can make a splendid circuit following the Pennine Way down the valley to Muker. It is a rough stony path but wonderfully rewarding, taking you along the rim of the deep valley, where the often harsh edge contrasts with the rich green and silvery glint of sparkling water down below. And, having done the hard bit, you can return on a gentler path up the opposite side of the valley past the old mines of Crackpot Hall and the rush and tumble of the Kisdon Force waterfall. The round trip is about five miles, but even those who do not fancy the walk should venture just a little way into this narrow valley to sample some of the best of the Dales scenery. The road south goes over the high Buttertubs Pass, which gets its curious name from the pot holes by the roadside. It is said that farmers on their way to market in summer would pause here for a snack and lower their butter into the cool depths as a sort of natural refrigerator. Now people simply stop, look down the holes rather cautiously, and move on to the town of Hawes. This is one of the most popular tourist centres with wide cobbled streets and narrow alleyways and a river rushing through the middle. It also has a working life of its own: they make Wensleydale cheese here and rope, but it is on market days that one sees Hawes at its best as an important local centre. Tourists then take second place as the serious business of buying and selling cattle gets under way.

Hawes can definitely get overcrowded in summer, but in no time at all the crowds can be left behind. The caravans nose each other along the main road but leave the winding, hilly cross-country routes alone. So if you want to get away, take the road through Gayle. This is scarcely separated from Hawes yet seems a world away, a place which you could describe as austere, bleak even, but a place of character. Like all the best Dales villages you cannot imagine it existing anywhere else but here, on the edge of the rough fells beside the beck which cascades over a series of broad ledges down the hillside. Had the ledges been a few feet higher they would have been waterfalls and coach and car park would have been built alongside: they are not, so no-one much comes here. Journeying on, the point is soon reinforced that Dales valleys generally run west to east, so if you are travelling north to south it is going to be all up hill and down dale. The road helps by putting in a few wriggles to ease the gradient. Only the Roman road that crosses your path on its way down to Bainbridge refuses all compromises with nature.

Langsthrothdale brings relief from the switchback. It is a great favourite with families: broad greens by the river, rocky pools and little waterfalls, an ideal place to paddle, perfect for building dams. Perfect, that is, except after heavy rain when the gurgling, bubbling stream becomes a torrent stained by the peaty moors to the colour of motor oil. Yockenthwaite is one of the few hamlets in the Dale, though you might not recognise it as such – just a few stone farmhouses, a bridge and a web of walls. Hubberholme is scarcely larger, though it does at least have its old pub. The surprise comes with the little church. It is basically as plain and as simple as you would expect from this quiet rural area, but what makes it well worth stopping for is the elaborately carved rood screen and loft. These divide the choir from the nave, the loft being a gallery where the cross or rood is set. It was often used on special occasions by choristers, hence the alternative name of 'singing gallery'. The modern pews are clearly the work of a craftsman and have in fact been 'signed': look hard enough and you will find a carved mouse, which shows them to be the work of Robert Thompson.

Turning south again, Langstrothdale gives way to steadily broadening Wharfedale and with it comes one of the distinctive features of Dales scenery, the limestone escarpments. These become ever more prominent, ruling a white, shining edge to the hills. They mark the return of the once busy lead-mining area, now visible in little more than the dribbles of spoil and an occasional glimpse of an old smelter chimney. But they have also left behind the big villages that grew on mineral wealth, Kettlewell and even grander Grassington. This is one of those regions where every single view seems to have a story to tell. It may be a tale of natural forces, eating away earth and rock to create the brutal overhang of Kilnsey Crag, or the pattern of shelf-like patches on the hillside that mark the field pattern of Celtic settlers who came here before the Romans. And then as one goes further south to the edge of the Dales, so one comes upon the medieval past at its most romantic, mixed in with the artifice of the picturesque.

It begins with the ruins of Barden Tower. Built in the eleventh century as a fortress, it was the home of the tenth Lord of Clifford in the fifteenth century. He was one of the those rare aristocrats who had little taste for court life. He retired to Barden, built a chapel and a priest's house, contemplated nature and earned himself the popular name of The Shepherd Lord. Nothing much happened then until 1657 when Lady Anne Clifford, an indefatigable enthusiast for all the Clifford possessions, paid to have the tower restored. Her successors did not share her taste for draughty, lonely medieval towers and it now crumbles gently into dignified old age. For the next few miles the Wharfe, which had been quite sedate, begins to busy itself forcing a way down a rocky gorge. It makes a tumultuous passage through a tight stone mouth, known as The Strid, and emerges again to broad grassland and one of the few great monastic buildings that can rival Tintern for the beauty of its setting. It is a somewhat confusing place, for the village is Bolton Abbey but there never was an abbey, only a priory. The priory church suffered less than many others for the nave was retained for use as a parish church, although the rest of the building was simply allowed to decay around it. The former priory gateway became Bolton Hall and very fine it is too. But it is the setting that makes the scene memorable and the area so very popular. The wide, flat grassland also bears another message. We have nearly reached the edge of the Dales.

The road east from Bolton Bridge soon develops a very different character. As it reaches Blubberhouses Moor, you find the brilliant white of limestone giving way to the dark grey of millstone grit. It is an altogether more sombre landscape, though there is a sudden, quite lighthearted moment at Blubberhouses itself, which with its little church backed by woodland has an almost alpine air. The rock, hill and moor are eventually left behind for something more polite, even genteel: the town of Harrogate. Having been brought up in Harrogate and having gone to school in neighbouring Knaresborough, I find it difficult to be objective about the place. I preferred Knaresborough then and still do now. Harrogate has its obvious charms. It is a very open town, thanks to The Stray, an area of grassland that all but surrounds the centre. It developed in Victorian times as a spa: visitors can still taste the waters, and there is a theory that anything that unpleasant must be good for you. Nowadays it caters for the conference trade rather than the gouty old men and vaporous old ladies, but somehow it still has about it the air of the palm court and afternoon tea. Knaresborough has its basis in more traditional beginnings. The castle on the hill, a rotting tusk scarcely distinguishable from the crag on which it stands, is the point around which the market town developed. Now it has one of the most famous river views in Britain, a sight that has graced a thousand calendars, and all thanks to the Victorians. When the railway came, a tall viaduct was built over the Nidd – not very well built as it happens. The first version collapsed, blocking the river and flooding the town. The replacement still stands and in deference to the castle it too is castellated, as thoroughgoing an example of railway medievalism as you will find. Between the two are the cliffs and the hilly streets lined with old houses. Cobble and stone create the first impression, but in amongst them is timber-framing and brick. Knaresborough provides the evidence that the world of the Pennines is also now almost at an end.

On a clear day, it used to be possible to look out of my classroom window and see the towers of York Minster. It really is quite an abrupt change to come out of the hills and deep river valleys to Marston Moor and the Vale of York, where nothing rises up to disturb the view. The road offers as few obstructions to travel and hurries you along to the capital of the North. Almost everyone knows about York's historic importance – the central role it has had in English history from the time of the Romans to the coming of the Vikings and on to the medieval period. It was only the rise of the industrial towns that sent ancient cities such as this slithering down the measuring stick of national importance. But decreasing importance eased the pressures for change. There is less need to knock down the old when there is no desperate urgency to supply the new. Not that everyone showed great respect for ancient York. When the railway engineers first arrived they brutally punched a hole straight through the medieval walls to build a central station which then proved inadequate anyway, so that it had to be replaced by another outside the walls. In spite of such shenanigans York has retained, to an extraordinary degree, the form and feel of the medieval walled city. On the basis of that it has become one of the most popular places for visitors in Britain. The trouble is that, knowing that, one has a tendency to turn one's back and go off in search of more esoteric pleasures. That is a mistake, because this really is a city with a unique atmosphere. The popular tourist sites were not put there to appeal to sightseers, but are an essential part of the historic fabric of the place. They are as potent now as they ever were, and it would be foolish to be deterred from going to see them just because thousands of others are doing the same.

One way to approach York is the one used at Chester, a walk round the walls. It works just as well here even though there is no complete circuit. This is not due to vandalism on the part of the city fathers. There never was a complete circuit for it was not needed. From the Red Tower to the Layerthorpe Postern was an impassable swamp through which the Foss made its way. Now the area is drained and built up for industry while the Foss, once a major trading route to the city, is an almost-forgotten backwater. You can see what it once was from the magnificent redbrick castellated warehouses. But to return to the wall itself – the main features are the entrances such as Bootham Bar and Monk Bar, but the best views come from the walk down the eastern side. You look out over red brick and pantiles to the minster. It looks impressive from whichever angle you view it, but there is something particularly awe inspiring in being able to look down on the city yet still having to look up to the minster. The obverse is equally intriguing, for those prepared to pant up 275 steps – to look down from the tower at the close-packed streets that follow a pattern laid down in medieval times.

The minster dominates everything in a most remarkable way. Great churches will always impress even if by size alone. Sometimes they are set apart, creating what might be called the cathedral city separate from the lay city. In other places they almost are the city. York is recognisably great in its own right, yet the minster still dominates, is always the inescapable presence. The sense of power it creates is, if anything, enhanced when one goes inside. The church we see today dates from the rebuilding that followed a disastrous fire in 1137: other, almost equally disastrous blazes, seem to punctuate its history. But the nave itself was not begun until 1291 and took half a century to complete. It seems taller, more resolutely vertical than other cathedral naves and this is because it breaks with tradition. Earlier naves generally had three tiers: a row of high arches and above that smaller arches of triforium and clerestory. Here triforium and clerestory are combined, so instead of looking up at a diminishing perspective, it is almost as if a whole new building had been piled up above the nave. Such a deliberate effect at impressing the congregation, overwhelming them

137

by scale, could easily seem coldly, almost brutally authoritarian, not so much leading the eye upwards in imagination as bearing down upon you. But what saves it is the glass, the rich, dense glass that warms the whole structure, touching and softening the hardest edges and colouring the severest details.

The minster is a great place for contrasts. Nothing could be further away in atmosphere from the austerity of the nave than the intimacy and ornate patterns of the chapter house. It is polygonal and the intricacy is increased by setting the canon's seats back in niches so that it seems that the whole wall is a ripple of undulations. And there is humanity here as well in the carved heads on the canopies. A rather plump lady scratches her chin as if trying to solve some niggling problem in the household accounts. Jack the Green and his May Day queen look down cheerily and confidently pagan, as happy to find a place among the Christians as they were in the older religions.

York has no shortage of lures for the tourist. There are museums in plenty and the newest, the Jorvik Viking Centre, is an undoubted success judging by the daily queues. I have to confess to a personal distaste for being mechanically propelled around exhibits, told what to see and how long to spend seeing it – even if it is all beautifully done. Inevitably one's view of museums is coloured by personal preferences. The National Railway Museum, however, is a place which never seems to fail. Even the sceptics who go in declaring they have no interest in the subject tend to come out as enthusiasts. It is, in its own way, not unlike the minster, in that you are bowled over by the first sight of the place. Everything is just right. The main building was the old motive power shed and contains two great turntables on which stand the engines, big and small, new and very old. Some are quite simply beautiful. The Stirling Single has the most amazingly sensuous lines which carry through the whole structure. In contrast, the monster built for the Chinese railways is almost brutal in its impact. It is only when you start to go around the exhibits that you begin to realise just how much material there is here. It is not just a locomotive collection: there are carriages and rolling stock, signals and posters. The museum tells a complete railway story.

There is more to York than its well-publicised attractions. It is also a great city in which to wander. Different areas have their own charms and you soon discover that things are not always

138

what they seem. If you want to get to one of the city gates you might expect that a street called Castlegate would be sure to get you there: but 'gate' is simply the Norse name for street, so the historical connection is there in a different way. In fact, York's gates are not called gates at all but bars. There are famous streets of medieval houses, notably The Shambles, but there are others which never feature in guide books but which are full of interest. Down by Fossgate you will discover a street to delight bookbrowsers for example. As is so often the case it is the sudden view that you find for yourself that turns out to be the one you remember. York seems to be full of them.

The way out passes through Walmgate and brings you back to the flat plain. It is somehow difficult to think of this as the same Yorkshire as the Yorkshire of the Dales. It is not just the flatness, but the neatness of everything. Near Kexby Bridge you can look across to a farmyard so trim in red brick it could have been set up as a model for a child's picturebook. You can scarcely imagine real live mucky animals ever being allowed into the yard.

The main road tends to go round places rather than through them so you have to make a definite detour if you want to see anywhere. Pocklington is a tidy little place, ordinary enough you might think but it has one really curious feature. The little cinema in the market place now houses the Penny Arcadia. This is a collection of the sort of penny-in-the-slot machines that used to be found on seaside piers. They play music, give you a butler's keyhole vision of the maid's bedroom and perform magical tricks. There is an innocence, even about the faintly naughty ones, and they are infinitely more amusing than their modern electronic counterparts, with their whirring lights, hooters and clanking coin releases. Pocklington also has a canal. Actually, the canal never quite reached the town. It stopped short just by the main road. It is not a particularly grand canal, for it only reaches a few miles back to the Ouse and it is not even fully open for boating, yet it provides a lovely calm environment. If nothing else, the end of the canal with its old lock, reedy banks and scuttling moorhens is a pleasant place to sit and ponder for a while.

Market Weighton marks the end of the flat lands and a gentle climb up to gentle hills. The changes create no real differences and this remains an area as cosy as the Home Counties. At Bishop Burton the village pond is surrounded by whitewashed buildings that seem made for the sketch pad. It is a landscape that lulls you into a warm, but by no means unpleasant, complacency. It cossets you, comforts you and seems to promise you no unpleasant shocks. On the contrary, it appears to offer civilised delights – and delivers the promise. Beverley could be thought of as a sort of York in miniature. It too had its bars, the town gateways, though only one survives. It has its minster and its ancient friary and many buildings of quality. Yet the impression it gives is quite different. Beverley belongs squarely in the countryside. The approach has town and country all mixed in together, houses looking out on a common where cattle still graze under the shadow of the old windmill tower. That, in turn, is balanced by the very sophisticated racecourse and once inside the North Bar, passing with impeccable logic from North Bar Without to North Bar Within, one arrives at one of those Georgian townscapes which could be anywhere but which positively reek of urbanity. The contrast continues through the town. The market square with market cross is balanced by a Victorian arcade, now very antiquey. In one matter at least Beverley and York are as one. The focal point is the minster.

Visitors to Beverley should beware. While the church fabric is well preserved, no similar enthusiasm has been extended to the lighting and this is a church that absolutely demands to be seen in detail. Beverley is packed with wonderful carvings full of the vitality of bustling life. Bagpipers puff furiously, peering out at a gentleman who has clearly had one too many; a falconer is just on the point of releasing his bird, while two nuns piously tell their beads, but the glint in the eye of the goatish devil behind them suggests that more than a touch of hypocrisy might be involved. But best of all are the misericords, a flavour of which can be given by quoting some of the bald descriptions in the official guide.

A pelican feeding its young with the blood of its own breast.
On left, an eagle; on right, a pelican picking up a serpent.
An ape on horseback, followed by a man armed with a
club. On left, a monkey combing a cat; on right, a boy
riding a pig.
The old pig plays the bagpipes, and young pigs dance to
the music; on left, a pig saddled; on right, a pig playing a harp.

What on earth is one supposed to make of this riot of anthropomorphism? And can one possibly contemplate the notion of

140

anyone putting such carvings in a church today? Even the more naturalistic scenes have an oddly surreal touch. A man wheels his wife in a barrow with a broken wheel, while she pulls at his ear. What makes them so touching is that the craftsmen who carved them clearly made no distinction between sacred and profane. They simply offered up their best work, and just as simply took their subjects from everyday life and common fables. Beverley's misericords bring us closer to an experience and understanding of medieval life than any conventional museum exhibit could ever do.

Beverley takes some following: Hull manages it with ease. It is situated on a borderline between Yorkshire and the north and East Anglia and the south and is a city in transition. Once the docks reached into the heart, but now the working life has gone from them. The innermost dock has been built over to create a supermarket on stilts; the outer docks are a marina, the last remaining big warehouse has been converted into a hotel. The planners must be kicking themselves: if not, they should be. The docks were designed by Jesse Hartley, the man responsible for Albert Dock in Liverpool, and his work was just as good here. But the bulldozers moved in, and one can admire what is left but grieve over lost opportunities. It is not that there is anything intrinsically wrong with the new schemes as such, but they could have been so much better. Happily, that is not the end of the story, for the River Hull presents a totally different picture. The river is crammed with barges and lighters, and if this were a roadway, traffic wardens would collect a fortune for double parking. When it seems impossible for anything else to move, somehow another laden vessel finds space to edge down the narrow strip of water towards a berth. The satisfaction of such a scene is immense: mooring lines sag under their own weight into perfect curves, bollards are worn by age and use to sculpted shapes and the barges themselves have a wonderful dichotomy, heavy and ungracious, yet moving with ease in their natural element of water. And it is the water itself, reflecting, distorting, doubling a shape in mirror image and throwing a metal hull into a dancing sparkle of ripples, that gives the scenes animation.

If the wharf area represents the best of the city, then it is only just so. Look down the alleyways and arches between the warehouses and you glimpse the wealth that was built up on the trade of the past. Some of the houses are really remarkably grand and none

141

more so than that where the abolitionist William Wilberforce was born in 1759. There is something especially poignant in finding memories of the slave trade displayed in such an opulent setting. Hull is a curious mixture of a place, though that is usually not Hull's fault. The main shopping centre is dull as can be, the result of rebuilding after the devastations of bombing, and the other new buildings are generally little better. But you do not judge a city just on one part, or even just on its buildings. If sometimes one might feel that there was something a touch precious about the over-neat villages in the surrounding countryside, no one could ever make that claim about a city that boasts not one but two professional Rugby League teams and has, in Hull Truck, one of the liveliest theatre companies in the land. And if you think that suggests a swing too far the other way to flat hats and braces, and 'ee by gum', you cannot label a place as too down to earth which has a street called The Land of Green Ginger.

8
Hull to Bath

The one complaint one can level against the Humber Bridge is that once it was opened the old ferries, paddle steamers such as *Lincoln Castle*, stopped running. Otherwise, it can be admired as a magnificent example of modern engineering. It takes you to an area which is divided from the north bank of the river by more than just the physical barrier of water. On the south bank, everything seems to change – buildings, landscape, everything.

Across the river is New Holland, where the ferries once ran, and it is an altogether appropriate name for this watery land, drained by dykes. The road itself clings tenaciously to the very edge of the rising ground to the east, scrupulously following each twist of the contours. The villages are attractive little places. Saxby All Saints is a place of brick and pantile, occasionally dignified by stucco and colour washes, but it too sticks to the margin to keep its feet dry. The view to the west is dominated by the straight lines of the ditches which converge on the smoking chimneys of Scunthorpe steel works. It is not especially impressive by day but at night the furnaces set the sky ablaze. Between the steel works and the road you can make out the forlornly winding River Ancholme, deprived of its power and its own chosen path, its main stream diverted into the ruler straight New River. The Wold may not represent much in the way of hills, but in this context it seems positively mountainous, and the few patches of trees make a far more varied landscape than that of the valley – or that which lies ahead.

Brigg really marks the beginning of an increasingly flat land-scape. The highest hill along the way, grandly named Owersby Top, just clambers over the hundred-foot mark by a few inches. Make the most of it, for it is the last hill you will see for a while. But that would suggest that 'flat' must necessarily be synonymous with dull and boring. It need not be so. What is lost in interest on the ground receives compensations up above, a sort of permanent

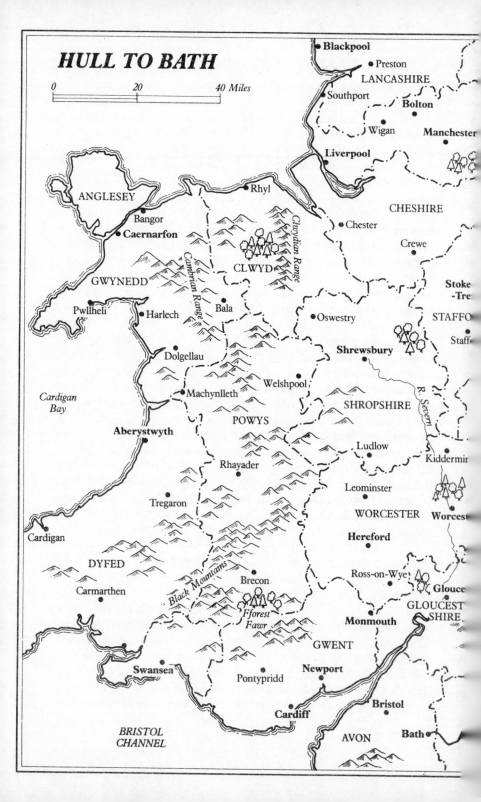

religious metaphor. There must be a rational explanation for why the skies of Lincolnshire seem so immense, why the procession of clouds has a majesty that cannot be matched elsewhere, but explicable or not the phenomenon exists. The effect is certainly enhanced by the ditches and dykes which lead away in narrowing perspective to the horizon, a pointer to the endless parade of the clouds. This is not a landscape for dull grey days, for without the overhead procession what is left is too often a dreary succession of wide fields, denuded of hedgerows and all interest. There is, however, variety in the roads themselves. Why does the road south of Market Rasen proceed through a series of right-angled bends when there are no physical features to prevent it taking a course as true as a Roman way? The answer lies, as so often, in private property. The road makers bowed to local pressures and made their convoluted way around, it seems, every field in the county. There is, however, one feature which grows ever more dominant with each mile travelled: the cathedral at Lincoln.

Lincoln is a city with two quite different personae, one part scarcely seeming to have anything in common with the other. The old city sits on the end of a ridge above the River Witham, with the now familiar focal points of castle and cathedral. The area involved is really quite small, just a few streets crowded together, some of which seem to have fallen off the edge. The naming of streets may not show much imagination, but Steep Hill is an inarguably accurate description. In this close-packed community are some of the oldest houses in the country. The city was once noted for its tolerance, and a large Jewish community developed, which thrived until anti-semitism grew rampant in the late thirteenth century and the Jews were expelled. But some at least of the buildings they occupied have survived and the Jew's house and Jew's Court are probably the finest examples of early domestic architecture that we have. The old city certainly has its attractions, including a pie shop that sets one drooling: a pork, plum and celery pie had place of honour in the window – irresistible. But almost everything here seems geared to tourism. The everyday life has moved off down the hill to spread itself outside the confines of the ancient walls. That still, however, leaves the cathedral.

The splendours anticipated on the journey towards the city materialise when you actually arrive. This book was never intended to be a guide to ecclesiastical architecture but cathedrals are so dominant in so many cityscapes that one simply cannot ignore them: you certainly cannot ignore Lincoln. Just pause on your way in and look up at the carving on the west front: at Daniel surrounded by some very ferocious lions, next to Noah about to be joined by a hare, frozen for centuries in the act of hopping aboard the ark. Then keep looking up to the top of the crossing tower, and you will never again have to ask anyone why architecture of this period is known as Decorated. When you go inside you can see the wonderful pattern of diamonds and stars of the vaulting ribs that are not really there to hold up the tower roof but to create an effect. This is only a sample of what the cathedral has to offer and one thing you soon discover is that the cathedral gives you a stiff neck. You are forever looking up at the details overhead, from the decorative roof bosses to the carved angels and the curious Lincoln Imp smiling down from the middle of their seraphic ranks.

Down the hill, Lincoln seems disappointingly like any other large town or city, but is partly redeemed by the river running through the heart of it. The river was the making of Lincoln: boats were coming here to trade in Roman times, but now it has lost its old role and has only partly found a new one. Riverside walks are rather limited, though at least there is the Glory Hole where the buildings continue on across the bridge. There is, however, one last glimpse of Norman Lincoln on the way out, St Mary's Guildhall, where on the rare occasions it is open to the public you can see down below the floor the actual surface of Roman Fosse Way, complete with two-thousand-year-old wheel ruts. Something of the history of the area seems to have percolated through to modern developers. The A46 still follows the line of the Fosse Way between Lincoln and Newark, so when it came to building a shopping precinct what better name could you have than The Forum and what other decoration would you choose but a colonnade? The result is a hilarious mismatch of styles. Still, it is better to get something hopelessly wrong and add to the store of life's amusement than to be merely halfhearted and dull.

Newark is everything a provincial town should be. Before the motorway age it was simply a nightmare, a permanent traffic jam as all the north-south traffic tried to fight its way through. Now that even the A1 is banished to the outskirts you can stop here for pleasure rather than necessity. Like all the best towns it has a most satisfyingly complex character. Its importance developed from its position at the meeting point of two major transport routes, the Great North Road and the River Trent. It makes sense to begin any exploration down by the river. Here is the castle, much damaged by Cromwell's men, for Newark was on the losing side. It looks good standing over the water, where a little oriel window strikes an oddly domestic note, but when you have seen this imposing facade you have seen it all. The rest is a ruin. The castle is not the only imposing building down by the water. A little way out of town is a huge sugar-beet factory, nearer at hand are old maltings and close by the bridge Vincent H. Dobson Limited announce that they can provide 'pumps, compressors, generators, plant equipment all makes types and sizes and wet mix pig food equipment'. What the pigs and their feed have done to deserve special attention remains an unsolved mystery. On the water itself, a large motorised barge has had an extensive superstructure added in garish yellow and has become a floating pub. At once one has that rather sad feeling that yet another inland port has died, leaving memories, conversions and a marina. But it is not yet true. The warehouses by the lock may not be bursting with goods, but commercial traffic still does use the Trent and here at least the atmosphere of the working river remains alive.

The town comes down the steep hill to meet the river in seemingly haphazard, building-block piles, but the heart of the town lies at the top of the hill. The market square is the real thing, a genuine centre overlooked by the magnificent town hall, designed by John Carr in 1773. It was a building with which I had looked forward to renewing acquaintance but it was surrounded by scaffolding and swathed in plastic. Presumably it will emerge from this chrysalis, butterfly bright. There is, however, a variety of alternative delights in the square. The Job Centre is housed in a very good thirties building with typical geometric decoration, and a plaque round the corner showed the origins. The stone was laid, it said, by Raymond Montague Burton. Almost next door was the old office of the publisher who printed Byron's first poems, 'Fugitive Pieces', in 1806. Around the square is what must once have been a superb inn, the fifteenth-century White Hart. Across the facade are rows of carved heads, set in niches covered with Gothic canopies, and inside one can see the original timber framework exposed. But at street level there is modern plate glass surmounted by the plastic fascia of the Nottingham Building Society. It is hard to imagine a more monstrously inappropriate transformation. Really, they might just as well have knocked the whole thing down and be done with it. Happily, there are other old coaching inns, which even if they have lost their original functions have at least maintained their integrity, and a number of other old houses.

The other inescapable presence is the parish church, with its spire shooting high over the roof tops. But to reach it you have to pass down an alleyway past an isolated tall chimney, like a miniature mill chimney without a mill – very odd. The church itself is one of the grandest parish churches in the country, a building that has grown with the centuries. Inside, Early English blends seamlessly into Decorated and that in turn merges with the Perpendicular. The tower was built in 1230, but the spire was only added a century later, yet it is now impossible to imagine the one without the other. The detailing is marvellous, from the famously macabre Dance of Death to the grinning gargoyles high on the wall. Newark is the sort of town that could turn the adjective 'provincial' into a compliment.

Leaving Newark, you pass the earthworks and redoubt of the old Civil War defences and discover that what you thought was the Trent at Newark was actually the Trent Navigation, not the river itself at all but an artificial cut. The genuine, meandering Trent splashes along a few miles away through Kelham, a place with an extraordinary Gothic fantasy of a hall in liverish brick. What appears to be the spire of a chapel turns out to be the stable block, grander than most people's houses.

Southwell is another town dominated by its church. The minster looks as if it has strayed across from France, a Norman church that appears from the outside to be genuinely from Normandy. The effect is created by the pyramidal spires that top the matching pair of towers, with the immense doorway in between. Once inside, the typical brooding atmosphere of ponderous columns seems to confirm the feeling, and then you come to the chapter house and an astonishing transformation. The passage from the choir is lined with columns that sprout exuberant foliage, not just generalised leaves but recognisably from English trees and plants. The chapter house itself is even more lively: oak and ivy, buttercup and hop bring the freshness of the hedgerow to the church. It is a gloriously light building, octagonal but with no central pier to support the roof vaulting. It might have been plain, but instead it is as though it had been abandoned and the plants took over before being miraculously petrified. The eagle lectern in the choir came originally from Newstead Abbey. The monks threw it into the lake at the Dissolution to save it from destruction, and it finally found a resting place in the cathedral in 1805. Newstead Abbey itself became a house and its most famous occupant, Lord Byron, was a frequent visitor to Southwell. His mother rented Burgage Manor between 1804 and 1807 and it was during his visits here that friends persuaded him to go and see the publisher in Newark. Inevitably one seems now to be drawn towards Byron and Newstead, but not before making just one diversion.

Papplewick Pumping Station could well be called a temple of steam. In what looks like an ornate water garden, there stands a building like a minor Transylvanian castle. Push open the massive doors and inside, bathed in the warm light filtered through stained glass windows, are two mighty beam engines. They are a delight to all lovers of Victorian engineering, gently nodding giants that rumble and hiss as they work. What makes the place exceptional is the decoration. The columns of the chapter house at Southwell were decorated with leaves; here brightwork fishes swim through brassy fronds up and down columns topped by solemn ibis. The watery theme is carried over to the windows, each one a stained-glass picture. It is reminiscent of the chapter house in another way as well. The latter was never intended to be seen by the general congregation, but was for use by the cathedral chapter; here too the only ones who saw this splendour were mechanics and engineers, the high priests of the new machine age. Now Papplewick is a show place restored by enthusiasts. The real work of water supply is handled quite adequately by an electric pump in a dull brick shed.

Papplewick speaks volumes about Victorian confidence, the absolute certainty that material progress was altogether a thoroughly good thing. After all the Byronic hints along the way, one somehow expects Newstead Abbey to be similarly illuminating about its most famous owner. In the event, it seemed to have little of that author's spirit about it. Perhaps it was the result of visiting the place at the fag end of a dully oppressive afternoon that made it seem to have so little to do with either the passion or the brilliant wit of Byron. The grounds are splendid, the house that grew out of the monastic ruins undoubtedly romantic, and there are parts of the church itself still standing. It is probably best to forget Byron and simply enjoy the place for what it is, but somehow the Byronic voice keeps whispering in the ear. One seems to hear him commenting on his neighbours:

> For what were all these country patriots born?
> To hunt, and vote, and raise the price of corn?

He declared that the notion of his body being returned to his native land 'would drive me mad on my death bed', but with splendid irony he was delighted to make his own contribution to the estate. He buried his dog here, under an impressive tomb embellished with his own verses.

It is odd how journeys seem to pick up themes. One visits a succession of places noted for their magnificent churches, and then literature starts to take over – and not just the popular literature of fable which makes the name of Robin Hood an inescapable presence when journeying through the last vestiges of Sherwood Forest. Up ahead lies the birthplace and early home of D. H. Lawrence. You might think that there could scarcely be a greater contrast than that between the aristocratic Newstead Abbey and the miner's son of Eastwood. Yet both shared a distaste for the hypocrisy of their age. Byron's lines might be matched by Lawrence, on the subject of the 'beastly bourgeois':

> What a pity they can't all be kicked over
> Like sickening toadstools, and left to melt back, swiftly
> Into the soil of England.

Less style perhaps, and certainly more bile, but Byron would surely have recognised the viewpoint. What one would dearly like to know is what Lawrence himself would have said when confronted with Lawrence Park, an estate of 'executive houses' on the edge of town.

Lawrence's birthplace in the town is an unremarkable house in an unremarkable street. In fact the family moved on when young David Herbert was just two, so that it tells you something of the circumstances of his family, but sheds little light on anything he

151

himself would have used in his writing. It is now a museum, a recreation of what the house was probably like but it inevitably lacks the personal touch, the intimate details that would bring it alive. It could be 'miner's house circa 1880' at any theme park or open-air museum. But Lawrence enthusiasts can follow a walk around the town that takes in other houses where the Lawrences lived and many of the places which he knew and which find their way into his fiction. One non-Lawrencian name certainly catches the eye. Round the corner from the birthplace is Scargill Walk: Lawrence and Scargill, an unlikely combination. But then, as Lawrence noted, this is an unlikely landscape, an odd mixture of rural England, farmland and woods and the manmade hills of old colliery spoil heaps. The industrial world will now become a dominant theme.

Even the industrial world has different faces. Old industries have now developed quite romantic associations, have become wrapped in gauzy films of nostalgia. Crich was once a centre for lead mining and quarrying. George Stephenson built a tramroad here in 1842, along which trucks full of stone were dragged by horses. Now trams of a different sort run on the quarry site – electric street trams, once such a common feature in British towns and cities. Many people now regret their passing, not from any feelings of nostalgia, but because we now see them as a very sound and practical transport route for clogged city streets. Up at Crich, however, memories of the past rule as visitors ride off on one of the clanking veterans. You do get a good run for your money here, with a grand send-off from outside buildings that started off as the assembly rooms in Derby. The journey itself brings splendid views across the countryside of the Derwent valley.

This is a region of which I never tire, one which can claim, along with the Severn gorge at Ironbridge, to be the site of some of the key events of the industrial revolution. It also has the advantage that the scenery can be enjoyed for itself alone, by those with absolutely no interest in the industrial past. But, for me, the great appeal will always be that it is an area where you can enjoy the best of both worlds, get out into superb scenery and still keep in touch with the past. The centrepiece of it all is Cromford. You approach on a typical hill-country route of twisting roads, with views of stone-wall straddled hills, and then you reach the river valley, where everything happens with a rush. First comes the railway and Cromford's unlikely chateau-styled station, then you move back to the eighteenth century to the canal wharf and, across the road, Arkwright's mill. It was here that Richard Arkwright came to establish the first water-powered cotton mill. He arrived at what was then a remote and wild corner of Derbyshire, attracted partly by the water power and partly because it was well away from the traditional spinning and weaving areas. He was starting a process which was to take textiles out of the familiar world of the cottage industry and push it into the factory. He assumed, quite rightly, that what he was going to do would be bitterly resented. But a factory needs workers and workers need houses and Arkwright provided them. In doing so he created the first mill village.

The village is the place to start. North Street is virtually as Arkwright built it, terraces of sturdy stone cottages, a long way from the popular image of jerry-built back-to-backs that disfigured so many later industrial towns. Things, however, are not quite as they seem. You can still see the long windows on the upper floors, where the men worked at their looms, so that a third of each house was workshop. It was the women and children who went to the mill. From here you can look across the valley to Willersley Castle, the grand house Arkwright built for himself from the new, profitable enterprise. It is difficult now to get much of an impression of what the first mill was like, but it is worth nipping up the road to Matlock Bath to see another Arkwright mill, built in 1784. It looks like an unusually large Georgian house. The original mill itself has suffered sadly with the years, though an extensive restoration programme is under way.

Cromford's success set in train a whole series of events. The canal was built to the town, and you can still travel a section of it by trip boat and visit the very excellent museum that has been built at the Cromford end. But the most remarkable feature was the railway that ran right across the Derbyshire hills: the Cromford and High Peak. Now it is a walkway and cyclepath – though some sections are very daunting on wheels. The railway began down by the canal, and there is a museum in the old maintenance works which explains the system. It leapt up the hills in a series of inclines, with trucks being attached to cables and then hauled up by stationary steam engines. The walk is magnificent, with Derbyshire Peak District scenery at its very best, but the less energetic can sample it along the way. The road out of Cromford crosses the old line just by the Black Rock picnic area. Those curious to see how the system worked can go on up to Rise End, either on foot along the track or by road, and there they will find the Middleton Top Engine House, complete with its original steam engine. Cromford is a place it is hard to leave, but there are compensations in the next section of the journey.

The road through the hills has all the elements that one expects to find in this part of the world: the stone walls, scattered farms, the occasional outcrops of gleaming limestone, all very reminiscent of the best of the Yorkshire Dales. Towns, too, have the same pleasing solidity. Wirksworth has one or two particularly good buildings, but even they sit comfortably in their surroundings with no sense of ostentation. Then, as you move south, it all begins slowly but subtly to change.

Increasingly the countryside becomes dominated by big estates and stone begins to give way to a dark, rather sombre red brick. It is rural, but not obviously pretty: there is nothing chocolate boxey in this area. The real change arrives with the return to the Trent we last saw back at Newark. It is a river with a wide flood plain of meanders and lakes. It is seen at its best from the road on the south bank which takes a high-level route, giving good views, including a sight of that most typical of all Trent-side establishments, a power station. There is one point, not far from here, where you can see three at once. Power stations, however, must take second place, for up ahead is the brewing capital of Britain, Burton-upon-Trent.

Here are breweries of every type and size. There are giants such as Bass, where you visit the museum, which really is well worth the effort for anyone with an interest in beer. There are medium-size brewers such as Marston's, where the famous Burton Union is still at work. This is not a group bargaining over wages and conditions, but an essential part of the brewing system. Fermentation takes place not in huge vats but in row upon row of barrels. As the beer foams, the froth is carried up a pipe to a trough above the barrels and with it goes some of the yeast. In this way, the same strain is kept going year after year. It is a glorious sight to gladden the heart of the enthusiast. There is also Burton's smallest and newest brewery just by the bridge, hence the name Burton Bridge. The beer is made at the back of the pub and drunk at the front. It is exactly what a pub should be. First, and most important, the beer is excellent – and for those who want to try something different, have a go at the dark, slightly sweet porter. The atmosphere is friendly, the surroundings plain and comfortable. It is, in short, a proper pub with no pretensions to being wine bar, bistro or amusement arcade. It makes a great deal of sense to take an overnight stop in Burton – after all, who is going to volunteer to drive afterwards?

Once you leave Burton, it is very clear that the excitement of the hills is very much behind you, and that this is going to be a drive through what we now think of as typically rural England. Farms, fields and hedgerows set the scene. It is pleasantly undemonstrative and apparently timeless, yet you can see in the fields that it was all very different once. Time and again, a field appears like a great green corrugated sheet. The old pattern of open, ploughed fields is preserved as ridge and furrow beneath the grass. Sometimes change came comparatively recently, in historical terms – perhaps no more than two centuries ago. The medieval pattern was broken as sheep or cattle were put to graze where crops once grew and hedges were planted to divide up the old open fields. Historical musings are broken at Twycross, where shocking pink suddenly takes over from restful green as a bend in the road provides a glimpse of the flamingoes at Twycross Zoo. They seem all the more startling for being seen in such a very traditional countryside, surrounded by places with names like Norton-juxta-Twycross and Sheepy Wood.

The stone bridge over the River Amber takes you out of Leicestershire and into Warwickshire, while another bridge in Atherstone takes you across the Coventry Canal. There is a little wharf down by the locks, where with luck you may still see the old narrow boats being loaded with coal. There are few left and now, instead of serving industry, these canal boats are floating coal carts, selling sacks of fuel to householders along the way. The brightly painted boats now look as if they had been specially prepared to create a picturesque effect for the benefit of tourist cameras, but they were once commonplace. The painting brought vivid life and colour to what was, in other ways, a mind-bogglingly cramped living space. That small back cabin was home to an entire family – living room, kitchen and bedroom combined. The colours helped offset a grindingly hard life. Much the same sort of thing has happened to our view of the countryside. The timber-framed thatched cottage may seem idyllic now that it has been modernised; the fields of grain may seem to speak of a rural paradise. We do not see the appalling conditions and misery of the rural poor of Merrie England. Happily for us, all we see are the pleasant results: personal unhappiness does not put in an appearance in bricks and timber, any more than brightly painted roses and castles on a canal boat tell a story of hard work.

The scenery tends to lull one into a comfortable complacency, reinforced by a touch of rural artifice in the shape of a little octagonal thatched lodge. It makes the appearance of a vast working colliery among the fields and hedgerows all the more a visual shock. Suddenly, in place of Bentley Common and Tithe Farm, you have a signpost to Furnace End. It does not last long, as the road manages to keep an essentially rural character while sliding neatly between Coventry and Birmingham.

Berkswell is every bit a country village. It even has a well, beside which stands the very fine Well House. This is an area of brick and timber, but anyone wanting an ostentatious display of wealth usually managed to introduce a little stone to highlight doorways, windows and corners. The combination of brick, timber and stone even spreads to the church. It is a most surprising building. Basically, it appears as simply a conventional stone church, but a porch has been added – timber framed with brick infill and a little room up above. It is like a small cottage tacked on at the front. I very nearly missed the church's real glory. I was wandering around, when the lady who had come to do the flowers offered to show me the crypt. Down a staircase in between the pews is a perfectly preserved Romanesque building. It is severely simple, with a visual effect entirely dependent on the dramatic geometry of vaults and arches. The stonework is almost crude, but is undeniably powerful. Here you can see the origins of the phrase 'the weakest go to the wall' in the low stone seat for the very old and very young that runs round the chapel. Inevitably, this area is Midlands-commuter land, and the old essentials of country life are now reduced to the purely ornamental. Balsall Common windmill, a fine brick tower topped with a boat-shaped cap to which the sails are attached, now stands in a garden like a bigger version of one of those plaster mills that one finds surrounded by fishing gnomes.

Kenilworth is dominated by the castle, which looks exactly what it was, a mighty and powerful fortress. The immediate surroundings may be faintly suburban, but the building itself is overwhelming. At its heart lies the great tower built on an earlier Norman motte in the late twelfth century. King John added the frowning curtain wall which now looms above a high green bank. Once it looked even better, for the ground around the walls was excavated and flooded to create a lake, turning the castle into a fortified island. It suffered the fate of others of its kind in the aftermath of the Civil War, when it was left to fall into ruin and Cromwell ordered the lake to be drained. There are two schools of thought about castles: there are those who admire the ruins, left much as they were when the castle was still an important defended centre; and those who prefer the lived-in variety, often with an artificial medievalism reinforcing the emphasis of the original. For the former Kenilworth is as good as they come: the latter will probably want to hurry on to Warwick.

Warwick Castle comes with all the trimmings. In itself it is magnificent. The setting above the Avon is perfect; the entrance of massive gateway flanked by defensive towers a model of impregnability. Guy's Tower, one of the pair, has walls 10ft thick, while its partner, Caesar's Tower, makes assurance doubly sure with two sets of battlements. Inside the castle there is everything to appeal to the romantic, from dungeon complete with torture chamber to the Great Hall with its armoury and a resident ghost. The lily, however, comes heavily gilded. Medieval banquets are held, all very Gadzooks. A Victorian weekend party can be viewed – and not just any weekend party, but a royal one, courtesy of Madame Tussauds. And so it goes on. Those who thrill to Kenilworth will probably wince at Warwick. But the castle is not the whole town.

The main street runs from Eastgate to Westgate, helpfully defining the old limits of the town walls, and all suggestions of widening the gates to benefit motorists have sensibly been ignored. Warwick, unlike its castle, carries its age unselfconsciously, and it is remarkable how many ancient buildings survived a disastrous fire of 1694. Some of the replacements are themselves notable. The Court House dates from the 1720s and was designed by Francis Smith, an architect well versed in the practicalities of building as his father was a bricklayer. Church Street leads off as expected to the church and the market square. The church itself was one of the victims of the fire, though something of the old miraculously survived a heat strong enough to melt the bells in the tower. This is a church which seems dedicated to the greater glory of the Earls of Warwick. Even the chapter house is dominated by the rather monstrous tomb of Sir Fulke Greville, who was given the castle in 1604. It is a bizarre affair, a mixture of decorative devices from columns to obelisks. In a town of old buildings, the Lord Leycester Hospital is outstanding. This was originally the fourteenth-century Guild headquarters, but in 1571 the Earl of Leicester – then spelt Leycester – took them over, added a chapel above the gateway and created a home for old soldiers and their families. So it remains. It epitomises the special appeal of old timber-framed buildings full of odd angles and corners, gables and porches and with an ever-lively facade of windows and exposed timbers.

Nearby Stratford-upon-Avon also has its fair share of old buildings, but it is impossible to see Stratford just as a market town on the Avon, though sometimes one cannot help wondering what it would be like if Shakespeare had not been born here. But he was, and his presence is inescapable. It is not just the obvious Hamlet cafes and Much Ado About Nothing snackbars, but rather, as with Burns in Dumfries, the way in which every genuinely old building is judged by its associations with the man. The house where he was born, and the church where he was buried, are places of pilgrimage for people from all over the world, and quite rightly so. For here was a man for whom the well-worn epithet 'universal genius' is no more than a simple statement of fact. Yet for all his local associations, one can learn little from a tour of the sites, and the man himself remains at best a shadowy figure. But there is no point in complaining about the Shakespeare industry: it has been with us for centuries. In the eighteenth century they did a good line in selling chips off the Bard's chair, and one tourist calculated that given the number of pieces on sale it must have stood 20ft high. Stratford does, however, have one building that brings his genius to light in the best possible way, the Royal Shakespeare Theatre. Shakespeare lives in the plays, and the plays live in performance. Stratford at its best does Shakespeare incomparably well, and even productions that are not up to the very highest level still have a special aura, and high standards. As an actor friend remarked: 'When the script says "fanfare" they don't press a button on the tape recorder, half a dozen blokes with trumpets stand up and blow'. It makes a difference. To visit Stratford without seeing a play would be like visiting Salzburg and not hearing any Mozart.

There are other aspects to the town: the pedestrian bridge over the river once carried a tramway down to Moreton-in-Marsh, and one of the old trucks is preserved at the town end. There is boating on the river and boating on the canal, but it is the poet and playwright who insists on dominating everything. Once you leave Stratford, however, you soon find yourself faced with one of those changes in the landscape that reflects changes in the earth beneath your feet. Mickleton marks the divide, where the brick and timber of the Midlands begins to give way to stone. You have arrived at the Cotswolds. If ever there was an area whose charm depends on the vagaries of geology then this is it. The underlying stone is an oolitic limestone and the magic is produced because it is available in two forms – as a building stone and in slate-like slabs for roofing. It is a most beautiful stone, rich in colour and texture, and the combination of stone house and stone-slate roof is irresistibly appealing. Some are inclined to dismiss the Cotswolds as being rather twee, but this is not really so at all. The buildings themselves are beautiful but very robust. The fact that everyone seems to respond to them is not due to a sentimental attachment to some olde-worlde illusion, but a reflection of their intrinsic value. If you could wave a wand and remove every tourist from one of the beauty-spot villages, it would be easier to see it for what it is: a collection of buildings completely at one with the environment.

Chipping Campden is a case in point. It still has something of the air of the days when this was one of the principal market towns of the wool trade. It still has its fourteenth-century wool-staplers hall, its pillared market hall, quite a newcomer by Campden's standards, only dating back to 1627, and its church. Wherever money was made in wool it is reflected in the local church. But where in East Anglian towns such as Lavenham it is expressed in a wealth of rich decoration, here there is a sense of cool dignity. It might seem almost austere, but no building constructed of the local stone can ever be free of that touch of warmth and deep colour that the stone itself brings with it. The values at Chipping

159

Campden are spread throughout the Cotswolds. Just occasionally, very occasionally, things seem to have gone a little too far. At the top of the hill outside Broad Campden is the thatched cottage to end all thatched cottages, a beetle-browed building almost lost beneath its roof. Blockley, though, has everything just right and one oddity, a carved memorial to a pet trout. But just when the pattern of the country is getting firmly set on the eye, and you are complacently thinking that you know what to expect from the region, it throws Sezincote at you.

The grounds at first give no hint of anything unusual. The trees may be particularly large, the water gardens exceptionally decorative, but everything falls very much into the English landscape-garden tradition. But then you find a little garden temple, not as you might expect in the style of classical Greece but in the forms of moghul India. It is a hint of things to come with the house itself, which sports a grand onion dome and minarets, mixing a touch uneasily with home-grown Gothic. It is like wandering down a quiet lane and being confronted with the Brighton pavilion. Both buildings in fact have the same inspiration in British trade with India, and the style was even given a name which fits its ambiguities: Hindoo-Gothic. It is nothing to do with the Cotswolds at all; it is a one-off, an exotic fantasy. After Sezincote, it almost comes as a surprise to find traditional Cotswold styles returning.

The Cotswold hills are so gentle that one is scarcely aware of them being uplands at all except in winter, when roads are regularly blocked by snow. But there is something of the upland look to the scenery with its stone walls and swoops and dives to little valleys. Upper Swell is just the opposite of Sezincote, a practical place that gains its character from the land. Houses seem almost ready to tumble down the steep hillside, ready to go like a line of dominoes. And, at the bottom, a stream slides quietly past the old mill. Beyond it is Stow-on-the-Wold, a place which one suspects would be happy to slip into gentility and would have made it sooner but for its two invasions in May and October for the horse fairs. The place then simply bursts with life. There were people of all kinds, from the ladies in head scarves and green wellies to the gentlemen in greasy caps who seem reluctant to offer too many facts about the pedigree of the pony on sale – nor even to be very keen to say where it was the previous week. Smart horse boxes rubbed against old caravans, and the accents that could be heard above the background of bargaining and clopping hooves cover the whole of the British Isles. This was no tourist event but a genuine fair where real bargains were struck, where the streets steamed with the gently rising sweat of horses and echoed to the shouts of enthusiastic dealers. This was tradition as a live, vibrant thing: now they have moved it to Andoversford. Shame on them.

Wyck Beacon to the south of Stow is one of the few places in the Cotswolds where you do feel up in the world, a genuine hill with a view, and from here the road begins to wander down to the Barringtons and the Windrush valley. These villages are off the main roads and, it seems, off the tourist circuit, and one hesitates to mention them at all. Great Barrington is, as the name suggests, the larger of the two and sits at the side of a big estate hidden from the common gaze behind high walls. But Little Barrington is as near as you can get to the archetypal unspoiled Cotswold village. It sits up proudly on its own little hillside with houses of stone and stone-slate roofs facing out not so much on to a green as a little common of rough pasture. Between these two villages flows the Windrush. What a hideous disappointment it would be if a river with such a lovely name were not itself lovely but there is no disappointment. It wanders through the meadows, beneath trailing willows and seems in no hurry to get anywhere.

Burford brings you very firmly back to the popular Cotswolds. It is the sort of place where it is easier to buy a Georgian side table than it is to get a loaf of bread. Filkins, however, brings something which one thought had vanished from the area long ago, the Cotswold Woollen Weavers. The name does not really do them justice, for they are more than weavers. Here they start with the fleece and finish with the garment. There is nothing arty crafty about it. This is, in effect, a small industrial unit with carding engine, ring frame for spinning and power looms at work. Many of the garments, such as coats, make use of the beautifully soft, naturally blended colours of the wool from Jacob sheep. It is wholly satisfying to be able not just to see all the processes at work but to discover that there is a product of real quality at the end. It makes an appropriate end to the Cotswolds, for the road now runs down to Lechlade and the Thames.

This is now the head of navigation, the highest point that motor cruisers on the river can reach. It is still a quiet spot, because although holiday boats can come here, few do: they tend to stay with the more popular river below Oxford. Yet for many of us, this is the Thames at its best, peaceful and relaxed. There were moves to extend navigation, as it used to be extended, to Cricklade, but they came to nothing, so the Upper Thames seems very likely to remain the peaceful backwater it is today. With the crossing of the river, the countryside changes again, to what will be, in effect, the last major transformation of the journey.

South of Lechlade, the road heads off to the Vale of the White Horse and an area that is almost incredibly rich in reminders of the ancient past. At first there are few hints of what is to come, just a rather peaceful countryside with an air of wellbeing: Round Robin Farm just outside Highworth could almost be taken for a small village. Then you reach Uffington and get a sight of the white horse itself. It is carved out of the turf of the hillside, like the Cerne Giant, displaying the white chalk underneath. Is it really a horse or is it a dragon? It is highly stylised and sinuous enough to be a dragon. Whatever it is, it is a wonderfully lively creature that seems ready to set off on a gallop over the Downs. No matter how many times you see it, it remains amazing. No one is altogether certain about when it was first carved. It is set near an Iron-Age hill fort, and its shape is not dissimilar to that seen on Celtic crosses, so it may be that old. Others say that it was cut by an Anglo-Saxon leader to celebrate victory over the Danes. Whenever it was made, the riddle remains the same. How was it made? If you go up the hill and stand on the horse you get no idea of what it is, for it is simply too big. You can picnic on his eyeball. So how did the carvers know how to make the cuts to create an effect which they could not see?

The green-sea swells of downland now dominate the journey. Towns take what space they can in the narrow river valleys. Marlborough spreads itself as a wide high street down the Kennet valley. Its identity is plain, a market town happily situated on the main road from London to Bath. Its old coaching inns still look as if they could accommodate the fast mail should it turn up. But having had a taste of the ancient world, it is very tempting to hurry on to a group of sites which together are as extraordinary and impressive as any in Britain. There is no easy way to take them all in as they lie on a triangle of roads, but there is .a certain logic in going clockwise, since at least you keep going in the same direction all the time. It also brings the grandest of them all as a climax.

The first thing you see, and you really cannot miss it, is Silbury Hill, a great cone with a flattened top big enough for a football pitch. It is entirely artificial, involved vast labour in its construction and no-one really has the faintest idea what it is. There is no shortage of myths and theories, the most popular of which has King Sil dressed in golden armour and sat astride a horse at its heart. But probing and burrowing have revealed no king, no armour, no horse – nothing. It has been estimated that it would have taken five hundred workers at least ten years to build it, and all we are left with is a giant mystery. Across the road, a walk away, is another site which also dates from the Neolithic or New Stone Age. This is West Kennet long barrow, a huge burial chamber under a hundred-yard-long mound. The entrance is marked by tall stones, behind which is a passageway that leads deep into the mound to two burial chambers, roofed with stone. The tomb was actually used for burials for a period of a thousand years before it was filled in and the entrance closed with stone slabs.

Avebury, the third site, is a henge, a monument like a great arena surrounded by high bank and ditch. Originally the earthworks were even more startling than they are today for the ditch was as much as 9ft deep and would have shone out as exposed chalk. Inside the great work was set a large circle of standing stones and two other smaller circles. The site is big enough to encompass most of the present village of Avebury. It is certainly Neolithic, and certainly had religious significance. But were the alignments of stones significant? Did they tie in with astronomical calculations? Rather as with Silbury Hill, there is a definite excess of theories over facts. At least it gives the visitors freedom to let their own imaginations work on this extraordinary site. And this is not yet the end of the story, for on the way out the road runs by and, for a while, through an avenue of standing stones, a strictly formal, processional climax to the visit. The one sadness about Avebury is that The Sanctuary to which the avenue once led is no more.

Tumuli and ancient earthworks continue to dot the downland and there is even a second white horse, neither as grand nor as old as Uffington's on Churchill Down. You can compare it with the real thing, for the springy turf that overlies the chalk makes

163

this perfect ground for racehorses to be put through their paces on the gallops. This is virtually the end of the Downs, and as one comes down to the lusher ground and the Avon valley you soon find that much of the best landscape has been appropriated by the rich. Whole areas have been enclosed and turned into parkland. Even the local villages have had to conform to the tastes of the landowners. Left to their own devices, the locals could not be relied on to fit neatly into the carefully organised naturalness that surrounds so many of the great houses. The answer was to knock down the old and build a new village in a style suggesting a rural idyll. There is a splendid example of just such a model village at Sandy Lane, where every cottage is rustic stone and thatch. It is the orderliness of it all that gives it away as an artifice. It cannot compete, however, with the real thing, even if very much attached to a grand house and almost as orderly. For the real thing shows the subtle variations that come with centuries of use.

Lacock is approached via yet more parkland spiked with lodges and folly towers. They bring you down to the Avon and a long, low snaking bridge. The Coun.. ss of Salisbury founded a nunnery here in 1232, but it went the way of all such establishments in the reign of Henry VIII. It was bought by William Sharington, a man of taste who built himself a house on the site that managed to preserve much of the old. Later it came into the hands of the Talbot family, enthusiastic Gothicisers in the eighteenth-century fashion. The result is that Lacock Abbey not only still has some of its old ecclesiastical buildings standing, but contrives to retain its air of medievalism. Jane Austen's heroine, so disconcerted by the comforts of Northanger Abbey, would have had nothing to complain of here. She could have walked genuine cloisters and let her vivid imagination populate them with the ghosts of the past. What the cloisters do have is a set of carved bosses on a watery theme. There are the naturalistic – swans and ducks to match those on the river outside, and the fanciful – seahorses and mermaids. But the most famous part of the abbey is an unobtrusive oriel window, famous because it was the first subject to be photographed by William Henry Fox Talbot, the father of modern photography. In 1844 he published *The Pencil of Nature*, the first book ever to be illustrated by photographs. A museum at the entrance to the abbey shows Fox Talbot's work and changing photographic exhibitions. The village of Lacock is as neat and tidy as any model village, but one soon realises that the buildings cover a span of centuries. Grandest by far is the old tithe barn, but even that is going to be overshadowed by the next tithe barn met just a few miles ahead.

The towns of the Avon valley prospered on the wool trade, reaching a peak of prosperity in the age of the water-powered mill. It was the coming of steam power that pushed them into decline, as the industry became increasingly concentrated in the north of England with its extensive coalfields. In their day, towns such as Melksham thrived, but if you want to measure the real wealth of the trade, there is no better place to visit than Bradford-on-Avon. This is a town with a long history. It has a tiny Saxon church and an absolutely vast fourteenth-century tithe barn that once belonged to Shaftesbury Abbey. The Town Bridge is handsome and unusual in having what may once have been a small chapel, and was certainly for a time the lock-up, built into it. But what really impresses is the quality of the houses: splendid individual houses, once owned by clothiers, such as Westbury House, and whole terraces that create a lovely effect ranged across the hillside above the river. Middle Rank and Tory – no political significance – with their warm, stone walls and stone-slate roofs, full of odd angles and gables, are streets that would be memorable anywhere. They combine elements of the picturesque with a certain eighteenth-century formality, but what gives them an extra quality is their airy situation high above the river. There is another Bradford to see as well, the working town of mills straggling out along the river. Abbey Mill still dominates, even though it has not been used for woollens for very many years.

The final stage takes us down the increasingly dramatic Avon valley. The wandering river has carved itself a deep gorge and everything else has to cram in as best it can, including the transport routes – all three of them. Running almost side by side are road, railway and the Kennet and Avon canal. It is the latter which enjoys the best of the scenery and which has the most impressive structures. Forced by the narrowness of the valley to take his canal from one side to the other, the engineer John Rennie crossed the Avon via the Dundas aqueduct. It is a bold piece of engineering, an archway that strides high above the river, and it is also a magnificent example of classical architecture built in the local Bath stone. It can still stand comparison with anything that elegant city itself can put against it. The canal here is at its most beautiful, and is a joy to explore, either on foot on the towpath or in one of the day-hire boats available at the aqueduct. Those who stay with the road get only a few tantalising glimpses.

Claverton offers a choice between two wholly different attractions. Staying with the canal theme, one can turn down to see the pumping station. This is not as dull as it might sound. A weir crosses the river, making a surprisingly attractive feature by creating little waterfalls and pools. From here a channel leads water down to the pumps, for it is water that will do the work. An immense water wheel turns and drives a pair of beam pumps which shoot the water up the hillside to supply the canal. It is a mechanical marvel and on one glorious day in the summer of 1989 Claverton pumps were called on for something more than just demonstrations. Modern technology failed, the electric pumps packed up and for twenty-four hours the canal was kept going by the power of the waterwheel. The other attraction is almost equally surprising. Claverton Manor looks, and is, a typical, rather refined English country house. It is also a piece of America dropped down in these unlikely surroundings. On display are the decorative arts of America from the late seventeenth to the mid-nineteenth century and all kinds of Americans get a look in, from the Indians to those constructors of beautifully crafted furniture, the Shakers. Even the garden has an American arboretum. It looks just the place where one could stop for tea and biscuits on the lawn, but here tea and cookies is the order of the day.

Claverton is not a bad last stop before the end of the road arrives at Bath, for it has all the qualities that one hopes to find on a journey: beautiful scenery, places of interest and, perhaps most important of all, the element of surprise. Beyond is Bathampton where the river swings sharply to the west, taking the road along with it and there, spread out before you, is Bath once again.

9
Four Detours

For those who might complain about regions that have received too little attention on this journey, four detours are given in this chapter, any of which can be tacked on to expand the main route.

SOUTHERN ENGLAND

The first detour is for those leaving London by road and it begins when you head off the M4 for Windsor. This is one of those places which could well be just another small town. It stands on the river but one is hardly aware of that. The main street has, perhaps, rather more than its share of antique shops and wine bars, but would otherwise be unremarkable if it were not for the fact that at the end of the road is an incredible theatrical backdrop. The round tower of Windsor Castle rises up, a giant cylinder, closing off the view, immensely impressive, wholly romantic. In fact, this is the tower seen at its best. Close up you become aware that it, like a good deal more of the castle, is an elaborate fake, conceived in a period from 1824 to 1840 by Sir Jeffrey Wyattville. There is a real medieval castle lurking under the nineteenth-century fakery, and there is the glorious St George's Chapel, one of the finest Tudor churches in the kingdom. But somehow it remains an uneasy mixture, both home and castle, a toy fort grown up. Across the river one can see Eton or Eau Ton, the water town. There is a chapel that rivals St George's in its splendour and the playing fields on which, reputedly, the Duke of Wellington declared that the battle of Waterloo was won. I have always wondered on whose playing fields other battles were lost: Harrow presumably. To the south of Windsor the map leads you to expect a very countrifed route, liberally spattered with woodland open spaces, even if the towns are all quite close together. In the event, the trees are there in profusion and make a splendid sight, yet this remains a

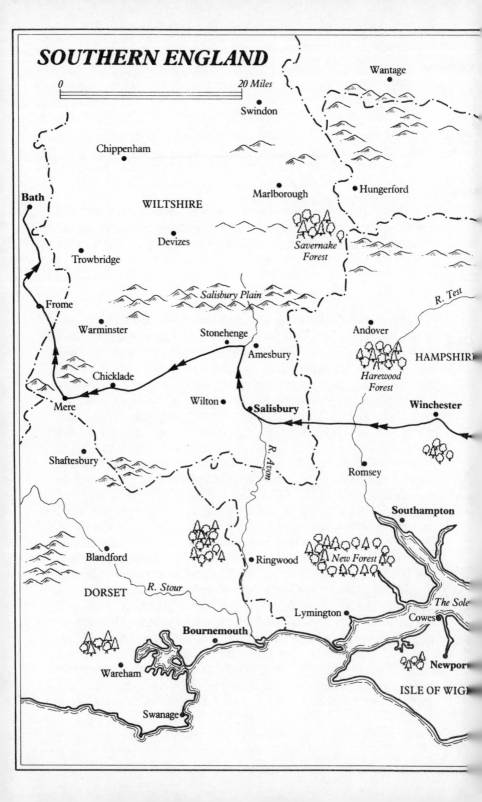

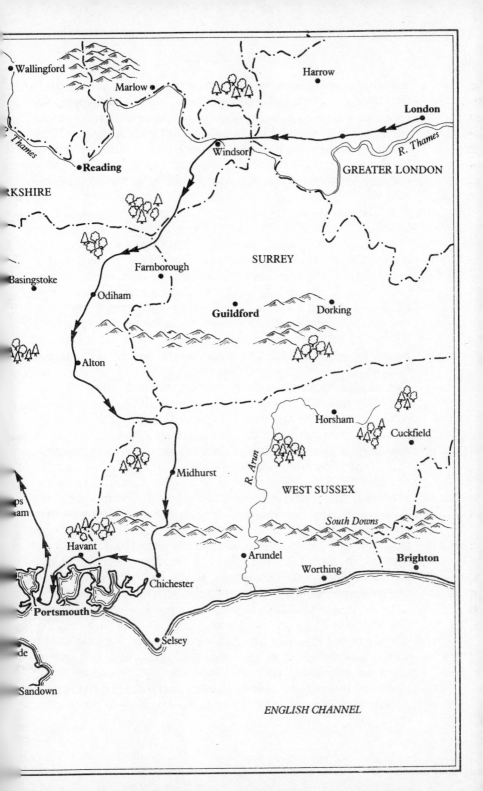

suburban countryside. You never quite get away from the houses, for they are not just gathered together in towns and villages, but continually crop up in isolated splendour, complete with two-car garages. There is a sudden opening up to wide spaces at Ascot Heath, but even this is not true countryside for it is dominated by the famous racecourse and the stand, which looks from a distance like a factory for the manufacture of washing machines. And when the racecourse ends the golf course begins.

In the woodland to the north of Camberley is a hill fort, known as Caesar's Camp – it is probably Iron Age not Roman, though a Roman road does also run through the woods. If it does nothing else it gives a sense of continuity, for Camberley is very much a military town. The Royal Military Academy lies just off the road, though it properly belongs not to Camberley but to Sandhurst, a couple of miles away. Increasingly, however, everything is becoming subservient to commuter developments. There is a rash of neo-Georgian building in this region, mostly unconvincing. One begins to think that this spread of commuter land will go on forever, but then one reaches a place which has its own identity firmly in place. Hartley Wintney still has at least the well-preserved memories of its rural past, with a wide, tree-studded green complete with duckpond. Perhaps the locals do all pop down to the station for the morning train to the City, but it does not show. It marks the start of an increasingly pleasant journey.

If Hartley Wintney suggests the rural life, Odiham Common provides the real thing. This is a genuine common of rough grassland, still grazed by cattle, though on this occasion the cows were not the familiar sloe-eyed, slightly mournful creatures that one usually finds, but rather frisky beasts with quite alarmingly long horns. The town itself is a quietly prosperous place, now bypassed by the main road. But if it has lost one route, it has gained another. The Basingstoke Canal has been restored, so that now you can wander down to the wharf, with its inevitable accompaniment of canalside pub, and enjoy one of those scenes which delight canal lovers. It is the simplicity that makes it; the easy curve of the bridge humped over the water, the little wharf, a tree that droops over the boats and the swans that gather expecting goodies. Even if no boats were ever to use the canal again, the restoration would have been justified, for it has turned a scene of dereliction into a thing of beauty. Beyond the town, a

170

sudden shattering burst of brilliant white appears at a chalk quarry, announcing the arrival of the North Downs. The woodland and common are left behind as the road climbs the slope of the dome to a countryside of fields and copses.

There is one last reminder of the rather anonymous southeast of modern times. Alton, at first glance, could be Croydon. It does, however, also have its own restored transport route as well, not canal this time, but rail. Out of Alton station at one end go the regular British Rail services, while out in the opposite direction go the steam specials of the Mid-Hants Railway. This preserved railway used to be known as the Watercress Line, which at least gives an idea of the pleasant country through which it passes but does not tell you that this is a line which, in railway terms, has mountains to climb. It huffs and puffs up to a summit and thankfully idles down the other side to Alresford. It is a line which offers the experience of travelling again behind locomotives which pulled main-line expresses in the days of steam.

Chawton offers very different pleasures. There are places associated with famous authors which seem to offer no real insights into their world. You can learn more about Shakespeare by spending five minutes with one of his plays then you can from an hour walking the streets of Stratford. Chawton is different. If admirers of Jane Austen had been asked to invent a place for her to live, then this would be it, so that when you get here you can scarcely accept it as real. This is precisely the world of the novels. The social niceties of the place can be seen: you feel you could walk from the house in the village across the fields to the big house; there is a garden for strolling in, for conversation. Chawton is as complete in itself as the world laid out for us in Jane Austen's fiction. She herself wrote some friendly lines just after her arrival in July 1809, ending:

And how convinced, that when complete
It will all other Houses beat
That ever have been made or mended
With rooms concise, or rooms distended.

It has to be said that she was guilty of a little playful exaggeration. The house is little more than a cottage, but neat, comfortable and attractive. There are few more poignant reminders of a writer's life than the little desk on top of a table in the diningroom. It was

171

here in these modest surroundings that she wrote the masterpieces. The house and the village now seem as much her creations as the words on the page. All lovers of Jane Austen's work will find at Chawton the shock of recognition.

Jane Austen took the life of Chawton and transformed it into fiction. The Reverend Gilbert White was content to record in meticulous detail the natural history of Selborne. The book appeared in 1788 and is one of the few undisputed classics of natural history writing, which can be read today with as much pleasure as when it was new. It is a book that nags at one long after it is finished, and particularly when one arrives here to spend a short time before dashing on to somewhere else. For White found all the world he needed right here in Selborne, constantly fascinating, always changing. All you need to enjoy it is the patience of the careful observer. You can visit his home, but a far better way to enter into his world is to walk up the zigzag path through the woods that White himself created with the help of his brother. It is at its best in autumn, when your slow climb brings you through a blaze of trees to look down on the little village, snug beneath the shelter of the hills. Sadly, you can never quite recreate White's world, for even here there is a background buzz of traffic, as irritating as a mosquito in a bedroom, but you can get close to it. To sit on the hilltop and simply watch is pleasure enough: to gain all the nuances that White gained here takes a little longer. Twenty years would seem to be adequate.

Down in the village there is another attraction, a Romany Caravan museum, a spot where every inch of space seems to be taken up by beautifully decorated horsedrawn vans. Driving out of the village, one passes a sign which suggests that the love of nature is still alive in Selborne for it asks you to take care not to squash toads. Perhaps they fare better than they did two centuries ago, for White recalls a time 'when a quack at this village, ate a toad to make the country people stare' – enough, one would have thought, to make anyone stare. I saw no toads, squashed or otherwise, but enjoyed a pleasant twisting road. The way beyond Liphook was even better, running through Linchmere Common, a woodland of silver birch through which the sun filtered to pattern a floor thick with bracken. This, you feel, is a genuine part of the old English countryside and so it would seem to be, for the land is marked out by high banks, defining ancient boundaries. Along the way is Shulbrede Priory, stoutly dignified with solid stone walls, richly coloured tile roof and tall brick chimneys. It was one of the few buildings met along the way, but if there were not many people around the lack was more than made up for in pheasants. The birds are everywhere, pecking in fields, scuttling across the road or simply staring at the car, seemingly mesmerised. This is a heavy land of heavy soils, which was once all dense forest, and woodland still provides the dominant theme. Villages retain the air of occupying little clearings, and it is only when you reach the river valley that a sizeable town appears. A large mill stands by the Rother and across the bridge is Midhurst, a typical small market town where the one building that really catches the eye is, surprisingly, the Catholic church.

Now the scenery changes again, for up ahead lies the steep face of the South Downs. It is tempting to go straight on to the top but it is well worth making a short detour into Cocking. Next to the bubbling, clear water of a spring stands the parish church. It is quite ordinary apart from its exceptional thirteenth-century mural. This shows the shepherds at the nativity. These are no Middle Eastern shepherds, but sturdy Sussex men straight off the Downs, with their old-style Sussex crooks and sheepdogs at their feet. To see the Downs themselves as they should be seen, you need to walk, and as the South Downs Way crosses the road at the top of the hill there is no excuse. The area is more heavily wooded than much of the downland, but if you walk west for just a little way you get one of those broad vistas which are such a feature of the area, and can look out across the trees and hamlets of the Weald.

Once up at the top, you can always be sure of a roller coaster ride over and round the undulating hills. At Singleton, in the heart of the Downs, you will find the Weald and Downland Open Air Museum. It occupies an enormous site, and is definitely not the sort of place to pop into if you have a few odd minutes to spare; half a day and you will just about get by. This could be described as an architectural rescue zone for buildings of worth threatened with destruction. They have been carefully dismantled and just as carefully reassembled here. There are buildings of all kinds and periods, each reflecting a different aspect of everyday life in the region – medieval houses, and a Tudor market hall, black-smith's forge and village school. There are more than thirty of them altogether and there are also examples of rural crafts and industries. The water mill brought to the site has been put back into working order, and a typical charcoal burner's camp has been recreated. The latter was once part of the main industrial life of the region, for until the eighteenth century charcoal was the fuel that fed the blast furnaces in which iron was produced. It seems odd today, that this peaceful corner of rural England lay at the heart of Tudor industrial life. It was down among the woods and streams of the Weald that the furnaces roared, producing iron for almost anything from nails to cannon. Now almost all that is left is a museum exhibit.

The downland stretches almost to the sea, and where the sea has bitten deep into the land there you will find the ancient city of Chichester. The basic plan is still the one established by the Romans. They built walls, quite modest affairs, in the shape of an eleven-sided polygon with the main street pattern based on a simple cross. A medieval wall was built over the Roman and much of it remains, while the street pattern too remains much as it was nineteen hundred years ago. So what better place could one start than in the centre, with the Market Cross given to the city by one of its bishops in 1501. It has seen changes but it is still a genuine centrepiece, startlingly ornate and an ideal meeting place. The most recent addition to it is the clock, which only arrived in 1724. But although Chichester is an ancient foundation and has a Norman cathedral, notable for some superb Romanesque carvings, it never seems to be that old. Round about 1700 a huge rebuilding programme began, not in the traditional materials of the area, timber and flint, but in newly fashionable brick. When an old house was not pulled down it was usually given a new brick facade to disguise its age. Almost everywhere you turn in the town centre you will find houses of extraordinary quality and finesse. Pallant House is as fine a brick building as you could hope to find. It is not just the overall effect, grand as it is, it is the detail that is so remarkable. Nowadays we tend to think of a brick building as a series of bricks, piled course upon course until they reach a height when the roof can be popped on. Not here: look, for example, above the windows, where the bricks have been cut to create a waving edge like a softly folded curtain, and a brick emblem stands proudly in the centre. It is craftsmanship of an extraordinary order, and this is only the best in a street of quality where any of the other houses would seem remarkable in less exalted company. Anyone who enjoys eighteenth-century architecture is in for a feast at Chichester.

Chichester also has its curiosities. St Mary's Hospital looks exactly like a church, walk inside and it still looks like a church, with an immense roof of oak trusses. There is a chapel at the end of the 'nave' but the 'aisles' actually consist of a set of little rooms, still in use as almshouses as they have been for seven centuries. St Peter's shopping arcade also looks like a church, and once was. When it became redundant the shell was kept intact and a number of small shops built inside. The surprising thing is that it actually works rather well. But to see the oldest surviving building from Chichester's past you have to leave the centre and head out to a suburban estate, the unlikely setting for the Fishbourne Roman Palace.

The palace was begun towards the end of the first century AD with, as the adverts have it, no expense spared. Part of the site had already been built over when the remains were discovered in 1960, but what can be seen gives a notion of just how luxurious it once was. The original was actually destroyed by fire in the third century, molten lead from the roof spattering over the floors. Over the centuries, the stone was gradually removed for other buildings and the old floors covered by earth and vegetation. But once that was cleared away a set of superb mosaic floors were revealed: a winged cupid rides the waves on a dolphin, sea monsters cavort and a Medusa head hisses with concentrated evil. A unique feature is the garden, a very formal affair which has now been replanted to grow just as it would have done when the Romans walked the pathways.

The main road to Portsmouth can be tediously crowded, and a detour on the B road provided a route which seemed far too wide and handsome for its lowly status. It also provided an extraordinary sight near Funtingdon. An old airfield contained what looked from a distance like row upon row of miniature hangars. These little corrugated arches were home to literally hundreds of pigs, porkers stretching away to the horizon, a sea of snuffling, grunting pink. The actual approach to Portsmouth is not quite what one expects, for it begins with the seaside resort of Southsea. But the navy seems to have had a hand in almost every development in the area, and this is no exception, for the resort began as a smart suburb for naval officers and their families. In any case, the military presence soon asserts itself with Southsea Castle built on the orders of Henry VIII, and probably the first fortification to be built primarily to act as a gun battery. This is the true start of Portsmouth, the heavily defended city with its curtain wall defying would-be invaders. Old Portsmouth itself has great charm, but the real lure is there in the glimpse of a ship at the end of a street, or the sight of a mast climbing high above the rooftops. The attraction is irresistible for here one can see three great warships spanning a period of development of over three centuries. Each is in its own way remarkable.

Those who saw the remains of the *Mary Rose* being lifted from the waves in 1982 could be forgiven for wondering what the fuss was all about. It looked like a large piece of driftwood. It seemed an appalling anticlimax to an extraordinary story. The ship was built around 1510 but sank off Portsmouth in 1545. Warships in that day were floating fortresses whose main function was to bring the rival forces close enough together to fight with bow and arrow and cannon. That day *Mary Rose* was laden with around seven hundred men and heavy ordnance – in the event too heavily laden. The waves came through the gun ports and she sank before ever reaching the enemy fleet. Her discovery and salvage ranks as one of the great feats of underwater archaeology and now that the remains are on show we can see that it really was worthwhile. The 'piece of driftwood' turns out to be almost the whole of one side of the vessel. Constantly sprayed to preserve the timbers, she seems to float up out of the mist towards you like a ghost ship. What one sees though is very recognisably a warship, from the gently flowing lines of the hull to the sudden upsurge of the sheer walls of the sterncastle, which was literally what its name suggests, a wooden fortress at the stern for the fighting men. Almost as remarkable are the aretefacts: the machines of war, cannon, longbows and arrows; navigational instruments that any deep-sea yachtsman could still use today and, most poignantly, the small personal relics left by the drowned men.

The next and most famous of the warships brings us forward to 1765. HMS *Victory* was thus already somewhat aged when she had her finest hour at Trafalgar in 1805, and after years of refits and repairs it is doubtful if many of the original timbers now survive. She represents the end of an age of great wooden sailing ships with their banks of cannon. She is an undeniably impressive sight, lording it over the naval dockyard, but when you go down to the gun decks with their seemingly endless row of cannon, you do wonder what life must have been like for an ordinary seaman in Nelson's navy. *Victory* had a ship's complement of 850 men and most of them lived in spaces such as this; sanitation was virtually non-existent, conditions incredibly cramped. The ship may have been glorious in battle, but as a home on the sea must have been little better than a floating slum.

The trio is completed by the latest arrival, HMS *Warrior*. The story of this vessel's restoration is almost as remarkable as that of the *Mary Rose*. When I first saw her in 1981 she was a hulk and restoration was just getting under way. She was still recog-nisably a fine vessel but without masts and rigging, and below decks there were just one or two pieces of machinery. Now she is as grand as when she first set sail in 1861. This is the first of Britain's ironclads, the first of a new generation of battleships. By the mid-nineteenth century, the rifled gun, firing shells, had replaced the old cannon, and the new armament could rip the old wooden walls apart in seconds. *Warrior* was the answer, with the hull built as a sandwich: the iron hull itself was covered by a layer of teak, outside of which was iron armour plating. This was not the only change, for although she still carried sail, she also had a steam engine. Now, everything is restored, from the spoons on the captain's table to the slowly turning cranks of her engine. It is difficult to believe that only a decade ago this was Milford Haven Oil Hulk C77.

Leaving Portsmouth involves a long slog through the suburbs that spread out all the way to Waterlooville, but once clear you are back to the gently swelling hills of the Downs and a place of pilgrimage for all true lovers of cricket, the village of Hambledon. The cricket club was founded in 1760, and it was not long before the game had become sufficiently popular for the village team to challenge not the next village, but the rest of England. What those men of Hambledon would have made of the modern game, of test matches played around the world, one cannot imagine. But they would surely recognise the Sunday-afternoon game of village cricket as essentially the sport they began and fostered. The rules may have changed, even the bat and ball have been altered, but the event itself is basically the same. One of the great virtues of village cricket is that it still has room at some level for the hopelessly inept enthusiast – as the author can testify. For some of us, a score greater than one against Little Piddington-in-the-Marsh second eleven is a triumph to savour for weeks. There are many reminders of the cricketing past in the village itself – even the post office has its cricketing sign – but the real shrine is on Broadhalfpenny Down. Here is the field itself with its thatched pavilion, its stone monument and, just as important to the enjoyment of the game, the Bat and Ball pub.

One of the pleasures of travel in this part of the world is to discover the changes that come as you leave the hills to follow the river valley. Here the road dips down to join the narrow meanderings of the Meon, a little river strung with villages. There are no great sights, no spectacular views but there are quiet pleasures to enjoy. A stop almost anywhere reveals something rewarding. Droxford church is not notably grand, but is full of good details. It has the fundamental solidity that characterises Romanesque architecture and lovely features such as the carved heads that form the stops at the ends of the arches, so lively that they must surely have been portraits of local people. Warnford provides one glimpse of the watercress beds that are a feature of the valley, but beyond that it is back to the Downs. There is a satisfying contrast in shapes and textures, where the smooth, rounded hills have been broken down, falling away into rough, scrub-covered escarpments. Chalk paths appear as white streaks through the springy, sheep-cropped turf. The high point is reached at Cheesefoot Head, a summit marked by a prominent clump of trees. From here you can look out over the South Downs, over to the Itchen valley and the city of Winchester.

It was only on entering the centre of Winchester that I realised this is a place I have passed literally dozens of times on the bypass that swings round to the east. Bypasses are both the curse and the saving grace of modern travel: a curse because it is all too easy to use them to speed on your way to the next objective, a blessing because they have preserved many a place from the horrors of incessantly pounding traffic. Now, at least, I found out what I had missed. The presiding genius is Alfred the Great, who looks down on the city from a high pedestal. It is hard to believe, however, that this was once the capital of the kingdom of Wessex, harder still to think of it as joint capital

178

of all England. The first view does not necessarily prove very enticing. The Guildhall, modelled on the medieval guildhalls of Europe, contrives to look less like a piece of medieval opulence and rather more like a poor man's Bradford town hall. So one begins with an uneasy suspicion that the genuine ancient heart of Winchester might have been lost. It has not. The real centre is not here, but the Cathedral Close.

The cathedral itself is not one of those buildings whose outer magnificence draws you inside; it seems almost to be coyly denying its true grandeur. Yet once you do get inside, the effect is overwhelming. The nave is basically Norman, but Norman transformed by a master craftsman and for once we can put a name to this man of genius, William Wynford. He took the basic fabric and elaborated on it, much as a composer might produce variations on a simple theme. Plain columns here become clusters; the roof a complex lierne vault, in which the main ribs are linked by secondary ribs, which do more than just strengthen the structure, for they give it a brilliant geometry. The cathedral seems almost organic, as if decisions were never taken by individuals, but emerged as part of a process of natural growth. The extraordinary elaboration of the various chantries, where no surface is left undecorated, sits quite happily alongside the medieval carvings of the choir stalls. And anyone who believes that the Victorians were merely borrowers, dabbling in pseudo-medievalism, should be brought here to see how well Gilbert Scott's screen fits into the pattern of the building. One of the strongest memories of Winchester cathedral is as the last resting place of the great and the good. Qualifying on both counts, William of Wykeham rests here in effigy. The son of a peasant, he became bishop in 1364 and did more than anyone to shape the cathedral. His tomb and chantry chapel are as grand as anything the building has to offer. Centuries later, Jane Austen was buried in the north aisle. The tombstone is simple, notable for its beautifully carved lettering. It begins: 'In Memory of Jane Austen youngest daughter of the late Revd George Austen, formerly Rector of Steventon in this County', and you can read to the end and receive not so much as a hint that this is the grave of a literary genius. The omission proved too much for her Victorian admirers, so they supplied a Gothic brass which one suspects would have horrified the lady herself.

William of Wykeham's other contribution was the College,

which was intended to take young boys until they were fit to claim a place at his other foundation, New College, Oxford. Boys continue to be processed for Oxbridge today. It is hard to escape the past in Winchester. The castle was a royal residence in William I's reign and the Domesday Book was kept here. Its finest monument is the Great Hall built by Henry III, but its curiosity value lies in the discovery that imitation medievalism was rampant even during the real medieval period. A great round table was built in memory of King Arthur, but hangs incongruously on the wall.

Winchester's ancient importance developed out of its strategic position on the River Itchen and later prosperity derived from the same source. It is now a backwater of life, but still helps to give the city its character and retains memories of former importance. The old mills are no longer at work, but have found new uses. City Mill, straddling its stream, was built in 1744 and is now a youth hostel, but has lost none of its old, rich character. The waterway itself, which was once vital to the economy, is now reduced to no more than a picturesque feature, but it is a role which it more than adequately fulfils. Ducks and swans float rather arrogantly through the city, seeming to sense that they have an inbuilt elegance that no mere earth-tied pedestrians can hope to match. There is one last glimpse of the distant past on the way out of Winchester. The Hospital of St Cross was founded in 1136 as a shelter for the poor and it has performed the same charitable function ever since. Changes have been few. The hospital itself was rebuilt in the fifteenth century, but the chapel remains unaltered – and the poor, alas, are as much in need of help at the end of the twentieth century as they were at the beginning of the twelfth.

The route taken out of Winchester was chosen almost arbitrarily. I wanted to take a look at Oliver Cromwell's battery but that turned out to be a somewhat undistinguished set of earthworks outside a shopping precinct. In the event, the route is probably immaterial, for all this network of minor roads between the Itchen and the Test valleys seem to have the same characteristics. The countryside is a maze of these lanes and tiny dotted settlements in a peaceful landscape of hill and woodland. Even the Test turns out to be no mighty river but a gentle stream of waving leaves that look like the scrawls with which children indicate water in a drawing. Trees droop over the river's edge, swans glide and the meadows spread lushly away from the banks. This seems a most English river with its cool greenness deepening to an almost purple denseness in the shadows, the whole enlivened by the quick flashes of light that wink out with each wind-stirred movement of the surface.

The medieval monks seem always to have had a good eye for a location, and a priory was established here in the twelfth century. At the Dissolution it went to William, Lord Sandys, and in exchange the king got two villages on the outskirts of London, Paddington and Chelsea. Not much doubt about who got the best value in cash terms, but otherwise – well, those who come here must make up their own minds. The priory became, typically, a grand house with little outward evidence of its origins. Such of its old identity as had survived was hidden from view behind a polite Georgian-brick facade. But one remnant can still be seen, the solarium or store, a moody, vaulted room below the house. And some records of the old Mottisfont Priory have survived, including a rent book of 1340, a beautifully written and illustrated document.

The road into Salisbury winds through mixed woodland. Driving there in autumn is an interesting experience, as one is bombarded by acorns that bounce off the car with a merry rattle. For once there is little to be gained by hunting out back-road approaches: the old road simply provides a view of suburbia that the new misses out. If ever there was a city dominated by just one building this is it. The spire of Salisbury cathedral is a giant exclamation mark demanding attention. It is quite literally incomparable, a unique triumph that soars majestically, yet with great delicacy. The spire itself has only the simplest decoration in comparison with the tower from which it springs, but such decoration as there is perfectly matches the basic patterns of the ornate tower, so that the unity of the whole is never in doubt. That same unity is carried on throughout the whole building, for Salisbury, of all the great cathedrals, most closely preserves its original plan. The nave has a beautiful clarity of expression. For once, one can see exactly the effect the medieval builders wished to achieve, with no complication from later additions. The first response can be one of vague disappointment at the cold sparseness of the design; there is even a fleeting thought that it might all be fake. You feel that you have seen it before, but this is because what you see in Salisbury is the original model which spawned a horde of Victorian copies. The differences soon shine through. This is the real thing: there is an insistent rhythm here that the copyists never quite match. After a while, you begin to contemplate even the notion of elaboration with horror. One finds the passage from the cool interior, out into the equally cool cloisters and on into the cathedral close to be an effortless, scarcely noticeable transition.

Salisbury Close is a town within a town, entered by its own gateway, protected by battlemented walls. Inside is a wealth of good buildings and not just the more obvious showpieces such as Mompesson House. Not that even the house can compete with the Mompesson memorial inside the cathedral. Here lie Sir Richard and his wife, Dame Katherine, in technicolour splendour surrounded by heraldry, beset by vine-entrailed column and flanked by obelisks. Angels pray over a couple as grand in death as they ever were in life. Outside the close, Salisbury has other delights to offer. It abounds with old buildings. Inevitably, it seems, in these situations when you find something called The New Inn, it turns out that it was actually new several centuries ago. But, as at Winchester, it is the river that seems to offer not just the pleasures of walking by the water but a chance to stand back and enjoy the city. The Town Mill looks across at the great west window of St Thomas's Church – the church itself having been built to serve the spiritual needs of the army of workmen who came to build the cathedral. But the best and most famous view is across the water meadows from the medieval Harnham Mill. This is the view painted by Constable, and it is remarkable how little the basics have changed. Yet if you had stood here when Harnham Mill was first built in the twelfth century it would have been very different. Salisbury, for all its fine old buildings, is a relative newcomer in the landscape, for when the mill was new it simply did not exist. It first appeared in the thirteenth century as New Sarum, challenging the supremacy of the older settlement of Old Sarum.

Old Sarum itself lies to the north of the present city. You drive up the main road, turn off to climb a steep hill and there it is. The first obvious features you meet define this as the site of an Iron-Age hill fort, for the road cuts straight through the massive ramparts. Inside these defences is the equally distinctive motte of the castle and the foundations of the first Salisbury cathedral. Church and military were not happy neighbours, which is why the clergy decided to move to the new site in the valley. The move was decisive. Old Sarum withered but lived on into notoriety. Long after it was depopulated it was still returning members of parliament, and was the most famous of all the rotten boroughs – the Accursed Hill, as the reformer William Cobbett preferred to call it. The curse has long since been lifted, and now one can enjoy it for its superb views across the Avon valley and out along the old Roman road that once ran to its door.

The road north has nothing of Roman straightness about it, scrupulously mimicking every twist of the winding Avon valley. Sometimes it climbs a hill, but never stops for long on the high ground before returning to the waterside. So all the time one is getting glimpses of the river with its little stone bridges and bordering meadows. The whole route is almost embarrassingly picturesque, too good to be true, with its aged cottages with thatched roofs and a grand house, its walls chequered with squares of flint. To complete the air of unreality, the road at times comes so close to the water that the languid swans drifting on the stream seem to be peering in at the window. The landscape may seem unreal, but once it was commonplace. It is just that the age which created it has gone, will not come back and cannot be recreated.

The river is pleasing, but is certainly not the sort of waterway that one associates with transport. Yet around four thousand years ago, at a point near the present village of West Amesbury, eighty tall blocks of stone from the Preseli mountains in Wales were almost certainly brought here by raft and taken down a processional way defined by banks and ditches, still visible today, known as The Avenue. These were the bluestones that form part of the complex of Stonehenge. It is the most famous and the grandest of all the prehistoric monuments of Europe. Sadly, it has been diminished by the demands of tourism. Where once the monument stood starkly alone on Salisbury Plain, now it is closed off behind a chain fence, giving the whole place the air of a prison camp. The approach down a concrete tunnel no doubt makes bureaucratic planning sense, but does nothing whatsoever to increase that sense of mystery which should surround the monument. It is in danger of becoming just another stop on the

183

circuit: pay your money, look but do not touch. But you cannot quite destroy its special aura, though what the present regime has done is to lose its sense of size and spaciousness.

Ideally, one should come in down The Avenue, past the Heel Stone to the outer edge of the henge. This sarsen stone, unmarked and left in its natural state, stands just outside the bank and ditch of the first henge, probably laid out around 2000BC. Some three centuries or more later, the bluestones were brought from Wales and arranged in a pattern of rings. Finally, huge blocks were brought from Marlborough Downs, carefully shaped and arranged in a horseshoe to form The Sanctuary at the centre of the henge. You can see the care that went into the work. The outer sides of the uprights are actually curved to fit the shape of the ring. On these are placed lintels, held there by mortice and tenon joints. To complete this new and last phase, the sacred bluestones were all taken down and reassembled, some inside the Sanctuary, others in rings outside. The alignments are clearly connected in some way with the summer solstice, but Stonehenge is not easily explained. It may also have connections with phases of the moon and movements of the planets. Two popular mythologies can be dismissed. The midsummer sun does not rise over the Heel Stone, and will not do so until the year 3260. The monument has nothing whatsoever to do with druids, who only appeared in Britain many centuries after it was completed. All one can say with certainty is that it must have been a site of deep significance to justify the immense labour of construction. Perhaps one day we shall find a way of bringing back the sense of reverence that should surround the stones.

One of the sad things about the isolation of Stonehenge is that it has taken it out of its context. Yet, as you leave, you can still see how the whole landscape is awash with reminders of the distant past. Barrows, prehistoric burial mounds, are to be seen on every side – the round humps of the Bronze Age and the rarer long barrows of the New Stone Age. The, literally, outstanding monument is rather more recent. Yarnbury Castle is an Iron-Age hill fort which may not top a very high hill, but more than compensates by its enormous earthworks with banks 26ft (8m) high. What now makes it all seem so strange is that where we now think of Salisbury Plain as an almost empty tract of land, there is everywhere evidence of settlements that were busy with people as recently as Roman times. Now, the sizeable places only exist on the edge of the plain. By the time you reach Mere the earthworks on the hillside are no longer prehistoric but strip lynchets, the cultivation terraces of medieval farmers. The village itself is the first large place you come across after leaving Salisbury. Now it is bypassed, but memories of its old main-road importance survive in the inn with its immense sign on an ornate wrought-iron bracket.

Turning north off the main road brings you the best of the Plain scenery, very reminiscent of the downland to the east – the same mixture of rough grass and smoother turf, the same rounded hills often climaxed by little clumps of trees. It also brings Stourton and Stourhead, the village happily incorporated into the great estate. The house of 1721 is typical of its period, but it is not what one remembers. Stourhead is famous for its grounds, not the work of one of the great landscape gardeners such as Capability Brown, but very much the design of the house's owner, Henry Hoare. His model seems to have been the classical landscapes of the French painter Claude. This is the cool view of the classical world: temples are there not for significant religious rites, but to provide the focal point for a view. It is a garden which has taken the outer forms of ancient Greece and Rome, stripped away the passion and turned them into objects to contemplate at leisure. And the result is wholly successful. Never for one moment does one question the right of buildings, originally designed for the clear skies of the Mediterranean or the Adriatic, to stand in northern woods, beside a cloud-reflecting lake. What is even more remarkable is that elements from other cultures, such as King Alfred's Tower, a typical folly, seem to fit with little hint of incongruity into this perfectly ordered landscape.

Stourhead marks the end of the downland. Increasingly views are closed in by woodland, the countryside is emparked and inti-macy replaces the wider vistas. It brings other worlds closer. Frome was once one of the major textile towns of the west of England, and early in the eighteenth century Daniel Defoe forecast that it would become 'one of the greatest and wealthiest inland towns in England'. It never quite lived up to those high expectations, but it certainly knew prosperity. You can still see the old weavers' houses near Trinity Street and the mill buildings down by the river, but none are working now. Industry appears again as you approach Radstock, with its surroundings of grassed-over spoil heaps as a reminder of the once active Somerset coalfield.

Those who prefer more obviously romantic spots can carry on to Faulkland, with its stocks on the village green and ancient church. Thirsty travellers have two splendid choices ahead of them. Tucker's Grave is one of those old-style pubs which began as a cottage and would have stayed as a cottage if someone had not decided to entertain the neighbours to beer and cider, and make a modest profit at the same time. It still has much the same air, with barrels on the windowsill of beer and the sort of cider that accounts for the mulberry noses that one sometimes meets in these parts. It is a place blissfully free of pretension. Down the road, the George at Norton St Philip is equally unpretentious, miraculously so really. This building has been an inn since the fourteenth century, when wool merchants came here to trade. The Duke of Monmouth stayed here, very nearly permanently, before the Battle of Sedgemoor: a sniper saw him at the window and just missed his mark. It was a short reprieve and his men fared little better. They were held after the battle in what is now the Dungeon Bar. A local, thinking it would be a kindness to doomed men, held open the gate on the morning they went to execution. It is not always a good idea to show sympathy with rebels who have lost: he was bundled along and executed with the rest. But even if no event of interest had ever happened here, it would still be a memorable inn; four-square stone and solid as a mountain with a galleried courtyard, cosily hemmed in by low-eaved roofs. The George has that special quality that comes from continuous use. Its appeal is what it always was: good food, good beer and pleasant surroundings.

The final stretch provides a brief glimpse of the stone-walled uplands of the Mendips and one curiosity. Roebuck's folly is a castellated building in the shape of the ace of clubs said to be the card which made its owner's fortune. The road rejoins the main route just south of Bath.

THE SOUTH WEST

The route begins at Honiton, with a brief dash down the main road before turning off for Ottery St Mary. As soon as you reach the minor road, the essential nature of the countryside seems to shout at you. The rich colours of the earth reappear in the buildings of the village of Alfington, where red soil translates into red brick that blends imperceptibly in with weathered sandstone. Then you leave the village up a road little better than a lane, sunk deep between banks and hedges, even passing briefly through a little sandstone cutting. Roads such as this shut out everything that lies beyond their own boundaries, so that it comes as a shock to find a town suddenly appearing in front of you. Ottery St Mary would have been a shock in any case. On the map it looks a typical situation for a market town based on a river crossing – one expects quiet charm, and little more. Instead, one finds a lady in her finery, dressed for the ball.

Ottery St Mary owes its splendour to its own natural beauty, set on a hillside above the rich valley of the river Otter. John de Grandisson was enthroned as bishop of Exeter in 1327 and declared his intention of founding a collegiate church. By 1334 he had decided on Ottery. The church of St Mary was so grand that the name of the town itself was changed to acknowledge its new-found importance. What was created was very like a cathedral in its close, for the church was surrounded by its own buildings – school and library, houses for priests of all kinds and for choristers. It suffered at the Dissolution, but still retains much of its splendour, notably in its carvings. The former Bishop Grandisson looks down from a roof boss above the crossing, but everywhere you look there seems to be some sort of figure: dignitaries watch you from corbels, heraldic devices abound, but the oddest thing to find in a Somerset church must be the elephant waving its trunk above a column. The clock is said to date back to the church's foundation and is certainly medieval, with its rotating moon and sun telling off the days and hours. But quite the strangest time in the church's long history must have come in the eighteenth century, when John Coleridge was vicar. He disapproved of all biblical translations and scrupulously read the scriptures in Hebrew to his congregation of Somerset farmers and clothiers, who seem

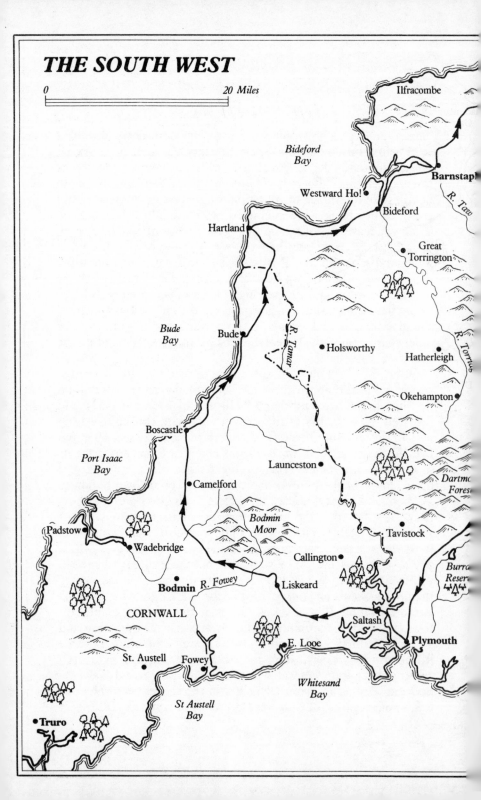

THE SOUTH WEST

0   20 Miles

Ilfracombe

Bideford Bay

Westward Ho!

Barnstapl

Bideford

R. Taw

Hartland

Great
Torrington

Bude Bay

Bude

R. Tamar

Holsworthy

Hatherleigh

R. Torrid

Okehampton

Boscastle

Port Isaac Bay

Launceston

Dartm
Fores

Camelford

Bodmin Moor

Padstow

Wadebridge

Tavistock

Bodmin

R. Fowey

Callington

Liskeard

Burr
Reser

CORNWALL

Saltash

Plymouth

St. Austell

Fowey

E. Looe

Whitesand Bay

Truro

St Austell Bay

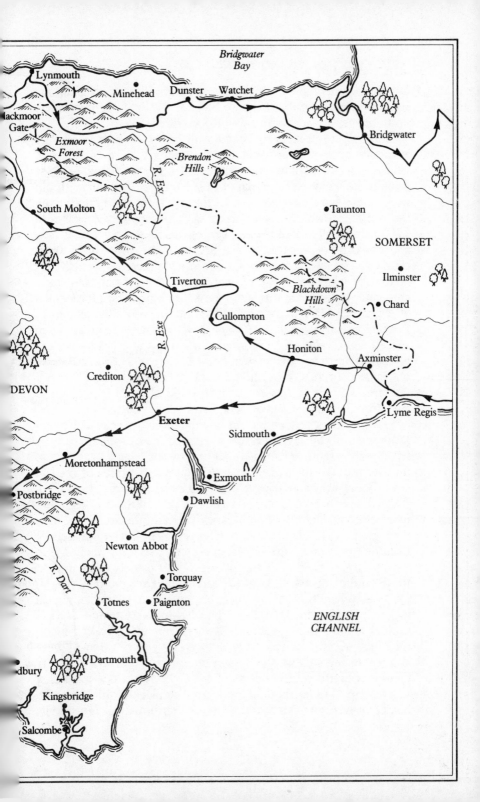

to have sat uncomplaining in bland incomprehension. It is not too surprising perhaps that his son, Samuel Taylor Coleridge, grew up to be one of the country's more eccentric poets.

Nothing ever seems to be quite ordinary here. It is all very attractive but one keeps noticing the oddity that creeps in. The village stocks stand in the churchyard but are roofed over, as though the locals were prepared to see miscreants punished, but were not so hard hearted as to let them get wet if it rained. Even the working town has its strangeness. The factory was begun in 1789 as a woollen mill making serges. It was not a great success and was turned over first to silk then to engineering. In its earliest days it was water powered, but there is no conventional water system here. There is a long leat, originally bringing water to a corn mill, but outside the factory is a 'tumbling weir', into which water vanishes like an oversized bath draining down the plug hole. But if you really want to see Ottery St Mary at its most bizarre, you should come here on November 5th. Everywhere has its bonfire night, but here they go one better: not a fire that is lit and stays put, but instead barrels of burning tar are rolled and carried through the streets. This is a town which it would always be a delight to visit, but its quirkiness gives it an extra edge of attraction.

Exeter too has its delights, but as with most cities you have to wait for them until you have cleared the suburbs. The twentieth century has not been kind to Exeter. It suffered in the 'Baedeker raids' of the Second World War, deliberately aimed at places praised in guide books – the aim being to demoralise the country. They failed. Then the postwar planners had a go and proved themselves rather more effective than the bombers, carving an inner ringroad right through the city. There is still much to enjoy in Exeter, but getting from one bit to the next is less entertaining. What you choose to look at is very much a matter of taste, but I usually head straight for the old dock complex at the head of the Exeter Canal. It is an area which has its notes of grace, but one where the chief appeal lies in solid, functional values. The Customs House of 1681 is undeniably handsome, yet there is something equally satisfying in the range of old warehouses, built of great blocks of stone. There is a reassuring solidity about such buildings. You could feel very confident that if your goods were stored there no-one was going to break in. Trade has died away, but the place is still alive with boats, for here you can find the Exeter Maritime Museum and its amazing collection of vessels from around the world: a Chinese junk rides next to a steam dredger, a Portuguese fishing boat winks an eye from its high prow towards a Danish tug. It is a museum for all who delight in diversity. There are museums in which everything has been nicely calculated to fit a pre-ordained pattern, to illustrate a wholly logical line of development. There may be such a pattern here, but I have never found it. One suspects that behind it all stands an obsessive, who seeing an interesting, attractive vessel simply cannot resist it, no matter where it comes from or how it relates to its neighbours. It is a delight.

Climbing up the steep hill to the city centre, the lane runs beside the stream that once served a number of small mills – you can still see ruined water wheels along the way. But once you get to the top, there is the racing traffic cutting you off, forcing you into underground passages. So, if one is going to go underground in Exeter, one might just as well do it properly. The city was once supplied by a complex of conduits, and one of the stranger experiences is exploring this underground maze. At times you are reduced to a sort of Groucho Marx crouch in order to get along but it is a fascinating experience seeing the foundations of the old city walls and gateways, as well as catching occasional glimpses of shoppers overhead.

Exeter seems often to be at its best when one is looking at its old working life. There are memories too of the wealth brought by the old trades. Tuckers Hall is home to the Guild of Weavers, Fullers and Shearmen, a place of richly carved panelling that almost smells of tradition, but which has its origins in the old wool trade.

Architecturally, the greatest work in the city is inevitably the cathedral. The nave seems to have grown from the soil, a great flowering of ribs to create the majestic vault of the roof. The effect of great richness carries all the way through the church, right down to the details of carvings. Near the musicians' balcony in the north transept, a strong man, his face contorted by the effort, seems to be carrying the whole weight of a vault on his shoulders. If the effect of the cathedral seems too overpowering, you can always turn for calm to the little church of St Pancras, marooned in a shopping precinct, or to St Nicholas Priory.

Getting out of Exeter is as bad as getting in, but the moment you shake off the last of suburbia, the transformation is absolute. The road turns downhill, twisting under an arch of trees and then shows you what lies ahead: the great heaved-up mass of Dartmoor. It seems as if you are almost there, but that is an illusion and there is some very different countryside to pass through first. The wide views are soon lost as the road slips between high banks, roofed over with leaves from trees that seem to spread to the horizon. Leaves you realise are not just green at all: there is green certainly, but there are shades which run from a cloudy blue to an almost iridescent yellow, changing all the time as the light changes. You almost lose the sense of where you are until the woods clear and through the trees the pale grey granite of a church tower rises up like a fingerpost pointing to the moor.

Just to the north of the road lies the little village of Dunsford, an almost-too-perfect example of a Devon village, with thatched roofs, drooping down over rough whitewashed walls. It stands on a hillside above the Teign valley, looking out over its wooded banks. This is just the sort of place that tempts one to linger, for walks by the river or a pint in the pub or, better still, both. Dartmoor almost seems forgotten, and even as you drive on the road wriggles and squirms so much that even a sense of direction soon goes. Then a turn brings you to a view of a green hillside, cropped by sheep and, at its climax, the tall slender tower of Moretonhampstead church. There is no question about it now, you have finally arrived at the edge of the moor.

Dartmoor has a sense of real wildness. There are just the two roads across it, so that one seems to see a trackless waste spreading out for ever. It is a place where the earth itself seems to be trying to break free, pushing up incoherent jumbles of rock that burst through the hilltops. If you walk, rather than drive, over Dartmoor the sense of loneliness can be almost frightening. Conan Doyle knew what he was doing when he set *The Hound of the Baskervilles* here. It is not difficult to imagine ghostly creatures on the wilder moors, and the great Grimpen Mire is not just novelist's exaggeration. There are bogs on the moor that can suck your boots off. Settlements are few. It was almost by accident that I came across a place that really delighted me. It was the name that caught my eye – Powder Mills Farm. It at once suggested quarrying and blasting in the days of gunpowder. I was not disappointed. At the end of the group of buildings is an old mortar, once used for testing the powder. The farm buildings themselves were originally workers' houses and are now partly in use as a pottery. The actual powder mills are a little further on down the track. They were begun in 1844 and this was an obviously sound choice for the works – convenient for the quarries that would use the powder, but far away from anything else. Gunpowder manufacture was a notoriously dangerous occupation, and when things did go wrong they generally went spectacularly wrong. The mixture of saltpetre, charcoal and sulphur was ground under big stone wheels, turned by water power, and the remains of the buildings can be seen by the stream. What is so appealing about the site is the way it brings so many Dartmoor elements together. The scenery is wild, a hill stream splashes down, trees bend at almost impossible angles, forced down by the strong winds. A simple clapper bridge of flat stones laid horizontally on piled stones is an obvious but satisfying device, while the ruined buildings serve as a reminder that man has been working here for far longer than he has been coming to enjoy the scenery.

The road passes the chillingly gaunt prison of Princetown, and for a time one can enjoy the special pleasures of the moorland roads, each rise offering a new prospect. All that, however, ends with the main road and the approach to Plymouth. There are really several Plymouths, each with its own individual character.

Much of the heart of the city was torn out by bombs, and in its place appeared a new scheme of wide avenues and shops. It is perhaps a mark of the quality of this postwar development that arguments about it are still going on today. Anything that arouses controversy has at least got a definite character. The main thoroughfare, Armada Way, seems to have taken for its model one of the great boulevards of Paris, perhaps the Champs Elysées. It has the same sense of heading inexorably to its grand conclusion, not the Arc de Triomphe but Plymouth Hoe. They still play bowls on a green overlooked by the figure of Francis Drake, though few of the present bowlers look as if they could see off an Armada. This is popular, seaside Plymouth, but there is still something of the Plymouth of Elizabethan seafarers to be seen. The Barbican is the area by the old docks from which the Pilgrim Fathers set sail and where the privateers who made their wealth from plunder on the Spanish Main dropped anchor and came ashore to spend their loot. It was almost lost for ever. Like so many old parts of cities it consists of narrow, inconvenient streets, old buildings, often allowed to approach dereliction, and was generally thought to be standing in the way of progress. At the eleventh hour, someone remembered that the stories of sea dogs and pilgrims were not mythology, but genuine history, even if overlaid with romance. Perhaps the old area was worth preserving, after all. It has been kept at least in part. One can still wander up the narrow streets, where Tudor houses lean across to each other as though enjoying a neighbourly chat. Mercifully, it has not fallen into the other trap of becoming a theme-park historic area, wholly divorced from reality. Fishing boats still unload their catches at the quay, people do live here and many of the preserved buildings still have the unmistakeable marks of former uses about them. Some are even still at work: Plymouth gin is still made at the distillery. True the knickery-knackery has crept in, but not enough to ruin the sense of old Plymouth the sea port.

Nowadays, the Pilgrim Steps are occupied by the trip boatmen offering tours of the bay and a view of the naval dockyard. There is probably no better way of seeing the city. This is a city of the sea, built to take advantage of the sheltered waters of the Sound. The boat takes you out past the sparkling granite of the defensive fortress, the Citadel, out past holiday Plymouth to the dockyards and their warships. You can still see the full range of development, starting where the colourful figurehead of King Billy presides over Number One Slip, the wooden building as astonishingly perfect in its way as a cathedral roof, and on to the new gigantic frigate repair docks. There is, however, another way to see and enjoy Plymouth. You can pop across on the Cremyll ferry to Mount Edgcumbe, a fine house with even better parks and gardens. It boasts two curiosities: a monument to a pet pig and a little folly tower. From the latter you can see all of Plymouth spread before you and watch the grey warships manoeuvre through the chicane-like passage marked by buoys that brings them through the narrows.

The Tamar marks the division between Devon and Cornwall, with the road bridge running next to Brunel's famous railway bridge. It was to be his last major work. The engineer did at least live long enough to see its completion. He was taken across on a specially adapted flat truck. The bridge was opened in May 1859 and by the end of that year one of the greatest engineering geniuses the world has ever known was dead. The bridge still bears his name on the arches, and it would be hard to imagine a more fitting monument. Once across the bridge and clear of

Saltash it becomes apparent that the differences between Devon and Cornwall are not simply a matter of lines drawn on a map. Cornwall seems altogether harder. The rich red earth and gently moulded rock gives way to splintered granite. The colour washes of Devon houses are replaced by unadorned grey stone; slate takes over from thatch. The sight of a distant engine house serves as a reminder of just how much of Cornwall's past was based on mining for copper and tin. The countryside at first has neither the drama of Dartmoor's open spaces nor the intimacy of sunken lanes, yet there is from the first an unmistakable Cornish identity. It derives in part from the nature of the landscape, but also comes from Cornwall's historic separateness, a Celtic enclave at the tip of England. You get a hint of the historic character in the Dark-Ages cross, known as King Doniert's Stone – though, to be honest, it is not wildly exciting, for its complex carvings have been blurred by centuries of rough weather. But the further you get into Cornwall, the stronger the sense of identity becomes.

St Neot seems in many ways to be a typical Cornish village. It sits beneath the slopes of Bodmin Moor in the shelter of a little river valley. It drew its old livelihood from the landscape around it: china-clay works, slate mines and farming, but now it looks more and more towards tourism. Many of the old stone cottages are let to holidaymakers; Carnglaze slate caverns are open to visitors but no longer work. Yet the essential qualities of the village have not been lost. The centre is still marked by the old focal points of pub and church. Old customs survive: each Oak Apple Day, a young oak tree is hauled to the top of the church tower where it stays all year. Inside the church is a splendid set of sixteenth-century windows, restored in the 1830s but still with a good deal of original glass. The biblical stories include Noah setting off in an ark not so very different from the *Mary Rose*, a recognisable Tudor ship. The church also relates directly to its surroundings: just look, for example, at the beautifully incised slate gravestones in the churchyard. The churchyard also has a modern sundial of bewildering complexity. Even the slate caverns, though not used, have lost none of their majesty: to go there is like calling in at the Hall of the Mountain King. These are not just vast caves, but astonishing examples of what man can create in a strange, dark, underground world. St Neot may be picturesque, but it is a place founded on the harshest realities of the working world.

195

Beyond St Neot the countryside offers startling contrasts. There are open stretches where you can see the whole pattern of farms and lanes, fields and walls, that cover the lower slopes of the moor. Then you dive down into a labyrinth of narrow lanes that run around the edge of Bodmin Moor. If initial impressions on coming into Cornwall are of leaving the deep sunk lanes of Devon behind, then those impressions are more than dispelled here. Any path it seems will be likely to get you lost, but equally any path will also eventually take you round the edge of the moor. It is simply that nothing outside the lane registers for most of the time. The glimpses one gets of Bodmin Moor are very different from the views of Dartmoor. This is an altogether more sombre presence. The lanes themselves have a far brighter atmosphere, especially in spring when they are spangled corridors of wild flowers. Places appear along the way, coming at you quite suddenly. Hellandbridge is a downhill dash to the river valley, a cluster of houses and, really rather surprisingly, a railway – or at least the remains of a railway, with level crossing, crossing-keeper's cottage and rails embedded in the road. It seems such an unlikely spot to build a line, that the one thing that is not surprising is to find that it is closed and has found a new role as a footpath. St Mabyn announces its presence rather more clearly with its tall church tower, and you have just about got used to the notion that you might be out in the open again when you are plunged in the narrowest, deepest lane you will ever meet, carved like a railway cutting or a miniature canyon through the rock. It is very colourful, if only because so many cars have left some of their paintwork on the roadside.

St Tudy enjoys the luxury of a village green, a real rarity in this landscape where most villages pack as much as they can into a limited space. All the time Bodmin Moor maintains a brooding presence, topped by the jagged outcrops of Rough Tor: strange to think that this windswept summit was a favoured site for settlers in prehistoric times. The remains of their simple stone huts are scattered across the flanks of the hills. In its own way, this area represents the changes brought about by the steady advances of technology. In pre-Roman times, it was the thin soil of the uplands that responded to cultivation with primitive implements; better techniques allowed the heavier, richer soils of the valleys to be farmed.

Camelford sprawls out along the main road, and has a most

attractive local history museum. It is one of those places which simply refuses to follow a pre-ordained logical pattern. Walk in and you see a Victorian loo perched between two vacuum cleaners of uncertain antiquity. In some ways, such museums are a much more accurate reflection of everyday life than more organised establishments. Real life is not compartmentalised and rarely follows a rational progression. The place reminds me of a country auction: not everything is worth having, but poke and pry and you are sure to turn up a real gem.

So far, the journey has taken us over a good deal of Cornish countryside, without a glimpse of the landscape for which the county is famous, its coastline. There are far worse introductions to it than Boscastle. This is one of the most attractive of all Cornwall's north-coast ports. The harbour was built as early as 1540 and was busy with trade right up to the 1930s. Yet how incredible it seems now to think of schooners tied up at the quay, having negotiated the narrow entrance with its wave-crashed rocks. It is a popular spot for sightseers, but to see it at its best you need to come on a wild day when the sea beats against the walls and foams down through a narrow, rocky passage. Even on a balmy summer day you can leave the crowds behind and walk out over Beeny cliffs to enjoy some superb coastal scenery. The route out brings you to Hennett and the beautiful Valency valley, a place which has its own real values to which rich associations can be added. Thomas Hardy came here in 1870 to work on the restoration of the church of St Juliot. It was a building of great antiquity, but far gone in decay and, although Hardy did his best, much of the old fabric had to be destroyed. What was left, what we see today, is a plain, but honest building which would probably attract little attention but for the Hardy connection. For Hardy found more than just the church to occupy him. He met Emma Gifford and together they walked and picnicked by the valley stream, fell in love and married.

Why go to Saint-Juliot? What's Juliot to me?
Some strange necromancy
But charmed me to fancy
That much of my life claims the spot as its key.

Cornwall now became for Hardy a place of magic, the mystic land of Lyonesse from which he returned 'with magic in my eyes'. Something of the magic still lingers in the valley.

The road tries to keep to the coast, but keeps being pushed inland. It arrives back eventually at Crackington Haven. This is a real seaside spectacular, where Atlantic rollers break on to a beach overshadowed by tall cliffs. It is one of the places much favoured by surfers. The spectator feels inclined to echo the words of Hamlet: 'What a falling off was there'. The surfers paddle laboriously out to deep water, wait for that one perfect moment, crouch and spring to their feet. For a moment they are Poseidons, rulers of the sea, then – whoops! – down they go to being mere floundering mortals. The coast around here offers, briefly at least, a sense of wildness that continues until you get near the accessible sands of Widemouth Bay: caravan park and suburbia on sea. There is a real dilemma here. There are a lot of people who want to enjoy the beauties of the Cornish coast, but the more that want to come the more scenery disappears. Everyone wants a little place with a view of the sea, and in meeting those wishes the view itself becomes less and less worth having. You cannot institute a sort of aesthetic entrance examination to see who is 'worthy' to enjoy it. Perhaps the best solution is simply to abandon some areas to wholesale development and apply really stringent rules to others. There are places away from the crowds, particularly for those prepared to use their feet instead of their motors. The other answer for anyone who really wants to enjoy the beauty of this coast is to avoid the summer. Widemouth Bay, deserted by all but the busily nibbling wading birds at the sea's edge, seen at sunset when a highway of light leads the eye away to the faint smudge that separates sea from sky, can be a place of magic.

Even at its busiest, this is not the most popular part of Cornwall. Bude suffered badly, as far as tourism was concerned, by being late into the railway age. By the time the trains arrived, in 1898, the town had been well and truly left behind in the popularity stakes. Somehow, one always feels that Bude has never been too keen anyway. The town keeps itself well away from the water, and it is quite easy to pass through without even realising you are by the sea at all. Yet this is not only an attractive spot, but one full of interest. It even has a canal, poking its lock gates out towards the waves. Its very lack of success in developing as a major resort can seem a positive advantage.

Even the road out of Bude seems to suffer from the same sense of never having quite made it to the first division. The A39 tries

198

very hard to be a proper main road, but no sooner has it achieved a speedy little section of straight lines than the landscape deflects it. Hills elbow it to one side, steep valley sides force it to twist and turn. On the other hand, once you do turn off it you soon decide that it was not that bad a road after all. Hartland, and even more Stoke, helped to dispel the notion that there is something rather twee about Devon villages. Here one finds the same dark sternness that one saw around the fringes of Bodmin Moor, a mood that fits the countryside itself. There is nothing conventionally pretty here. The Abbey river carves out a narrow green strip, a mere suggestion of meadows, before the heavily wooded sides hunch up over it. The woodland is almost forbiddingly dense, the road a green tunnel, and then you break out to a seascape even wilder than the countryside through which you have travelled.

Hartland Quay has a little museum much preoccupied with shipwrecks. One is not surprised. The cliffs rear up above a stony beach and send out spurs like spiky dragon tails into the sea. The little port provides some refuge, but only expert seamanship could ever bring a large seagoing vessel safely into this harbour – but then it was founded by men who had just that expertise, the famous Elizabethan captains, Drake, Raleigh and Hawkins. It is only when you reach the sea itself that you realise how dominant it is; even the tower of Stoke church is now seen not as ecclesiastical grandiosity, but as having been built as a tall landmark for sailors. This is an unforgiving coast, with a noble savagery to it. The land itself seems as prone to spasms and upheavals as the sea, for the exposed strata on the cliffs show the stresses of a buckled and twisted surface. Hartland Quay can seem a place of thinly veiled violence where one half expects the ground to move once again and where the sea can be a threatening presence. Perhaps if one came on a different day in different weather the mood would change, but it will always be a spot that carries with it a charge of excitement.

Clovelly, by contrast, is overwhelmingly picturesque, with steep cobbled streets leading down to the harbour. Yet it is still a most extraordinary place. Where else in Britain is there a main street so steep that local shoppers regularly use sledges to carry their groceries? The harbour itself is a joy, full of wonderful shapes, rounded stone, set off by mooring chains, the curve of a time-worn step. No amount of planning or artifice can ever create the same effect. It is a mark of just how few shelters there are on this wild coast that it was worthwhile building harbour and village in this cramped, vertiginous spot.

The road to Bideford gives glimpses of the sea, with the whale-humped shape of Lundy rising out of the channel. The town itself climbs up the hill to meet you. First come the lace-curtained Sea View villas, then the older, severely squared-up stone cottages, and finally you arrive at the river and the medieval bridge, striding away, arch after arch after arch. Below it is the quay, still used by seagoing vessels, including the Lundy ship which takes passengers and supplies to the island. Bideford may be some miles from the sea, but it is the sea that gave it an existence and memories of the sea are everywhere. A wander round the parish church – a Victorian building which has at least one reminder of the past in a screen made up of carved bench ends – reveals the tombstone of Captain Henry Clark who died in 1836. On top is a delicate carving of a cutter, and below a long and rather charming verse and a sad one. The captain spent his money but scorned the poor house.

The Blackbirds whistling Notes at Break of Day,
Used to awake him from his BED of HAY.
Unto the Bridge and Quay he then REPAIR'D,
To see what SHIPPING up the River steer'd.

OFT in the week he used to VIEW the Bay
To see what SHIPS were coming in from Sea.
To Captains Wives he brought the Welcome News,
And to the Relatives of all their CREWS.

At last poor HARRY CLARK was taken ill,
And carried to the Workhouse gainst his Will.
But being of his mortal Life quite tired,
He lived about a Month and then expired.

The simple lines keep the memory of the old captain more alive than many a grander monumental tomb could ever do.

To get to the true sense of the seagoing tradition, you really need to go a little further down river to Appledore, and the best way to do that is to wander down the riverside path under the new road bridge. It is a pleasant walk, and you can look down and see the skeletons of old vessels lying in the mud at the water's edge. You reach Appledore at the shipyard, and they still build ships here, anything from dredgers to container vessels. There is a long tradition of shipbuilding and Appledore was once famous for its schooners, international vessels that were constructed in Canada, where timber was plentiful, and then sent here for rigging and finishing. The Appledore story is told in a wonderful little museum, but you can still see it all around you, in the narrow streets and the old shipbuilders' sheds and slips. The town itself spreads right down the river, but it is worth persevering to the end, when you can reward yourself with a decent pint in a pleasant pub looking out across the estuary. And anyone feeling footsore can come back by bus.

There is now a new road that links Bideford to Barnstaple, but the old A39, now relegated to B road status, is more interesting, offering views across to Appledore. After Bideford and Appledore, Barnstaple itself is a little disappointing. It has some features in common with the former, with its quay and multi-arched bridge. Here the quay has extremely fine light standards around which dolphins curl, and they take you back to an earlier stop on the journey. They were cast at Coalbrookdale. The local museum has paintings which show Barnstaple as it was in the days when it was a busy port. Merchants then settled their bargains on the tome stone in the colonnade of Queen Anne's Walk. The walk was first used in 1609, but was rebuilt in 1713, hence the name.

The journey does at least have a fitting climax, passing through a landscape like a patchwork quilt, single lines marking out the squares of fields, double hedges indicating the deep lanes. It looks more like a map than real landscape. At Shirwell a pair of classical gatehouses appear but do not seem to mark the entrance to anything at all. The next grand entrance, however, just by an attractive thatched cottage, leads to Arlington Court. The actual house of 1822 is really a little dull, but its contents make up for that, particularly the model ships. The grounds are best of all. Grazed by Shetland ponies and Jacob sheep, the park is surrounded by woodland and occupies a lovely position over a winding river valley. After that there are a few more hairpin bends to negotiate back on the road, and a good deal of swooping and climbing before the main route is rejoined at Blackmoor Gate.

NORTH WALES

The route begins with the main road that runs past the end of the great Pontcysyllte aqueduct and along the Dee valley to Llangollen. There is a real sense of being in a different country, something indefinably Welsh. There is of course the language: for a long time I wondered why there were so many signs pointing to a place called Llwyber Cynoeddis, until discovering that it was Welsh for public footpath. Names such as the Owen Glendower Hotel reinforce the impression, but there is something more fundamental than that. As is so often the case in Britain, geological changes are reflected in the buildings, with red sandstone giving way to sombre greys and red-tiled roofs replaced by slate. This could result in a certain drabness were it not counterbalanced by a liberal use of bright colour: a Welsh terrace is unmistakable. Roads no longer seem to wander at will, ranging haphazardly over the landscape, but stay rooted to the valleys until they are ready to climb over the pass to resume their way down the next valley. Hills are already straining to become mountains.

Llangollen, once a working town with a flannel mill, is now very much tourist territory, very tea-shoppy, but there are one or two things to see all around it. The canal that leapt the valley at Froncysyllte has now become a narrow, hill-clinging waterway almost lost among the trees. You can climb the hill above the town to the ruins of Castell Dinas Bran, though they turn out disappointingly to look better from the valley than they do when you eventually puff and pant your way up there. But the view more than compensates: the surrounding hills with their headband of pale crags; the shining thread of the canal far below. The less energetic can visit Valle Crucis, the Vale of the Cross. In the ninth century, the Pillar of Eliseg was set up here, to a man noted perhaps not so much for piety as for reclaiming Powys from the English 'by fire and sword'. It was, however, considered a holy place and the abbey was founded here in 1201. The holy vale, however, seems to have lost some of its sanctity: a caravan park now occupies the space between the ancient cross and the church. The abbey itself, however, is majestic, seen at its best across the old fish pond. The east wall is a strange design. Buttresses rise up between the lancet windows, then branch out to allow space for a second tier of windows actually to be set within the buttresses. The result is like a set of giant tuning forks on the facade. It is, though, nowhere near as strange as Llangollen's most famous house, Plas Newydd, home of the equally famous Ladies of Llangollen.

The ladies caused quite a scandal in their time. Lady Eleanor Butler and Sarah Ponsonby ran away from Ireland together and in 1780 set up house in what was then a plain Welsh cottage. They themselves looked, apparently, somewhat freakish. They cropped their hair, always wore riding dress and looked in old age like 'superannuated clergymen'. Their plain cottage became less plain with each passing year as more and more decoration was piled on. Their great love was carved wood: subject matter immaterial. Cherubs look at lions, Hindu gods sit down beside ancient Greeks. If a surface could be decorated it was, inside as well as out. And visitors who came around with carvings were always sure of a welcome – and anyone and everyone seemed to visit them, from Wordsworth to the Duke of Wellington. The spirit of the ladies still lingers around their extraordinary house.

The deeper you go into the Dee valley, the more you become aware of the character of the land. It seems a surprisingly empty landscape, at least as far as humans are concerned. Even by the main road houses are few and the hills that rise all around seem to have only a spattering of farms and cottages. Corwen is the nearest thing to a town after Llangollen. It has one really handsome building, now a craft centre, yet surprisingly it turns out to be the old workhouse. For an Englishman like myself Wales often seems more foreign than, say, France. I learned French at school, but know nothing of the language of my nearest neighbour and so am left looking at, say, Gwalia stores, uncertain whether Mr Gwalia owns them, they sell gwalias, whatever they may be, or whether it is a simple bilingual sign. There is nothing, however, to prevent one enjoying the villages for themselves. Cynwyd is typical, all bunched together in a comfortable little hollow with a tributary of the Dee rushing through the middle under an old stone bridge.

Beyond Llandrillo is an area of old woodland, tall pine trees mingling with venerable oak. There is a very particular sense of place here. Buildings are built for rough weather, plain and simple, with solid stone walls – often whitewashed – and slate roofs. They are at one with the landscape. Crossing to the north bank of the Dee

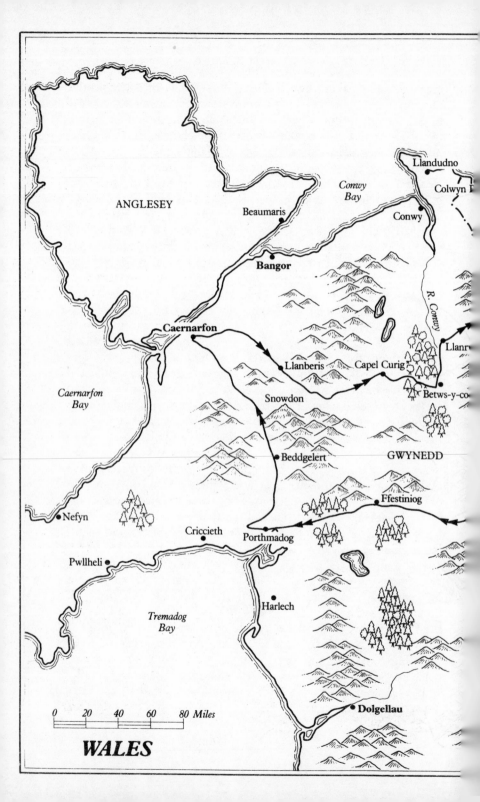

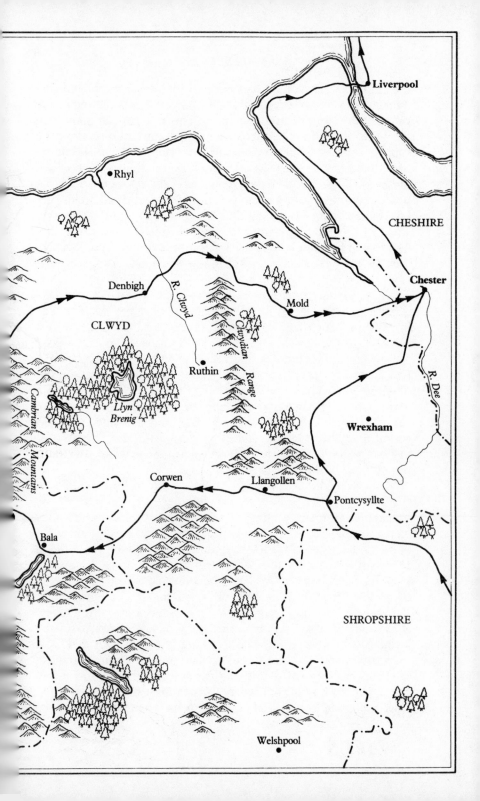

the road runs between walls of massive boulders, with the bustling river never very far away. Bala brings a pause, a widening of the valley at the head of the Bala Lake. This is a popular spot, with the added attraction of a narrow-gauge railway that runs along the southern shore. Originally this was a conventional line and in the days when it was run by the Great Western Railway one of the directors of the august company lived on the opposite shore. To be a director was to be a person of importance, and he had his very own halt, still known as Flag Station. When he required a train to stop, a flag would be run up the flagpole and the director would be brought by launch to take his place on the train. On his return the flag was raised again as a signal for the launch to appear. That is what one calls travelling in style.

The road up from Bala is pure delight. It follows the little Tryweryn river, a gurgling hill stream, full of mossy boulders like pin cushions surrounded by gently waving lace. There was once a railway up here as well, and what a joy it must have been to travel – though probably not if you were in a great hurry. It climbed to a height of well over a thousand feet into some of the wildest scenery of any line in Wales. The last passenger travelled this way in 1960, and it is never going to reopen. The line was flooded to create the reservoir Llyn Celyn. One can see why the locals must have felt resentful as the water was not for them, but for the English over in Liverpool. Perhaps it is mere fancy, but the new lake still looks out of place in the landscape.

With the lake left behind one is really in the middle of the hills, the flanks dotted with boulders rising up from the bracken as though waiting for collection. And collected they were, for the same stone reappears, roughly dressed in walls, barns and houses. And for anyone with any doubt about being really up in the hills, a lonely petrol station proudly announces itself as the highest in Wales. Then the moorland ends as you drop down into the vale of Ffestiniog, though the grandeur of the scene is enhanced rather than diminished. Beyond the valley, the mountains rise like a theatrical set in a series of planes, each a touch paler than the last. Everything is tinged with grey, and everywhere you look you see slate: slate on houses, in walls, slate piled up as heaps of debris and exposed on the mountainside. Some people find it oppressive, this touch of darkness on every side, but come here just after a rainstorm when the clouds have parted for the sun, and it becomes astonishing. The valley gleams as if floodlit.

Almost everything you see here has its origins in slate. Porthmadog was developed in the early nineteenth century when a Lincolnshire member of Parliament proposed building an embankment, The Cob, across the estuary and reclaiming the land behind it. The next stage was to build a narrow-gauge railway up to the slate mines at Blaenau Ffestiniog and develop the port. In time it also became an important shipbuilding centre: I recently saw a Porthmadog vessel gently rotting away on the shore of Port Stanley in the Falkland Islands. So three themes meet here: ships, rails, and slate. The maritime museum deals with the first, and quite the best way to see the other two is to travel the line.

When it first opened, the Festiniog Railway – the second 'f' is a recent addition – was worked by horses. Early experiments with steam locomotives were not a great success, but then no one had ever tried running engines on such a line, with its sharp curves and severe gradients. Success came when Robert Fairlie introduced his double-ended locomotives. These were mechanical equivalents of Dr Dolittle's Pushmi-Pullyu beast, looking like an unfortunate accident in which two locomotives backed into each other and then stuck. The cab was put in the middle, with two boilers, one at the front, one behind. Each had its own set of wheels on a bogey, so that there is ample strength in the two power units, but the engine could still cope with tight curves. There are twists on this line when the front wheels and the back wheels can seem to be going in opposite directions. These unique engines are still in use, along with more conventional locomotives.

The journey is spectacular. It starts with a run across the Cob, but soon the climbing has to begin. The line rises over seven hundred feet on its way to Blaenau Ffestiniog, not in a steady ascent but in quick dashes alternating with furious twists and turns, culminating in a great U bend round the valley head. This is known as Tyler's Curve, named after a Board of Trade inspector who, perhaps a little to everyone's surprise, approved it. This is a line that simply goes on getting bigger and better the further you travel. It brings you Welsh mountain scenery at its best. The line, however, is not quite what it was. It too disappeared in part under a reservoir, so a new deviation had to be built to climb to an even higher level on the mountain. It rises in a spiral like an approach to a multi-storey car park. But having got all the way up there, it has nowhere to go but down into Blaenau Ffestiniog. Travelling this line is quite unlike travelling the railways of the Scottish highlands. A narrow-gauge route seems altogether more intimately connected with the landscape. Rocks seem almost to touch the carriage windows; the little trains can cope with hills in a way that no standard gauge could ever do. So instead of a succession of deep cuttings or great viaducts, the train just keeps puffing its way on and up, twisting round a rocky headland here, riding high over a valley there.

At Blaenau Ffestiniog itself, the effect of slate seems almost literally overwhelming, for mountains of shattered material rise up above the houses, and this is just the discarded rubbish left behind after the good slate has been sent out down the little railway to the waiting ships at Porthmadog. Now, just as the railway has moved from freight to passengers, so too the mines and quarries have turned over to the new industry of tourism. There are two main sites. Gloddfa Ganol is a vast enterprise. You look at a mountain from the outside and it seems solid enough, but turns out to be more like a Gruyere cheese, riddled with cavernous holes and tunnels. This is more than a mine, it was a whole industry in which extracting the slate was only the first stage. It was followed by the skilled work of splitting and shaping, so the mine developed a complex of buildings to match its labyrinthine underground workings. Llechwedd Slate Caverns give visitors an underground train ride as well as a chance to explore on foot. Gloddfa Ganol offers a reasonably plain tour and, given the immensity of the site, no frills are needed; Llechwedd has sound and music, lights and action. It is a matter of taste as to which the visitor prefers.

One might expect that anything that followed a ride on the Ffestiniog Railway would come as something of an anticlimax, but not the road north from Porthmadog. For much of the way, the road keeps to the foot of tall cliffs as it threads a passage to the mountains. At Llyn Cwellyn, the hills rise up sheer from the water, while over to the east stands Snowdon and the dark, brooding cliffs of Clogwyn d'ur Arddu – cliffs which have an almost mythic appeal to rock climbers. They offer a variety of routes – all arduous, all long and all exposed. You have to be good to attempt even the easiest route on the face, because the easiest is not easy, just a touch less difficult than the rest. Fortunately, for the majority

208

of people, there are alternative ways of getting up the mountain which do not involve suspending yourself by your fingertips from minute cracks in a sheer rock wall.

The mountain road seems to end too soon, and even the distant prospect of the sea seems a poor substitute for the constantly shifting perspectives of the hills. Then to find yourself slowing down for a roundabout seems a horribly banal ending. But it is not quite the end: up ahead is Caernarfon Castle. It is both a fitting and a logical climax. The mountainous region of Snowdonia may be powerfully scenic, but it offers little in the way of comfort for settlers. It is certainly not an area one would choose for easy living, but in medieval times it was to become the last stronghold of the Welsh, an enclave from which they could watch the advance of the English. In the summer of 1283, Edward I defeated Llewellyn, the last of the Welsh princes, and threw a cordon of fortresses around Snowdonia. Caernarfon Castle is the mightiest of them all. Its importance is obvious as guardian of a major port. There is still a sense of excitement coming through the passes of Snowdonia, though in winter they may be closed. Seven centuries ago when there were no roads worth speaking of in the region, the advantages of having an open sea route were enormous. The castle stands high above the quay, with an entrance directly on to the harbour. It looks if anything more imposing from the outside than it does from within, but if you really want to understand its importance, you should stop off on your way here at the Roman fort of Segontium by the A4085 on the edge of the town.

Segontium served the same function as the castle. It protected the harbour and acted as headquarters for the cavalry. The lower courses of the walls still stand. Edward I saw himself as part of an imperial tradition that stretched back to the Roman occupation or, at least, he tried to persuade the Welsh of this continuity of power. So Caernarfon had to be the administrative centre for Wales in Edward's time as it had been for the Romans, and when he came to build the castle he brought to it more than a hint of Rome. The bands of coloured stone are a very Roman touch, reminiscent of the great wall of Constantinople built by Theodosius II, which Edward had seen on the Crusades. The castle is more than a defence, it is an imperial gesture on the grand scale. So the imposing exterior is no accident: it was meant to impress as well as to resist attack. Edward did not live, however, to see the great work finished, but he did see it survive an attack by Madog ap Llewellyn in 1294. And at his death its final form was at least firmly established. A walk around the castle reveals its monumental dominance: the great gates, the three pinnacles of the Eagle Tower, the formidable walls. Inside it is more domesticated, with green lawns and a peaceful air that belies its martial surroundings.

Caernarfon itself follows an easily recognised pattern, of encircling walls running out from the castle, the market place at the castle gate. The port has an attractive little harbour office of 1840 with a weather vane topping a lantern. A latter-day Welsh hero looks out over the town centre. Lloyd George strikes a suitably declamatory pose, but the heroic gesture is rather diminished by the dribbling white cap provided by the local seabirds: a not wholly inappropriate response to political rhetoric.

From Caernarfon the way turns back to the heart of Snowdonia. Llanberis presents a strange mixture of natural and manmade scenery. The mountains have been hacked away into shining terraces of slate; new cliffs have been created in place of the rounded flanks of hills. The result may not always be beautiful, but it is mighty impressive. There is yet another slate museum, but one with a very different character from those of Blaenau Ffestiniog. The Welsh Slate Museum is based on the works of the old Dinorwic Quarry, and everything has been left much as it was. The concern was almost wholly self-sufficient. When machinery in the quarries needed new parts they were made on the spot at the foundry or forge. Power came from an enormous water wheel, later joined by turbines. The museum helps one to understand the complexity of an industry which had rather more to it than simply blowing away lumps of the local scenery. It is a place full of intriguing features, such as the craftsmanship on display in the pattern-making shop. To cast in iron you must first make a pattern in wood, so here is a fine assortment of cogs and wheels – and even the wooden patterns for the building's own windows. A little steam railway runs from here along the shore of Llyn Padarn, but a more famous railway can be found across the road, the Snowdon Mountain Railway.

This always presents something of a dilemma to those who feel that a visit to the region is incomplete unless you have stood on the summit of Wales' highest mountain. Do you let someone else do the work, and simply sit back and enjoy the scenery, or do you make the effort and use your own two feet? There is, in some of us, an awful form of puritanism that says that the view from the mountain top should be earned. I have been up the mountain by rail but felt quite guilty, and convinced that the walkers passed along the way were sneering at me. On the other hand, it is a memorable ride, with immense views, plus all the special pleasure of travelling the vintage railway. The walk is still preferable – it is not really very arduous if one takes the easiest routes. The path from Llanberis is the longest, following much the same route as the railway, others such as the Pig Track are shorter but steeper. It all begins, in fact, quite gently, but has its moments of pure wonder. There is a long steady pull towards the crags of Clogwyn du'ur Arddu, then the path suddenly steepens as you near the ridge. The most disheartening thing that can happen to you as you pant up, stopping occasionally to 'enjoy the view' – it never has anything to do with being out of breath – is to be overtaken by a horribly fit young person *running* up the mountain. But the steep part provides its own, superb reward. You come out under a little railway bridge to find yourself at the top of the ridge, looking out to the whole Llanberis pass spread at your feet. After that there is a rocky way up to the summit where you meet the railway passengers, cool and unflustered, while you are hot, bothered but more than a little smug. There is, however, one thing that must be stressed. Snowdon is not a low hill, it is a mountain and subject to mountain weather. Even in spring, the summit may be clad in snow and ice and a summer's day can cloud over, enveloping you in a cold, clammy mist. No-one should set off up the mountain without checking the mountain weather forecast – not just the general forecast but the Snowdonia special. Equally, no-one should go without proper walking shoes or boots and protective clothing. Some may think this is all a bit namby pamby: the people who are killed each year on the mountain probably thought so too.

The good news about reaching the top of Snowdon is that it is a lot easier going back. And the view from the summit also shows you something of the splendours of the scenery of the next stage of the journey. First there is the ruined castle of Dolbadarn, stuck out on a headland and raised up on its mound. Built by the princes of Gwynedd it is small, uncompromisingly defensive. Even on a sunny day it seems a comfortless place; when the clouds sit low over the mountains, it appears positively miserable. Beyond it, at the entrance to Llanberis Pass, is Llyn Peris, a milky green pool reflecting the shattered slate faces which rise above it. The pass itself is like Glencoe in that it is as thrilling in bad weather as good. It can become positively Wagnerian, when thunder echoes from rock to rock and you tunnel through the oppressive clouds, a poor insignificant little thing tied to your narrow thread of road. Good weather enables you to enjoy the wider views, the shapely rock peaks, but I am not sure that, paradoxically, the bad days are not really the best.

At Pen-y-Gwryd, the barren rockiness gives way to a richer, greener valley with great colour contrasts. If you came upon this valley anywhere else, you would exclaim over its wild scenery of rough moorland and rocky outcrops, but after the high drama of the pass it can go almost unnoticed. At Capel Curig you join the main A5 road by an old toll house. This was, and is, the Holyhead road, the main route linking London and the ships to and from Ireland. It is one of the great pieces of early-nineteenth-century engineering, largely the work of Thomas Telford. Today, it can be an infuriatingly slow, wriggling-up-and-down sort of route, but given the terrain through which it has to pass it still seems remarkable. Nevertheless it always seems a good idea to get off it when you can. The little minor road to the south of the river is even less direct but you are much more likely to have it all to yourself, and it has a lot to offer. It passes the site of a Roman camp, which is just about still visible, but the real attraction is the river itself. One of the consolations of wet weather is that it fills the mountain streams and rivers until they positively boil round the rocks, and here the water is a constant companion. You may not see the Swallow Falls, the famous beauty spot, but you can enjoy this river scenery without the trappings of tourism which you find at Betws-y-Coed. Peace returns again when you turn north, off the main road and up the Conwy valley, and the scenery changes yet again. Now it is altogether gentler, a lush valley of green windings through the hills. It brings you to Llanwrst, an unpretentiously attractive spot sitting comfortably and contentedly in its sheltered hollow, but not without its sense of history. Gwydir Castle is a Tudor mansion built round a fourteenth-century hall and set in beautifully restored formal gardens. The chapel built for the house in 1673 has a superb painted ceiling and has borrowed several features from earlier buildings, including Aberconwy Abbey, left to decay at the Dissolution. It is said that the body of Llewellyn the

212

Great was also brought here, in a stone coffin, from the abbey.

If the road into Llanwrst is gentle, the way out is a long climb up a steep hill, and the views get better as you go. By the time you come out of Pandy Tudur you really have a feeling that the transformation is complete: the barren mountains have ended, to be replaced by hills which seem all the richer by contrast, almost an emerald green after the grey of rock and the dark bracken. It is still very hilly, a convulsed landscape, never still, all hump and hollow, through which the road twists in highbanked lanes. A sign at Gwytherin proclaims it 'best-kept village in Wales'. It would be interesting to compare it with its equivalent in England. One suspects that the latter would be rather more obviously picturesque. Gwytherin has no really blatant charms on show – a simple church, a pub, a scattering of cottages and a farm. Its appeal lies in the fact that there is not a false note struck anywhere. It is all of a piece with itself and the land that surrounds it. The buildings are in a simple vernacular style, the materials local, the decoration restrained. There is no rhetoric here, and no need of it.

This is an area that is difficult to characterise. A procession of hillocks seems endless, each separated from the next by its own valley, cut by stream and river. No driver need get bored on this route, for it scarcely gives a moment's rest as it rises and falls, twists and turns. The landscape is never monotonous, but there are no really dominant features until you reach Denbigh. No doubt about the main feature here for the castle dominates the town: reaching it seemed more of a problem. Each access road appeared to have a 'no entry' sign, and the centre of Denbigh became rather more familiar than I could have wished, but in the end the effort and frustration were rewarded with success.

Denbigh was another stronghold of the Welsh resistance to Edward I, but once the battles were over Edward followed his usual practice of building a fortress to try to ensure they stayed that way. He was not entirely successful, for Denbigh was taken by the Welsh before it was completed, but recaptured by the English. It has an airy position above the town and something of its old might and majesty survives in the massive triangular gatehouse with its three towers. It was to prove its worth some centuries later when it withstood a siege of six months by Cromwell's men in the Civil War. It was never captured: the Royalists surrendered when it was finally clear that no-one was coming to their rescue.

The parish church offers a rather more peaceful scene for contemplation, and has a most unusual double nave, each topped by a hammer-beam roof.

Denbigh still has something of the feel of being on a border, marking the edge of the hills that reach their climax at Snowdon. The Clwyd has a broad valley, and the road just touches the end of the Clwydian range. Here in fact is a very old border indeed, Offa's Dyke, which divided Wales from England long before the reign of Edward. Beyond it, towns and villages start to appear with far greater regularity. Industrial sites appear along the way, and all around Hendre are the unmistakable signs of mining – disturbed ground, spoil heaps. In this case, the mineral was lead and was still being worked just a few years ago. Somehow, the arrival at the actual border on the outskirts of Chester seems of minor consequence: the transition in terms of the sense of place has already been made.

EAST ANGLIA

The first sight of the East Anglian landscape that you have on leaving Lincoln might be enough to turn you back again. Everything has gone in the name of efficiency: hedgerows demolished, trees rooted up, until all that is left is a drab, featureless plain. Villages and towns seem forlornly isolated, touched by a melancholy of emptiness so that their own personalities scarcely register. It is a landscape that numbs the visual senses and it needs a powerful stimulant to arouse one's enthusiasm. Tattershall Castle provides it.

A very bald description might suggest that this is just another medieval fortress, a great tower surrounded by a moat. But this tower is not some monumental edifice of stone, it is built almost entirely of brick. It seems an incongruous material for a castle, for it was no mere piece of romantic fakery. It was built by Ralph, Lord Cromwell between 1430 and 1450, in the middle of the dynastic struggle between the houses of York and Lancaster, an age when defences might well be needed in earnest. There was an older stone castle on the site, but that was pulled down to make way for the splendid new tower. Cromwell did, however, look to his defences. The old moat was retained and a new outer moat added with defended gateways. Nothing, however, can disguise the fact that Tattershall Castle is a splendid characterisation, not of military power but of the power of wealth. Cromwell was treasurer of England, and you will find the purse motif used as decoration in the chimney pieces. This is wealth ostentatiously on show.

Tattershall was a very important building, a trendsetter. It was one of the first major buildings in England to use large areas of bare brick, uncovered by plaster or paint. In those days, when bricks were handmade and fired in quite crude kilns, they showed great variations and real richness and depth of colour. No-one could possibly call the brick wall of the castle dull. Inside, the plan is simple, each floor centred on a single large open room, and a vaulted basement at the foot. The chambers are rather daunting in their echoing emptiness, but around them are smaller rooms with delicate vaulted ceilings and everywhere the details are superbly executed. Just look for example at the handrail of the staircase, constituted as a continuous spiral of carved stone recessed into the

215

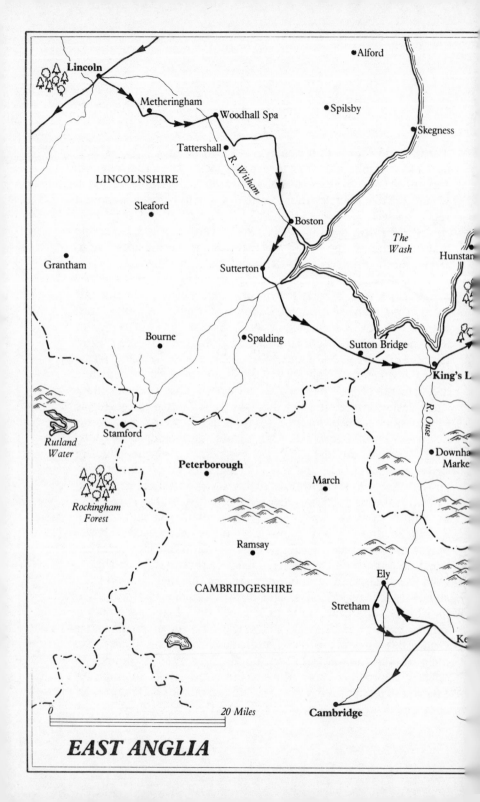

Lincoln
Alford
Metheringham
Spilsby
Woodhall Spa
Skegness
Tattershall
R. Witham
LINCOLNSHIRE
Sleaford
Boston
The Wash
Hunstan
Grantham
Sutterton
Bourne
Spalding
Sutton Bridge
King's L
Stamford
R. Ouse
Rutland Water
Downha
Marke
Peterborough
March
Rockingham Forest
Ramsay
CAMBRIDGESHIRE
Ely
Stretham
Ke
0   20 Miles
Cambridge

EAST ANGLIA

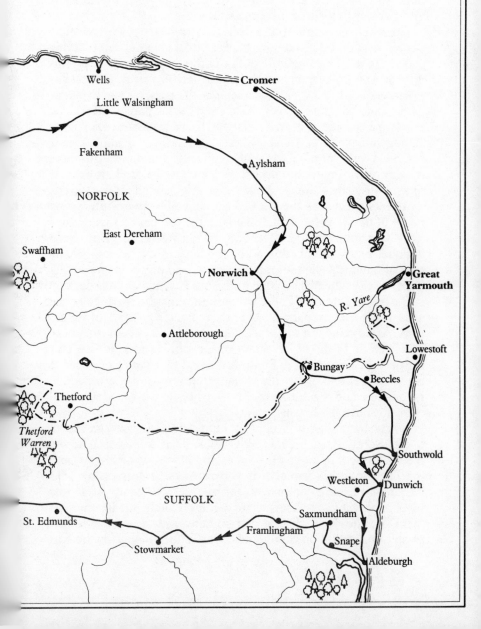

wall, both elegant and practical. One thing that one can say about this part of the world is that if you do manage to gain any height at all then the views are immense. From the battlements one can look out across to Lincoln cathedral. Castles may turn one's mind back to thoughts of medieval warfare, but at Tattershall you are likely to be jolted out of your reveries by the warplanes roaring into Coningsby airfield just across the river.

Cromwell also endowed a college of priests and a collegiate church next to the castle is particularly interesting. The first thing you see is an intriguing little notice at the front: 'Please close this door at 4 pm to keep bats out'. Inside there is a clear division between choir and nave. The former was the preserve of chaplains, clerks and choristers, screened off from the lay parishioners. The graveyard outside is a great spot for those who like rummaging among tombstones. An apothecary and surgeon's tomb comes complete with a particularly grisly skull and crossbones. And there is a curiosity to note. For such a well-endowed church, it has one note of austerity – the clock face is merely painted on the tower.

Tattershall marks the start of an altogether more interesting phase of the journey, though the fact that you pass a sign to New York has nothing to do with it. The old fenland has long since been drained, but is still chequered by the lines of ditches so that the glint of water is never far away. It comes to take an ever-increasing importance as ditches become wider, until eventually they develop into navigable drains. There was a time when the produce of the area was carried in barges plying this complex network of waterways. At Cowbridge a whole set of locks and sluices come together, as a prelude to the main watery theme which grows in intensity as you near Boston. The Drain is crossed by a series of pleasing brick bridges and one really elegant iron bridge, while the scene is completed on the outskirts of town where a five-sailed windmill rises up above the houses.

Boston has a slightly foreign air, but even so one does not expect to discover this is an inland port which still has connections across the North Sea. In among the shops and offices you will find both the Danish and Norwegian vice-consulates. It is in many ways a difficult place to summarise, for there are so many influences here. The gabled houses seem vaguely Dutch but in amongst them is a purely English jettied building with ornate pargeting, plaster decoration on the theme of the Tudor rose. It is the sort

218

of place which has few really outstanding buildings, but where it is well worth keeping your eyes open. The river frontage has its workmanlike scene of old warehouses and shapely bollards, just by the wharf a former corn merchant advertised his presence by a three-dimensional metal sign in the form of a bag of grain, and practically next door is a lovely little thirties cinema. The town is famous, however, for its one really grand building: the church, the tower of which, the Boston Stump, is the best-known landmark in the region.

East Anglia probably has more fine parish churches than any other area in Britain and this is one of the biggest and grandest in style. The claim, it should be said, is not undisputed: how do you define 'biggest' – floor area, volume, height? Biggest or not, it is immense, nearly 300ft long and 100ft wide. It is perpendicular architecture at its most impressive, with an altogether magnificent window above the west door. Tracery from one of the church windows was taken for Trinity church in the other Boston in Massachusetts. It is a church which appeals both for its overall splendour and for the wealth of its detail, and the misericords are as good as you will find anywhere. There is the usual mixture of mythology and domesticity, fable and piety. The carvers recorded the quirkier aspects of human life: a hunter coming home empty handed is being beaten over the head by his wife; another wife is chasing away a fox which has seized a cockerel. There is a satire on the bagpipes: jesters with cats tucked under their arms are biting their tails to make them squawk. Animals feature largely, and a somewhat macabre scene shows Sir Yvain galloping into an enemy castle and not quite making it: his horse is chopped in two by the falling portcullis. There are sixty misericords altogether, so no-one should find a visit to Boston's parish church dull.

Churches are the most important feature in the landscape. Coming out of Boston you are soon back to the flat lands, across which spire and tower announce the presence of the next village. Some are more interesting than others. The spire of Fosdyke church appears to be crooked, but then the angle changes and it appears perfectly normal again, and one is left wondering whether it might not be simply an optical illusion. The spire was, in any case, soon forgotten because just as one had become accustomed to the agricultural landscape, masts appeared on the horizon, where a coaster lolled on a mud bank by the Welland. One is soon, however, back to the sense of travelling between churches. It is very rare that their prominence is challenged. At Gedney, the water tower does its best, rearing up like a giant Olympic torch, but it cannot really compete. The church itself stands back from the road but its huge clerestory windows – and here one is tempted to use the alternative spelling of 'clear storey' – give it an oddly insubstantial, fragile appearance as you look straight through it to the sky beyond.

Sutton Bridge brings another of the major navigation routes that slice deep into the land. It crosses the Nene halfway between the old port of Wisbech and the Wash. The bridge swings to allow ships to pass, and the bridge keeper is provided with an ornate little cabin perched on high over the centre of the waterway. It gives the impression of practical, solid engineering to which someone has absentmindedly added a little summerhouse. It is slightly quirky, but all the time these crossings seem to be pointing the importance of the rivers that lead to the Wash and the open sea. This sense of maritime significance reaches its climax at King's Lynn.

This is a real port and an ancient one, which from medieval times has traded with Europe, trans-shipping goods on to the network of Fenland waterways. Its long history can be read in its buildings, for every stage of its development seems to have given the place something of quality. You know it is going to be special from the moment you reach the outskirts. You come in through the South Gate built for the serious purpose of defence in 1420 but made more of an ornate feature as peace came in the sixteenth century. Just inside is a well-designed Georgian terrace with a central archway for carriages, which looks across to a house blessed with a beautifully ornate wrought-iron balcony. But once in the town centre, the problem is not what to see but where to start an exploration of such riches. The obvious answer would seem to be by the river, but time has brought great changes to the town. As new docks were developed, so the old wide quays that once fronted the water were built over, which means that many of the older buildings are now hiding away down quiet streets. Nelson Street, however, seems to strike a suitably nautical note and it turns out to be the ideal approach to a most remarkable old building.

The Valiant Sailor was an inn in medieval times but is one no longer. It looks out on an even older building – Hampton Court. This was begun in the eleventh century and remodelled in the fourteenth as a merchant's house. If you want evidence that there was cash to be made in King's Lynn in those days, then here it is. The house has been added to through the centuries and is still lived in today. Just around the corner are the old warehouses of the Hanseatic League, built in 1475 but considerably restored. This was the English depot for one of the most powerful trading groups in Europe. Already something of the power and importance of the town is beginning to come across, and as you stroll on through streets and lanes, you are constantly astonished by the richness and variety of the buildings. But all the time, it is the water seen at the end of a street or the sudden arrival of a quay that act as constant reminders of the source of the wealth. At the end of Queen Street the river suddenly seems to dip a wet finger into the town, and there at the end of the quay is the Customs House. It was actually begun in 1683 as a merchants' exchange, which rose above an open colonnade, but that was filled in when it acquired its new status in 1718. It looks out on a battered old schooner, to the mast of which, on this occasion, was pinned a note explaining in some detail just what the owner thought of the local council – which could be summed up politely as 'not a lot'. The Market Square still has its glimpses of quays and its own grand buildings. The Duke's Head was built just a few years after the Customs House and is an extraordinary confection in pink and white like a strawberry gateau. The nineteenth-century Corn Hall opposite has a grandiose facade, but is spoiled by a plethora of obtrusive road signs.

It is only when you move away from the river frontage that the town begins to lose its special character. The High Street could be almost anywhere: the usual array of bland shopfronts and standardised plastic signs sent out by headquarters to be stuck up everywhere, regardless of the character of the building to which they are to be attached. But look up a bit and you will find, for example, The Lynn Drapery Emporium still being announced in elaborate Gothic script and alongside that a shaped gable dated 1898, followed by a brick and plaster building with a little turret. Shall we ever be clear of the standardisation of centralised design? It is a relief to get back to the old town, to the medieval cottages and the church with its curious moon clock and high-water mark showing where the floods of 1978 reached – you would have been wading waist deep during the worst of it.

Leaving King's Lynn one rather expects to be nodding one's head in agreement with one of Noel Coward's most famous lines: 'Very flat, Norfolk'. But you don't, because it isn't. It could not really be described as hilly, but having just left the genuine flat land of Lincolnshire one really appreciates its gentle undulations and the constantly changing views. There is not the same monotony of open fields, instead, beyond South Wootton you reach an area of sandy heathland, dotted with trees. That takes you on to Castle Rising which does indeed have a castle, with a twelfth-century keep. But it is not the keep that impresses, for it is almost overwhelmed by the truly massive earthworks that surround it. This is only a brief interruption to what is really a very attractive country road. Coming out at the other side, you plunge into very brackeny woodland that positively teems with life. Within the first hundred yards I was taking evasive action to avoid one squirrel and two pheasants. One would certainly not wish to demolish the birds which probably belong to the nearby Sandringham estate: heaven knows what the punishment is for killing the royal game. Sandringham, however, has nothing like the lure of nearby Appleton, one of my favourite slightly mad buildings. There is not much to Appleton, just a few houses, a ruined church – and the water tower. All a water tower needs is a tank high enough off the ground to provide a suitable pressure. That is what you have here, except that it is unusually ornate and the tower on which it stands was built as a home for the tower's keeper, and there is a little room at the top for viewing the world, the latter reached by a spiral staircase in a minaret-like turret at the side. It is a glorious mixture of the fantastic and the wholly practical – in the latter department, what could be more sensible than running the flue from the fireplace up through the centre of the tank, preventing the water freezing in winter? It was a bit of a cross-country diversion to see it, but well worth the effort.

The pattern of Norfolk buildings soon becomes clear. The traditional materials of the area are brick and flint. The latter can either be used as a rough stone in great, uneven nodules, or it can be knapped: split to show a smooth, dark, shiny face. You see its use in villages such as Stanhoe, which sits at a crossroads with houses grouped round the duck pond, and even the more modern additions have kept to the same basic materials. By the time you get to North Creake, however, another familiar East Anglian phenomenon appears, or rather disappears: we are back

222

to the land of vanished hedgerows. You can see what were once thickset hedges reduced to single bushes. They stand well spread out and have been cruelly cut back, so that they are flat-topped and shorn like crew-cut GIs on parade. Perhaps one should not be too dismayed. In a way, it is only completing a circle of experience. Just a few miles further on are the ruins of a little church, a green lane and a series of humps in the fields. This was once the parish church and village of Egmere. The medieval village would have been surrounded by its open fields ploughed into deep furrows, then crops went out in favour of more profitable sheep grazing, and the land was turned to grass. Now the open fields are back, the plough has returned – only the fields are that much more open, and the village has gone. The sense of the past being with you remains all the way to Walsingham, for the road runs between the ancient banks of field boundaries, their age proclaimed by the mature trees that still grow along the top of the banks.

Little Walsingham itself is a notable medieval village which grew to importance as a place of pilgrimage. In 1061 the lady of the manor claimed to see the Virgin Mary in a vision and established a shrine of Our Lady of Walsingham. The Reformation put an end to the practice, but in the 1920s pilgrimages were resumed. The crowds of worshippers have returned. The abbey is in ruins, but the shrine has been restored and there are now Catholic and Protestant churches in the village. In spite of its past, and reputation for piety, the most prominent object in the centre is the lock-up. Among all its medievalism Walsingham church is quite unexpected. Behind its old exterior lies a wholly new interior, for the entire building was gutted by fire in 1961. It has an almost startlingly bright interior and although the form of the old has been preserved it is all unmistakably new. Some bold decisions were taken, and none bolder than to add to the survivors from the flames not imitations and copies of what was there before but works by contemporary artists, including abstracts. On the whole, the new works sit quite happily in this bright and shining building.

A pilgrimage of a more secular nature took me off to Thursford. One of the happiest features of East Anglian villages is the name board. Thursford's decorated sign shows you what to look out for here: traditional heraldry is joined by locomotive, traction engine and plough. Thursford Green is the home of the Thursford Steam Collection. For the uninitiated anything powered by steam that

223

trundles down the road on big wheels is a traction engine, but that is not so. Traction engines were designed to haul farm machinery from place to place, but once on site they could be adapted to run the machines such as threshing engines, as well. Ploughing engines are quite different. These are not steam tractors, for these heavy monsters would do more damage than good if let loose on the fields. They worked in pairs, one at each side of the field, and hauled the plough to and fro by cables. But the kings of the road were the showmen's engines. The job they were required to do was mundane enough, hauling the fairground rides from site to site, and once in position they were used as generators to light up the scene. But the whole point about a fair is that it has to attract the customers and it must be gaudy. The engines became displays in their own right: canopies carried on barley-sugar twisted columns, elaborate designs, bright paintwork and gleaming brass turned them into works of art. At Thursford the engines are on show, and so too are fairground organs and a classic switchback ride. Each night in summer the Norfolk air hums with the breathy notes of the music and by day there is the equally enticing sound of the steam whistle as the 2ft gauge railway carries another trainload of passengers. Incidentally, although the men on the footplate of a railway locomotive are easily distinguished as driver and fireman, on a traction engine there is the steerer who twiddles the handle to move the beast around, but the driver is the one shovelling the coal and pulling the levers. A constant regret on leaving Thursford is that I have nothing more exciting to drive than a mundane motor.

Memories of the railway past turn up just outside Thursford, where the road runs by a disused line. The little crossing cottage is now just another home, but the old signal box has been converted into a splendid greenhouse cum gazebo. It is good to find that all is not lost and forgotten. A bit of the past that no-one is likely to let go appears soon afterwards. Blickling Hall is the very model of a great Jacobean mansion. You can see just how far the use of brickwork has advanced in the two centuries that separate this house from Tattershall Castle. Everything here speaks of riches, comfort and luxury, with no hint of defensive needs. The turrets are clearly there for show to balance the stately curves of the gables. Inside, the house was largely modelled in the next century, but one of its glories survives, the extraordinary elaborate plaster ceiling of the great hall. The new builders also added splendours of their own: a

224

soaring staircase inside, while outside they added the orangery and the temple. The formal gardens came a century later. The estate once belonged to Sir John Fastolf, said to have been Shakespeare's model for Falstaff. If so, nothing of that rumbustious knight's character has survived in this urbane establishment.

Aylsham is a town which exudes wellbeing, a place that has developed over the centuries on the sound basis of prosperous industries, wool and linen. It has welcomed innovators from Holland and Belgium, and something of their influence remains in the gabled buildings. It was served by the Aylsham navigation – long defunct, but there are still reminders of trading days in the area known as Dunkirk. The finest building of all is the old mellow brick mill overlooking a wide mill pond. It provides a suitably watery introduction to what will become a main theme, for the river Bure that flows through Aylsham is one of the principal rivers of the Norfolk Broads. You cannot really see the Broads at their best from the road; you cannot, in the opinion of many people, see them at their best at all these days. Popularity has brought a vast expansion of boat hiring, and where once that meant sailing now the motor cruiser dominates. There is a sad tendency on the part of many hirers to want to dash around furiously as soon as they get on board, whereas the whole point of boating in an area such as this should be to find calm, and relaxation. Personal prejudice enters here: on numerous broadland visits, I have yet to travel on any vessel with an engine in it. But at their best the Broads can still offer marvellous sailing days: stiff breezes, but not too stiff for comfort, sunshine on the water and, if you get off the more popular routes, peace. Those who say it is all spoiled are wrong. Even the busiest waters are not crowded all the time – nor all the year. There are still riverside villages such as Coltishall which are pleasant and peaceful, even if they are matched by Wroxham which, alas, is neither.

Norwich, too, is a city that grew up as the centre of the woollen trade that ultimately depended on water trade. Large vessels could and can come up river to load and unload at the quays. As the wool trade declined, so shoemaking and engineering moved in, to be replaced in their turn by big commercial concerns such as Norwich Union Insurance. This is a city that has adapted to changing times. Added to these were the industries that looked outwards towards the products of the countryside – maltings, breweries and the local speciality, mustard. All have left their mark with some interesting and sometimes impressive buildings. The finest of all can be found down by the river – the old Norwich Yarn Company mill of 1839, with its domed staircase tower. It is no bad thing to start with buildings such as this for they remind you of the continuity that holds cities together, the realities of change and adaptation. It is all too easy constantly to look back at the great buildings of the past, as though nothing of interest or importance has happened since. The past is important. It provides the foundation on which everything else has been built, and there are few places where one can see the might and confidence of Norman England more surely portrayed in architecture than Norwich.

The cathedral shows Norman thought throughout. It was Herbert Losinge, who became bishop of East Anglia in 1091, who began the work. He decided to move the see from Thetford, bought a large area of the city by compulsory purchase and proceeded to pull everything down. Something of that brutal determination survives in the fabric. The nave has the conventional three storeys, but the clerestory is insignificant, so that what one sees is great arch piled on great arch, with the shafts confirming the strong, almost overpowering verticality. Everywhere you look in the nave seems to emphasise the sense of power. It makes a marvellous contrast with the work of later builders who added such gorgeous decorative details as the elaborate vaulting of the choir. But it is the sense of brooding power that remains dominant; and the same sense carries over to the other great focal point of the medieval city, the castle. The Conqueror showed the same disregard for the locals as did the Bishop: a hundred houses were brushed aside to make way for the new castle. Henry I added the tower on the mound, again uncompromisingly solid, a giant box 100ft square with walls rising 70ft high, with only tiers of decorative arches on the outside to relieve the severity. When we talk about 'featureless blocks' these days we usually mean the modern offices of concrete and steel. Few modern architects would dare to suggest anything as overwhelming as this, so completely out of scale with its surroundings. Nowadays, citizens protest against the carbuncles of modern architecture; there was not much future for anyone who tried protesting at having giant blocks such as this imposed on the neighbourhood in the eleventh century.

The excitements of the city centre seldom extend to the suburbs:

the journey out of Norwich can seem interminable. But once clear, it is back to the same rather gentle countryside, which seems to have appealed to the local landowners, who pinched a surprisingly large amount of it for themselves to create parks. From Hedenham to Ditchingham parkland accompanies you virtually all the way.

There is something about some names that leads one to expect the worst. Bungay sounds flat and somehow dull – which makes the town itself all the more delightful. It turns out to be a place that one is surprised not to find established as a tourist centre and more than grateful that it is not. In fact, as a writer, I feel sorely tempted not to say anything at all about the place for fear that the heritage brigade set their lads on it and it starts springing little plastic kiosks, gifte shoppes and dubious antiques. At the moment it is simply a modest market town of uncommon character and charm sited on the river Waveney, straddling the border between Suffolk and Norfolk. Bungay is a town that grew on the river trade and the produce of the region and it proclaims its character almost at once, with a large malting rearing up above the water meadows far grander than the town's Norman castle. The elements that made the town have not changed that much for centuries, so one finds that it was important even before the conquest – the Domesday Book recorded five churches here. Two old churches survive, to which has been added a more recent Catholic church. Logically, one should proceed chronologically, but that is unlikely to be the order in which you encounter the buildings. In the town centre is the functional but not very enticing Catholic church and next to it a typical East-Anglian church of stone and flint, the centrepiece of an area of well-proportioned houses. It was once much larger, but was partly destroyed by fire and is now redundant. To wander in is to find curiosities in plenty, but inevitably everything has about it an air of gentle melancholy. Beside the altar is a typically grotesque Flemish carving of the resurrection, presented to the church by the novelist Rider Haggard. Rather more obviously appealing is a cupboard by the door, inscribed W. B. Bungay 1675, covered with naive carvings of bishops which, though crude, seem to register a real and genuine emotion. Close by is a plaque of 1792 to C. Cook and J. Sheppard Churchwarding and J. Cattermole, Plumber – appropriately for the latter it is in lead.

The next place came as a surprise to me. Not expecting another church I went off for a stroll and found the attractive little butter cross in the market place, an octagonal building with a domed roof. On this stands a blindfold figure with a sword in one hand and scales in the other, representing justice, but being set on a butter cross one had the irreverent thought that it might just be a blind grocer about to weigh out half a pound of the best creamery. The town inns feature immense signs on wrought-iron brackets and everything seems to have a sense of style, from the Georgian doorways with porches and fan lights down to the little Jacobean-styled fire station. There is a wealth of interesting things to see: a house which to save window tax blocked out the windows and painted on fake ones to preserve the symmetry, the Chaucer Press, and a house with a curious round porch fitted with two curved doors. It was only now, thinking that I had seen the best of Bungay, that I chanced on the third church.

John Betjeman thought it was worth cycling twelve miles against the wind to see the round tower and the woodwork of this Saxon church. He was right, because this is not quite the usual East-Anglian church. One gets used to certain motifs and a particular splendour: the motifs are here, but somehow all rather more homely. It has an angel roof, but here the angels are rather matronly types who seem to be wearing their Sunday best and looked justifiably apprehensive about their airy position, held aloft by very skimpy wings. The pulpit has extravagant Elizabethan carving and the organ loft looks like a balcony that acquired its organ as an afterthought. There is a most unusual font rising up on a fluted column. The whole place is a mixture of outward simplicity and quirky detail. One could say much the same thing about the whole of this enticing town.

From Bungay to Beccles the road follows the Waveney valley. It passes another round-towered church at Mettingham and a set of cultivation terraces on a hillside like a giant's broad staircase. Beccles itself grew up, like Bungay, around its river connections – now only a memory and a marina. The maltings were, in their day, the biggest ever to be found under one roof. Beccles is bigger than Bungay and has a quite different character. It stands high above the marshy land of the river bank, to which it is joined by a variety of narrow, steep lanes and steps. Coming into the town, the first building to hold the attention was, for once, modern. A house at the end of one of the sets of river steps had a curved roof topped by a weather vane in the shape of a wherry, the traditional sailing barge of the Broads and Broadland rivers. First impressions are of a wealth of mellow brick, stone being reserved for the more important buildings, notably the church. This is a rather odd building with a separate, blank-eyed tower and a graveyard with stone coffins set above ground. The macabre urge to peep in through the cracks is irresistible, but the inhabitants seem to have left. Ideally one would reach Beccles before Bungay, for it undoubtedly suffers by comparison. It does, however, still have a role as a port, not for sailing wherries, but for helicopters. You pass the heliport on the edge of town.

From here to the coast, the road is far more pleasant than you might expect. The countryside has not yet succumbed to the East-Anglian disease of prairieisation. The fields have hedgerows and the hedgerows have flowers; trees spring up from the boundaries and haphazardly dot the landscape. Villages cluster round the church towers that announce their presence. There is the added pleasure of seeing an old craft thriving. In the marshes north of Reydon, the reeds are still being harvested and you can see them neatly bundled by the roadside ready to be sent off to the thatchers. These are salt marshes that bring with them the first whiff of the sea.

There are few seaside towns more attractive than Southwold. It is not so much the beaches that make it so pleasant, for the shore line is long and featureless apart from the steady procession of groynes dipping into the waves and the rows of beach huts lined up against the sea wall. Nevertheless, it is the sea that adds the extra crispness to the air and provides a distantly rumbling accompaniment to the life of the town. Southwold is based on a series of greens and the first provides you with enough interest to satisfy the most demanding visitor – it has a lighthouse, a brewery and church. The lighthouse is the oddest, a curiously suburban affair rising up above the roof tops of neat little houses. The brewery is Adnams, a wholly traditional concern, and that tradition extends to the dray horses, such dignified animals, that deliver the ale. If anyone needs an excuse to visit Southwold, then the excellence of the local brew would provide it. This is beer at its best. The church is simply glorious: painted angels stare down from the roof, looking out over an elaborate choir screen to the yet more exotic carvings on the choir stalls, a menagerie of strange beasts. Southwold Jack is a man at arms who, when a rope is pulled, strikes a bell to mark the start of services and welcome brides to their weddings. Everything seems to be on the same scale of magnificence: the font cover has the proportions and elaboration of a Gothic spire; the pulpit rises from a fountain pedestal in red, green and gold.

Most places would be hard pushed to live up to such a beginning, but not Southwold. Outside the very grand Swan Hotel is an equally grand standard with cavorting dolphins. Houses are often very attractive, and none more so than those that look out to sea – one particularly delectable building is enlivened with pilasters topped by scallops. Then, just when you have become accustomed to all this grandeur, you find the Sailors' Reading Room and Museum. It is still used, but is a place of old memories as well. It is a corrective to the notion that the sea was put there to amuse visitors and improve the view, for it tells of the other life of the sea, of hard work, foul weather and disaster. This is a town which encourages one to linger and to explore. A pleasant way to do this is to walk the line of the old Southwold Railway, one of those quirky little railways which provided an often erratic service but which somehow inspired more affection than the bigger, more efficient neighbours. It brings you out to the River Blyth, still a working river with fishing boats lying alongside the yachts. It is a wholly unpretentious place with nothing to recommend it but water, jetties, boats and a few simple tarred huts for tackle. It needs nothing more.

The road out of Southwold has to take a great detour to get around the salt marshes. It is an area of gently rippling water and reeds fringed by pine trees that rise up from the sandy soil. The river crossing arrives at Blythburgh. You could dash by on the road and never know it was there. Up a lane are some extremely good examples of timber-framed houses and a church that could pass for a cathedral. Once this was a prosperous town and an important port but the meandering river proved an obstacle to the trading ships. When they no longer came, Blythburgh dwindled to a hamlet, with only the church as a reminder of what once was. It is an immense building in stone and flint, with a long nave accentuated by the buttresses that alternate with the elaborate traceried windows. Like so many churches in the region it too has an angel roof – though these angels have had their wings peppered by pot-shooting Cromwellian troops. During the visit made on this trip, the interior was swathed in sheeting and a complex of scaffolding, so a good deal of restoration work is in hand. Some things at least will presumably not change: the Jack the Lad, similar to Southwold's Jack, and the carvings on the pews. Those who have overindulged in Adnams may care to contemplate 'drunkenness', a miserable figure sitting in the stocks and clearly nursing a monumental hangover.

Having finally crossed the Blyth, the road now makes its way back to the coast and disappearing Dunwich. The sea is steadily nibbling away at this coast as it has been for centuries, washing away a bit of it here and depositing it again somewhere else. No point in looking for the church here: All Saints crashed to the beach in 1920, gradually followed by its graveyard and now just one memorial stone is left. Out under the waves lies Roman Dunwich and Saxon, Norman and medieval Dunwich, all succumbing to the inexorable advances of the sea. Not content with eating into the town, the sea reversed the process during a great storm in 1326, when it dropped a million tons of sand across the mouth of the river. An important port was a port no longer. Dunwich has no reason to be grateful to the sea. The story is all told in the excellent local museum where a model shows you what the waves have long since hidden from view.

Inland is a rather surprising area, mixing marshland with sandy heaths of gorse and bracken. The villages are usually enlivened by a very popular Suffolk technique of colour washing walls, usually in pink though this can shade down into a deep, full red. Another tradition reappears at Theberton, where the church has a distinctive round tower. Leiston, the first town of any size, has two claims to fame: an abbey which has almost vanished as completely as Dunwich, and Garretts. The Garrett family began working a forge in the town at the end of the eighteenth century, and soon became involved in making agricultural machinery. The decisive change in their fortunes came when they turned to producing portable steam engines that could be pulled along to a farm for use at harvest time. Eventually, the engines became self propelling and the traction engine was born. By 1851 the company was employing five hundred men, but was always on the look out for improvements. Richard Garrett III went to America to study new production methods, and as a result of what he saw he came home and built the Long Shop, nicknamed 'The Cathedral' and it is easy to see why. The company closed in 1980 but the Long

Shop and the surrounding works are now a museum where the glorious engines are on display.

The last visit to the east coast is to Aldeburgh, with its associations with Benjamin Britten and the poet George Crabbe, who was his inspiration. First impressions are of a spot that is more Peter Pan than Peter Grimes. Somewhat twee gift shops seem to have little to do with stories of grim struggles against the sea. Perhaps this is unfair. It is a handsome enough place, even if not as fine as Southwold, and the sea sucking at the shingle beach is real enough. You can still buy fresh fish from huts on the beach and perhaps if you came here on a stormy day you would also feel the darker mood of the place. In the sunlight, it is just another seaside resort. It is, however, an odd coastline. This is one of the places that the sea has chosen to deposit the land it has robbed elsewhere. It closed off the mouth of the Alde, which now runs parallel to the sea, separated by little more than a sea wall of gargantuan proportions, which seems more like a causeway. Near the end is one of those giant Martello towers which spread right round the southeast corner of England, built to guard against the advances of Napoleon.

Music lovers can pay their respects to Britten at the church, which has a memorial window by John Piper, or travel to Snape and the Maltings. The pleasant thing here is to find how well the place has retained its old identity. The buildings that front the road are a hotchpotch of different dates, but are all the more satisfying for that. Each has its own style and identity, yet there is an overall unity of purpose: the same covered hoists, the same rhythmic pattern of loading bays. Grain was brought to the stores by boat – barges can still often be seen at the quay – or by rail, and the barley then went to the maltings themselves. These are the buildings which now house the concert hall, the heart of the arts complex. They look out over river and marsh, and here the spirit of Britten really does seem to hover in the air. You can turn your back on the buildings and face a landscape of poignant loneliness, of woeful bird cry and the high, dry rattle of reeds. Even the large sculpture of Moore seems at home here, as though it had grown from the landscape. The slight shabbiness, the down-at-heel wear of the old industrial buildings, rather than detracting from the atmosphere provides a sense of continuity, prevents the maltings from seeming either arty or precious.

232

As soon as you turn your back on the sea, you become aware again of East Anglian flatness, of a countryside where the visual excitement is as likely to lie with the clouds overhead as with anything to be seen on the ground. It is not surprising that the greatest painter of cloudscapes, John Constable, was a Suffolk man. Anything that rears itself up from this level land is bound to make a strong impact. Framlingham Castle certainly does, but would probably do so anywhere. It has a great enclosing wall, 60ft high with thirteen towers set round the perimeter. Some years ago the walkway round the battlements was giddyingly open: now it is protected by railings, much more sensible but a lot less fun. It was to this castle that Mary Tudor fled to escape the forces of the Duke of Northumberland, who wanted to make his daughter-in-law Lady Jane Grey queen following the death of Edward VI. Northumberland's army never arrived, the revolt fizzled out and Mary emerged from the castle to be declared queen. The castle is all about majesty and power and the church repeats the theme. It is yet another church dominated by a richly carved roof. Equally extraordinary is the fourteenth-century font, energetically carved with wild lions and equally wild men. The dominant note, however, is struck by the memorials to the aristocracy, to the dukes of Richmond and Norfolk. It is difficult to decide which sends out the stronger message of the importance of earthly power, castle or church.

The landscape does little to stop the winds blowing across the land, which may not do much for creature comfort but makes it perfect for windmills, and none is finer than the mill at Saxstead Green. She – and sailing windmills like sailing ships are all female – is a post mill and a masterpiece of simple ingenuity. The weatherboarded buck which holds the mill machinery and to which the sails are attached, is mounted on a single central post, hidden from view inside the round house. The whole structure can be pivoted to face the wind, and the wind does the work for the miller. The precipitously steep steps up to the buck have a pair of wheels and a 'fantail' at the bottom. This acts as a giant propeller. When the wind catches it, the blades whirl round and drive the buck back to the right position. Once it is facing the wind, the fantail is fully sheltered and stops turning. The windmill has an obvious appeal as a picturesque feature, but is equally attractive as an example of how a simple

mechanical device can be as satisfyingly efficient as the most sophisticated machine.

The market town of Stowmarket gained its prosperity from its
situation at the head of the Ipswich and Stowmarket Navigation
and, as the age of water transport gave way to the dominance of
rail, it slipped easily into its new role as railhead. Round the
waterway, you can see the traditional industry of the region represented by old maltings, and the railway has a particularly grand
station in Jacobean style carried out in red brick. The town serves
a wide but mainly rural area which makes it an appropriate choice
as home to The Museum of East Anglian Life. Like other big
open-air museums, there are features which were there before
the museum opened, notably the thirteenth-century tithe barn.
Others were brought in, often as rescue operations. Alton water
mill would otherwise have disappeared under the rising waters of
a new reservoir. The emphasis is inevitably on the countryside
and its crafts, and visitors have the opportunity to compare two
forms of power – the resident Suffolk-punch working horse and a
pair of Burrell steam-ploughing engines, the latter well into their
second century. After a pleasant mooch around Stowmarket, the
exit seemed almost indecently hasty as the only sensible way on
to the next town is down the dual carriageway of the A45. One
advantage of this is that, after a long journey on minor roads, it
serves as a useful reminder of just how little enjoyment there is in
speeding down an 'improved' road. The other advantage is that it
brings you all the sooner to Bury St Edmunds.

The first monastery was founded here in the seventh century by
the first Christian king of East Anglia, Sieghert. In 903 the body
of King Edmund was brought here. Edmund was captured and
killed in the wars against the Danes, tortured, beheaded and the
head flung away. The head was later recoverd, and miraculously
reunited to the body. This was quite enough to gain the king
canonisation and St Edmund's shrine drew in crowds of pilgrims.
King Cnut was sufficiently impressed to endow the abbey and the
process he had begun was continued by the Normans. The site is
still a dominant feature in the town, even though much has been
destroyed. What remains is the Great Gate built in the fourteenth
century, at once defensive – you can still see the remains of the
portcullis – and highly decorative. The role of defence was real
enough. Town and abbey were by no means always on the best

234

of terms, and the abbey community was often glad of the shelter of its surrounding walls. Nothing else quite matches the grandeur of the gate, which now leads to not much more than a municipal park. The form of the abbey church was almost lost in the complex of houses which have literally built it into their own fabric. It can produce some bizarre effects for it seems as though it must have happened the other way round – houses being aggrandised by adding Gothic set pieces for dramatic impact.

It is pleasant at the end of a day when maltings have appeared with great regularity to find that here at least their product has been put to good use. Over the town drifts a sweetly rich scent of brewing, and an old copper on the pavement – a vessel in which wort is boiled, not an ageing policeman – announces the presence of Greene King, brewers of Abbot Ale. Beer drinkers have always considered that the presence of two breweries as good as this and Adnams is sufficient in itself to justify a visit to Suffolk. The argument is difficult to refute, particularly when there is an ancient pub right up against the brewery wall. The Dog and Partridge must have been constructed in the conventional way, with all its timbers at the correct angles, but over the centuries floors have sagged and ceilings drooped so that now there is not a right angle to be seen anywhere. It can be disconcerting after a few pints. It is the sort of place that could easily have been turned into an olde worlde inn, but thank heavens it remains a good honest pub that just happens to be very old and serve very good beer. The town is really a bit like that: created round a monastic foundation a thousand years ago, it wears its age with no undue ostentation. It is, one feels, a town to live in, not just to visit.

The A45 that zooms you into Bury St Edmunds also zooms you out again, and you have to watch what you are doing for if you miss a turn it may be miles to the next one. It is only when you do turn off that you get your first real sense of the character of the region. This is Newmarket area, and you have hardly joined the B road before the first stud farm appears, positively reeking of prosperity. The fields look fit for a Wimbledon final, not just for grazing horses. Everything is trim and spotless. A horse from such a background would surely feel deep shame if it failed to win. Humanity has also been well ordered. The road skirts Chippenham Park, politely bending round its corners to leave it inviolate. The estate village is perfectly regular, even down to the somewhat startling colour scheme, alternate houses in pink and mustard. It gives one an irrational desire to build something wholly inappropriate in the middle, just to break the too-perfect symmetry. But up ahead lie the Fens.

Downfield marks the beginning of the recognisable fen country in quite spectacular fashion. There is a splendid water tower complete with windows, louvred roof and weather vane and, just beyond, a tower windmill with ogee-shaped cap but just two sails. But already one other building is beginning to dominate the landscape. Ely cathedral seems to float above the fields like a mirage. Before the land was reclaimed, and Ely was an island, the effect must have been almost miraculous. When one finally reaches the building, one is not disappointed. The initial effect is stunning, a great nave bathed in rich light from stained-glass windows, whose depth and richness of colour is overwhelmingly intense. But the greatest glory came about literally by accident. In 1322 the Norman tower suffered the all-too-common fate of Norman towers, and collapsed. Its replacement is an astonishing feat of architecture and carpentry, an octagonal lantern that rises above a fountain of vaulting. It is impossible to tell that this is wood not stone, and that the lantern is not supported by the complex ribs of the vault but by hidden timber framework. The construction details may be fascinating, but what you see is an 8-pointed star of vaults with another brilliant star round about it, a tour de force. Even that is not the end of the story. The fourteenth-century Lady Chapel has the widest, flattest medieval vault in England: over 40ft wide it rises little more than 1ft in the centre. Below it is an almost Baroque richness of carving, of canopied stalls covered in decoration, statues, niches and foliage. It is sumptuous. In the end the memories one takes away from Ely are of contrasts, between the dramatic simplicity of the great forms of pillars and arches balanced against rich ornamentation, and of light, a wonderful complexity of shade and colour. After the cathedral, it seems almost impossible even to attempt to take in the surroundings for it is as dominant close at hand as it is among the wide skies of the fens.

It is tempting to try and imagine the 'unspoilt fens' but not very sensible. Change has been going on for centuries: banks erected against inundation, drainage ditches cut as long ago as Roman times. You get a hint of man's work as you cross the Great Ouse with its high flood banks, and if you look along from the bridge to the south you can see a building with a tall chimney. This is Stretham Old Engine House, the Victorian answer to draining the wetlands. Inside is a big beam engine that drives a scoop wheel that literally scoops away the water as it turns. But the engineers never quite completed the task of reclamation. They nearly did: the Great Fen once covered over two thousand square miles, but is now reduced to a few hundred acres. Wicken Fen is virtually the last of it. This is still an artificially controlled environment, but when the controls were allowed to slip strange things happened. Old fence posts literally took root to become flourishing willows. The droves, the paths once used by men who came to harvest reed and sedge, became dense, tangled thickets. Now the birds are the main attraction, thousands of them who come here probably not realising how closely they are being observed by the many enthusiasts. The main appeal of Wicken Fen to many is its role as a nature reserve, but it is also a fascinating glimpse into a carefully balanced environment. One feature is a wind pump, a seemingly fragile, pretty little windmill that drives a scoop wheel. Yet if it was set to work in earnest, the nature of the land would change to what you can see all around: the dark, peaty reclaimed fields. It is a minor miracle that Wicken Fen has survived at all.

Old villages developed wherever the land rose up, however slightly, above the morass of the fens. Burwell has gone on developing, spreading itself out along the road with a lot of new buildings. The church presents a very odd appearance. The windows are clear but tinted green, so that with the light behind it the effect is like looking into a giant aquarium. There is also a curious little malting, with a kiln that looks as if it belongs to the potteries. But none of this is half as odd as the churches of Swaffham Prior. The village itself is pleasant, but why does it have two churches in one churchyard? The answer is very complex. It began with the foundation of a Saxon church, St Mary, by the Prior of Ely, replaced in Norman times. But part of the village belonged to Norman knights from Brittany, who decided they needed a church of their own and St Cyriac and Juliet was duly built. In the seventeenth century it was decided that one church was enough and St Cyriac was demolished except for the bell tower. Then St Mary was struck by lightning, so a new Georgian nave was hastily tacked on to the old St Cyriac tower. Time then seemed to favour St Mary again. Restoration work began and St

Cyriac was again abandoned. There matters stand, but even that is not quite the end of the strangeness. The windows of St Mary were installed at the end of the First World War and all round the ancient church glassy bombs rain down, cannon roar and young ladies, instead of sitting piously at home, fill shells in a munitions factory. The other Swaffham, Swaffham Bulbeck, has charm with a road snaking round the village green but cannot really compete with the two churches of its neighbour. Lode, the next village, does however have Anglesey Abbey, rebuilt from the old monastic foundation around 1600. It is now a fine manor house with attractive grounds which, most unusually, still has its old estate watermill – still in working order and still occasionally put through its paces. Beyond that is the end of the detour, Cambridge.

Cambridge is city and university, inextricably intermerged. It spreads over a wide area, but at its heart is a complete unit wholly identifiable, its pattern plain. The river is the key to it all. The town did indeed grow around the Cam bridge and the main street, which bewilderingly changes its name as it goes, follows its meanderings but keeps its distance. It is that distance that gives Cambridge its unique atmosphere. Between road and river, the land seems filled with colleges, but not quite, for there are also the Backs, literally the back gardens though the name sounds much too provincial and suburban. The succession of bridges across the river and the view of the colleges has been shown in films, postcards and pictures and seen for real by millions of tourists. Yet nothing can diminish what is really one of the great sights of England; there is nothing quite comparable to the first sight of King's College across the water, with its famous Tudor chapel, leaving no-one in any doubt that it owes its grandeur to royal patronage. It is always tempting to avoid the obvious but it would be folly to visit Cambridge and not see inside its most famous building. Even if you were led in blindfold and then allowed to do nothing but stand in the centre of the nave and look up at the ceiling, the visit would be worthwhile. The intricate fan vaulting represents a final stage in the development of English Gothic at its purest. It gives an impression of immense richness, yet at the same time remains a wholly practical answer to a particular building problem – how to create a roof that seems to flow naturally from the columns and arches below. It can seem like a petrified forest.

The trouble with places like Cambridge is that one is so quickly overwhelmed by the profusion of grand buildings. You cannot do as at Ely – resolutely march into the centre, go to the cathedral and leave contented. On the other hand, one does run the risk of suffering from architectural indigestion. It is not a problem when spread over a long period of time, but for anyone looking for a retreat into a calm, equally extraordinary world but one quite different from that of the colleges, Kettle's Yard is recommended. It was the home of art collector the late Jim Ede and virtually nothing has been changed. This is not a gallery but the home of a man to whom art was central. He bought work which was then unfashionable – paintings by the Cornish primitive Alfred Wallis as well as more conventional artists, such as Ben Nicholson and Gaudier-Brzeska. What makes this so special is that the works are not separate from the house, but integral, an essential part of the everyday life of the place. Visiting Kettle's Yard is like calling in on a friend and browsing through his books and pictures while you wait for him to cook supper.

Cambridge is a most happy mixture of odd little places and the grandiose, universally admired collegiate buildings. It is not a place to dash round in a hurry. It also, on this occasion, marks the official end of this journey through Britain. For those heading for London, quite the best way is to get the train. In my case it was time to head for home, speeding this time – or at least travelling as fast as M25 traffic would allow. At the end, the one regret was that there was never enough time. This was a journey that could have been extended from weeks into months. It confirmed my initial feeling: that Britain is still a country of rich diversity, in spite of the spread of anonymous, neutral buildings that has characterised recent years. It also confirmed that there can be just as much interest in some little town or village, glossed over by a few lines in the guide books, as in a town which draws coachloads of tourists. Readers who follow all or part of this route will, I hope, get as much enjoyment as I did. They will also perhaps share with me a sense of dissatisfaction, of wanting more. The longer my travels lasted, the more I kept noting down places to go back to, areas in which to spend more time and to explore in more detail. Perhaps one should not think of this as the end of the journey at all: just the beginning of the next one.

239

The Route

1: BATH TO BRIDGWATER

Leave Bath on A367 Radstock road. Follow this to Radstock to merge in on left with A37 ½ mile after Oakhill. After just over 1 mile turn on to B3136 into Shepton Mallet. Leave Shepton Mallet on A371 and after 2½ miles turn left on B3081 to Wincanton. At Wincanton follow road which is parallel to A303 and at the roundabout turn left on to A357. About 3 miles beyond Stalbridge turn right on to A3030. After 1½ miles turn left on to B3143 and after 5 miles turn right at Duntish on to unclassified road signed to Cerne Abbas. After 3½ miles turn right to go down to Cerne. Detour to Giant involves right turn on to A352 and retracing steps to turn south towards Dorchester on A352. Leave Dorchester on A354 Weymouth road. After 1½ miles turn right and right again on to unclassified road past Winterborne Monkton along the base of Maiden Castle (on right). At B3159 turn right through Martinstown and when you reach A35 turn left. Continue on A35 for 2–3 miles and turn right on to minor road towards Compton Valence. After 1 mile turn left on to unclassified road and follow it through Powerstock and West Milton to A3066.

Turn left on to A3066 and at roundabout turn right on to A35 and remain on this until A3052, turning left to Lyme Regis. Leave Lyme Regis on A3070 and after 3 miles turn left on to A35 to go into Axminster. Stay on A35 and 1 mile after the railway station turn left on to unclassified road and turn right at Kilmington church to pass through Shute. Turn right on to B3161 at Shute and after 1 mile turn left on to A35.

Continue on this road to Honiton. Detour to South West starts here – see Chapter 9 p187. At Honiton turn left on to A30, follow it for ½ mile and then turn right on to A373 until M5 is crossed at Stoneyford. After motorway turn right on to B3181 and cross back over motorway through Willand. Turn right on to B3391 to Uffculme. Return to B road and turn right and left at church on to unclassified road across B3181. At junction with A38 turn left to cross motorway (road becomes A361). ½ mile after M5 turn left at roundabout on to minor road to go through Sampford Peverell. At Halberton turn right on to B3391 and stay on this road through Tiverton. At Tiverton turn right on to A396 by church and stay on this road for ½ mile. Turn left on to B3137 and immediately right on to the road to Calverleigh passing through Ash Mill. Turn left on to B3227 at Bish Mill for South Molton. Leave South Molton on B3226. Follow this road to Blackmoor Gate (end of detour to South West). Turn right here on to A39 and after 1 mile take left turn on unclassified road to Parracombe. Go through village and turn right at church to Churchtown. Turn left after old church on to A39 and follow A39 to Barbrook, where you take left turn to Lynton on B3234. At the bottom of the hill at Lynton turn right to rejoin A39. Turn right at junction and go back up river valley for 2 miles. Turn left on to B3223 to Simonsbath. Turn left and continue on B3223 and where road turns right continue straight on on B3224 through Exford to Wheddon Cross. Turn left here on to A396 to Dunster. At Dunster turn right on to A39. After 1½ miles turn left at Carhampton on to B3191 to Blue Anchor, and coastal route to Watchet. At Watchet turn left on to minor road along coast for 3 miles until A39. Turn left and stay on A39 to Bridgwater.

2: BRIDGWATER TO MUCH WENLOCK

Leaving Bridgwater head north on A38 and after crossing the river turn on to A372 to Westonzoyland. 1½ miles after Westonzoyland turn left on to minor road. After 1 mile turn left on to A361. After Greinton turn left to Pedwell on to minor road and first right. After ½ mile cross A39 through Ashcott and follow minor road to Meare. At Meare turn right on to B3151 to Glastonbury. In town turn left past church on to A39 and follow this road out of Glastonbury to Wells. Follow A39 through Wells until 4 miles beyond town and turn left on to minor road to take you to Priddy across the crossroads. Go through Priddy and across B3135 and B3371 and stay on this road to Charterhouse. 1 mile beyond Charterhouse turn left on to B3134 and after ½ mile turn right on to unclassified road to Blagdon. After just 1 mile turn left on to A368 and immediately right on to minor road along the edge of Blagdon Lake to Butcombe. In Butcombe turn left up hill and after 2 miles turn left and go for

½ mile to reach A38. Turn right on to A38 and follow this road into Bristol. Leave Bristol on A4 to Avonmouth and continue on A403 to junction 21 of M4 and cross Severn Bridge. Leave M4 at junction 22 and take A466 to Chepstow. Leave Chepstow on B4293, rejoining A466 to Tintern Parva. At Tintern Parva turn left on to minor road to Llandogo. Turn right after 2 miles and turn left on to A466 at Llandogo. Follow A466 along river valley to just outside Monmouth. Turn right on to A4136 and after ½ mile turn right to the Kymin for detour up the hill. Return to A466 and follow this into Monmouth. Leave Monmouth on B4233. At Llantillo Crossenny turn right on to minor road to visit White Castle and then return on this road to rejoin B4233 towards Abergavenny. Take A465 west out of Abergavenny but turn left on to Llanfoist road (B4269). Follow B4269 through Llanfoist to Govilon and turn left to rejoin A465. Immediately turn right to go through Gilwern and turn right on to A4077. Go on into Crickhowell, turning right across the bridge. In Crickhowell turn left on to A40.

After 2 miles turn right on to A479 to Tretower Court. On leaving Tretower Court turn right on to A40. Follow A40 to Bwlch and after village take right turn on to B4560. Follow this road up to Talgarth, turning left on A479 and then right on to A4078 (less than ½ mile). After 2–3 miles turn right on to A438 through Three Cocks. At Glasbury take right turn on to B4350 to Hay-on-Wye. At Hay-on-Wye take B4348. After 3 miles turn left on to B4352 and follow this road until it merges with A465. Go through Hereford on to A49 Leominster road. At Leominster turn left off A49 on to B4361 to Ludlow. Leave Ludlow on B4361, joining A49 temporarily for ½ mile before turning right on to B4365. At T junction with B4368 turn left on to it and then first right on to minor road. Follow this road to Ticklerton where it turns right and after 2 miles turn right on to B4371 toward Much Wenlock. Turn right on to A458 to Much Wenlock.

3: MUCH WENLOCK TO GRETNA GREEN

Leave Much Wenlock on B4376. After 2 miles turn left on to B4375 and after 3 miles turn left on to minor road which crosses River Severn to Ironbridge. Leave Ironbridge on A4169 through Coalbrookdale. After 3 miles turn left on to minor road to Little

Wenlock and follow this road round the base of the Wrekin for 6 miles. Turn right on to B4380 to Wroxeter. Follow B4380 and turn left on to A5 1 mile after Wroxeter. Stay on A5 into Shrewsbury and leave Shrewsbury on A528 to Ellesmere where you turn on to B5068. Stay on this road for 5½ miles to St Martins and turn left on to B5069. After ¾ mile turn right on to B5070 and after 1 mile turn right at roundabout on to A5 for Chirk. Detour to North Wales starts at Froncysyllte. Continue on by turning off A5 to right (3–4 miles after Chirk) and right on to A539.

After 2 miles turn left on to A483 and at crossroads turn left on to B5097. After 4 miles turn left on to B5426 to Minera. At Minera turn left on to unclassified road. Follow this road across B5430 and across A525. After 2 miles turn left on to B5102. Follow this road to Rossett, turn left on to A483 into Chester. Leave Chester on A540 and follow this road round the Wirral. This road becomes A533. Follow this until road tunnel for Liverpool is reached. Leave Liverpool on A59 and stay on this road until Preston. Leave Preston on A583 for Blackpool. Leave Blackpool on A586. At Poulton-le-Fylde take A588 for Lancaster. 3 miles after Cockerham take left turning to Glasson dock, B5290. Rejoin A588 and continue on to Lancaster. Take A6 out of Lancaster. Turn left to Levens Hall at Levens Bridge and turn left on to A590 after Levens Bridge. Take A590 to Newby Bridge and just beyond Newby Bridge take right turn on to minor road to Lakeside. Take left turn and follow minor road to Finsthwaite for visit to Stott Park Bobbin Mill. Return to road junction and take left turn north to B5285. At B5285 turn left for Hawkshead and Coniston. At Coniston turn right on to A593. After 6 miles turn left on to minor road to Little Langdale and across the passes. Turn right on to A595 and after Egremont turn right onto A5086 through Cockermouth and leave Cockermouth on A594 to Maryport. Leave Maryport on A596 for Carlisle. Leave Carlisle on A7 then A74 to Gretna.

4: GRETNA GREEN TO FORT WILLIAM

Take A75 from Gretna through Annan. Just after Annan turn left on to B724 and left into Ruthwell. Leave Ruthwell on B725 to Dumfries. Leave Dumfries on A75 towards Castle Douglas. 8 miles beyond Dumfries take right turn on to minor road to Shawhead, and Glen Kiln reservoir. At the far end of the reservoir retrace your route and then turn right on the minor road to the A712. At A712 turn left and continue until A75. At A75 turn right and follow this road through Castle Douglas. Just before Gatehouse of Fleet turn right on to B727 through Gatehouse of Fleet and back to A75. At Newton Stewart turn right on to A714. 3 miles after Pinwherry take right turn on to B734 and at Barr where the road turns sharp left go straight on to minor road for about 8 miles then turn right on to B741. After 5 miles turn left on to B7023 into Maybole. Leave Maybole on A77 towards Girvan and just at the beginning of Kirkoswald village turn right on to minor road to join A719. Turn right and, a few miles on, turn off for Culzean Castle on left. Follow A719 along coast road and take detour to left after Drumshang to Dunure. Road takes sharp left turn toward Dunure on minor road. Rejoin A719 to Ayr and then take A79 and A78 to Irvine. Leave Irvine on A78 and cut across to Ardrossan. Leave Adrossan on ferry for Brodick, Arran. Leave Brodick on A841, going south, to Lamlash. At Monamore Bridge turn right on to minor road. At A841 turn right to Blackwaterfoot. Leave Blackwaterfoot on B880. Turn left on to A841 for Lochranza, where you take ferry to Claonaig.

At Claonaig turn left on to B8001 and right on to A83 and carry on to Tarbert. 14 miles beyond Tarbert turn left on A816 to Cairnbaan. At Cairnbaan take left turning on to B841 following Crinan Canal. After 2½ miles turn right over canal toward Kilmartin (B8025). Turn left on to A816 and follow this road to Oban. Leave Oban on A85 and at Connel turn left on to A828 and follow this road to Ballachulish bridge where you turn left on to A82 for Fort William.

5: THE RAIL EXCURSION

Details of regular train services and steam excursions are available from British Rail or local tourist information centres. Bus timetables are available from Fort William and Portree, Isle of Skye tourist information centres.

6: FORT WILLIAM TO THE BORDERS

Leave Fort William on A82 and travel south through Glencoe. At Crianlarich turn left on to A85 to Comrie. At Comrie turn right on to B827. Follow this road until junction with A822 and turn right into Braco. At Braco take right turning on to B8033 and then right on to A9 to enter Dunblane. Leave Dunblane on A9 to Stirling. Leave Stirling on A907 to Dunfermline. At Dunfermline take A823 and then A90 to cross Forth Road Bridge into Edinburgh. Leave Edinburgh on A7 to Galashiels. After Galashiels leave A7 and turn left on to A6091 through Melrose to Newtown St Boswell. Turn right here on to A68 and follow this through Jedburgh to the Borders.

7: THE BORDERS TO HULL

Continue on A68 through Elishaw. 3 miles after Elishaw take B6320 to right to Chollerford. Turn right here on to B6318 and turn left on to minor road to Haltwhistle. Turn left on to A69. Turn right on to B6529 through Corbridge. Turn left on to A695 and continue on to A69 to Gateshead. Turn left on to A692 for Newcastle. Leave Newcastle on A692. At Sunniside turn left on to A6076. Beamish is a minor turn off A6076. Return to A6076 and follow to Lanchester, turning on to A691 just before Lanchester. At Lanchester turn right on to B6296. At Wolsingham turn right on to A689 and then almost immediately left on to minor road to Bedburn. At Bedburn take first right turn on to minor road and at Woodland turn right on to B6282. After 3 miles turn left on to minor road, cross B6279 and continue for 2 miles until B6278, turn left and into Barnard Castle. Leave Barnard Castle on A688 towards Bowes, but turn left after bridge across River Tees on to B6277. At A66 turn right and then left on to minor road towards Langthwaite. ½ mile before Langthwaite turn right across Arkle Beck on to minor road to Tan Hill. Turn left at Tan Hill Inn across Stonesdale Moor until West Stonesdale. At Park Bridge over River Swale turn left on to B6270 through Keld to Thwaite. At Thwaite take right turn on to minor road to Hawes. Turn right here at A684. Turn left on to unclassified road through Gayle, Oughtershaw and Hubberholme. Turn right on to B6160 at Buckden. Follow this to Kettlewell and then follow B6160 to A59. Turn left and follow A59 to York. Leave York on A1079 and at Barmby Moor take left turn on to B1246 through to Pocklington and at church turn right on to minor road. After ½ mile turn left and follow minor road until A1079 is reached at Canal Head. Turn left on to A1079. ½ mile beyond Bishop Burton turn left at roundabout on A1035 for Beverley. Leave Beverley on A1174 and at roundabout after Dunswell go on to A1079 to Hull.

8: HULL TO BATH

Leave Hull on A63 and cross Humber Bridge on A15. At first roundabout turn right on to A1077. At South Ferriby turn left on to B1204. At T-junction turn right on to B1206. Follow this to A18. Turn right on to A18 to Brigg and at roundabout here turn left on to A1084. After 2 miles turn right on to B1434 and follow this road until A46. Turn right on to A46 and follow this road to A631 (just before Market Rasen). Turn left on to A631 and after railway turn right on to B1202 Wragby road to Holton cum Beckering. Turn right here on to B1399. After 3 miles turn right on to A158 to Lincoln. (Detour to East Anglia starts here.) Leave Lincoln on A46 to Newark and at Newark turn right on to A6065 at roundabout and then first left turn after railway on to A617 to go through Kelham. 2 miles after Kelham turn left on to A612 into Southwell. Leave Southwell on B6386 and follow this road until 1 mile after roundabout junction with A6067 at Oxton. Turn right here at crossroads on to minor road. After 1 mile turn left on to minor road and after 1½ miles Papplewick Pumping Station is off to the left. Continue down this road until you reach A60 and straight across to Newstead Abbey. Return to A60 and turn left and then turn left again after ½ mile on to B6020. Follow this road for 3 miles, turn left on to A611 for 2½ miles and then turn right on to A608 to Eastwood. Leave Eastwood by turning right on to A610 through to Ripley.
Stay on A610 and 1 mile after crossing B6013 turn right on to minor road to Crich. Stay on this road after visiting Tramway Museum and follow it down to Cromford. At Cromford cross river and turn left on to A5012 into town and turn left on to B5023 to Wirksworth. Stay on B5023, cross A517 and after 1 mile turn right on to B5024. Turn left almost immediately on to minor road to Weston Underwood. At Weston Underwood turn left and after 1 mile turn right and follow road round Kedleston Park, through Kirk Langley, crossing A52, on to B5020. Stay on this road for 1 mile to Langley Common and turn right there on to minor road to Radbourne. Follow this minor road up to A516 and turn right to Etwall. At Etwall take turning after the church to Egginton. After 2 miles turn left on to A5132 and follow for 2 miles until Willington, where you turn right on to B5008 to Repton. Follow this road along river valley to Winshill and at A50 turn right to cross river into Burton-upon-Trent. Follow A444 out of Burton to Twycross and there turn right on to B4116 through Atherstone.

Turn off to left on to unclassified road abut 6½ miles beyond Atherstone, and then left on to B4098. Carry on until Fillongley and turn right on to B4102 across both M6 and A45 to Meriden. Just after A45 turn left on to unclassified road and cross B4102 at pond (straight across road) on to unclassified road to Berkswell. Turn right in Berkswell and left on to A452 to Kenilworth. Just on outskirts of Kenilworth turn on to B4103 to Kenilworth Castle and rejoin A452 just before the church. At church turn right on to unclassified road to join A429 to Warwick. Leave Warwick on A429, joining A46, and turn left on to A439 to Stratford-on-Avon. Leave Stratford-on-Avon on A422 across bridge. At roundabout take A34 but after 1 mile take right turn on to B4632 to Mickleton. At the end of the village turn left on to B4081 through Chipping Campden and towards the end of this village take unclassified left turning to Broad Campden. At the end of this village turn right on to unclassified road to arrive at Blockley. In village turn left then right on to B4479. After 2 miles turn left on to A44 and immediately right on to unclassified road. Follow this past Sezincote and at A424 turn left. Travel 1 mile and then turn right on to minor road. Turn right again and left past Donnington Brewery, and after ½ mile turn left on to B4077. 1 mile after passing through Upper Swell you arrive at A429. Turn right here into Stow-on-the-Wold and a mile after Stow take left turning on to A424. After 2 miles take right turn on to minor road to Great Barrington and turn left after River Windrush at Little Barrington, and left again after ¼ mile to follow road to Upton. Turn left on to B4425 into Burford and after ½ mile right on to A361 through Burford and straight across at roundabout following A361. 4½ miles after this roundabout take left turn on road through Filkins and then rejoin A361 to Lechlade. Follow A361 through Lechlade to Highworth and towards the end of Highworth take left turn on to B4000. After 1½ miles turn left on to unclassified road to the outskirts of Watchfield. At A420 turn left on to it and then after ½ mile turn right and immediately left on to unclassified road. After 1 mile cross B4508 and on to unclassified road. After 1 mile, turn left at railway into Uffington village and turn right towards White Horse on unclassified road. Turn right at B4507 and after ½ mile there is a road up to the White Horse with parking on left. Return to B road and follow this to Ashbury. Go straight across at crossroads on to unclassified road through Idstone and Bishopstone. ½ mile after Bishopstone turn left on to unclassified road and continue on this road across crossroads over M4 and across B4192. At junction with A345 turn left and follow road into Marlborough. In Marlborough turn right on to A4 and follow this through the town to Beckhampton. Turn right on to A4361 for Avebury. At Avebury turn right on to B4003 to West Kennet. Turn right on to A4 to Calne. Turn left at Calne on to A3102. After 3 miles turn right on to A342. After 1 mile turn left at Sandy Lane on to minor road for Lacock. At Lacock turn left on to A350 and follow this road into Melksham. At roundabout turn right on to B3107 to Bradford-on-Avon and in town centre turn right on to A363 (Bath road) and just after church turn left on to B3108 through Winsley to meet A36. Turn right on to A36 and follow Avon valley into central Bath.

SOUTHERN ENGLAND

Leave M4 at exit 6 and take A355 becoming A332 into Windsor. Leave Windsor on B3022 and turn left on to A330. Follow this road for 1½ miles and turn right on to A332. Follow A332 for 5 miles and turn left on to A322 through outskirts of Bagshot to turn right on to A30. Follow A30 through Camberley until 1 mile past Hartley Wintney centre (at Phoenix Green) where you turn left on to B3016, marked to Odiham. Cross M3 and after 4 miles turn left on to A287 and at roundabout turn right on to minor road into Odiham. Leave Odiham on this road and turn left on to A32 to Alton. At Alton stay on A32 then cross A31 and turn immediately right on to minor road to Chawton. Go back to turning and turn right on to B3006 and stay on this through Selborne. 3 miles after Selborne turn left on to A325 and at Greatham (½ mile after turning) turn right on to B2131 to Liphook. At Liphook stay on B2131 for 2 miles then turn right on to minor road through Linchmere. 2½ miles on turn left and after 1½ miles turn right at Fernhurst on to A286 through Midhurst to Chichester. Leave Chichester on A259 and turn right on to A27 and immediately right on to minor road at Fishbourne to visit Roman Palace. After 1½ miles turn left on to B2178 through East Ashling. After ½ mile this road joins B2146 to Funtingdon. 1 mile after village turn left on to B2147 to bring you down to A27 at Emsworth. Turn right on to A27 and after 6 miles turn left on to A2030. After 3½ miles turn left on to A288 to Portsmouth. Follow road through Southsea and turn right on to A3 to Waterlooville where you take left turning on to B2150 to Droxford. At Droxford turn right on to A32. At Warnford, 3½ miles on, take first left on to minor road and straight across three sets of crossroads to turn left at A272 6 miles on. After 3½ miles turn left on to A31 to bring you into Winchester. Leave Winchester on A333 and after 2 miles turn right at roundabout on to B3057. After 1½ miles turn left on to A3090 and after 2½ miles turn right on to minor road at Standon. After 2 miles turn left and continue through Lower Slackstead and Braishfield to Michelmersh. At B3057 turn left and immediately right on to minor road, passing Mottisfont Abbey on right. In village of Mottisfont turn right and immediately left. After ½ mile turn left on to B3084 and at railway turn right on to minor road. After 1½ miles turn right at Butts Green and after ½ mile turn left at Lockerley, following river valley. At West Dean go through village and take right fork to East Grimstead but turn left before village. At crossroads turn left into West Grimstead, go through village and turn right on to A36 to go into Salisbury. Leave Salisbury on A345 and after 2 miles turn left on to minor road to Old Sarum. Stay on this road, go straight across at river and follow river Avon on west bank up to West Amesbury. Turn left here at T junction and, ½ mile on, turn left on to A303. After ½ mile turn right for visit to Stonehenge. Return to A303 and continue to Mere. At Mere turn left on to B3092 through village and across A303 to Stourton for visit to Stourhead. Return to B3092 and follow it to Frome. In Frome turn left on to A362 Radstock road. After 6 miles turn right on to A366 through the village of Faulkland to Norton St Philip. At Norton turn left on to B3110 and follow through Midford up to A367 into Bath.

THE SOUTH WEST

Leave Honiton on A30 and after 3 miles turn left on to B3177 to Ottery St Mary. Leave Ottery St Mary on B3174 and turn left on to A30. Follow A30 to cross M5 and beyond this it becomes B3183 into Exeter. Leave Exeter on B3212. Continue on this road to Yelverton. At Yelverton turn left on to A386 and follow this road into the centre of Plymouth. Leave Plymouth on A3064 from Devonport and turn left on to A38 to cross Tamar Bridge. Stay on A38 to Liskeard and at first roundabout turn into the town centre. Turn right on to A390 and turn left on to B3254 just past school. After 1 mile turn left on to unclassified road to St Cleer. Follow road through village to the left of the church and up to the crossroads. Turn left here and follow road to St Neot. Go through St Neot and Cardinham. At A30 turn right on to it and immediately left through Helland, across B3266 to St Mabyn. In St Mabyn take right turn at church to St Tudy and in St Tudy take right turn at church. After ½ mile turn left on to B3266 and follow this road and A39 into centre of Camelford. In Camelford turn left on to B3266 Boscastle road. Turn right on to B3263 in Boscastle. Follow this road for 2 miles and then take right turn on to minor road to visit St Juliot's church, returning to B3263 to cross it at Tresparrett Posts. After ¼ mile turn left on to minor road to Crackington Haven and turn right here on to minor road. After 1 mile, at Coxford, turn left on to minor coast road and follow this road along coast to Bude. In Bude turn left on to A3072. After 1 mile turn left on to A39. After 15 miles turn left on to B3248 to Hartland. In Hartland village turn left on to minor road to visit Hartland Quay and return to village on same road. Rejoin B3248 for 3 miles and turn left on to A39 and immediately left again, taking B3237 into Clovelly. Retrace route back to A39 and continue on this road into Bideford. Leave Bideford by crossing over the old bridge and on to the B3233 through Instow to Barnstaple. Leave Barnstaple on A39 to Blackmoor Gate.

NORTH WALES

At Froncysyllte take A5 to Corwen. At Corwen turn left on to B4401 – cross river 1 mile before Bala and turn left on to A494. At Bala turn right on to A4212 until B4391 (Ffestiniog turning) on right, 2 miles after end of Llyn Celyn. Follow this road into Ffestiniog. Turn right on to A470 and almost immediately left back on to B4391 for 1 mile. Turn left on to A496. After 1½ miles turn right at Maentwrog on to A487 to Porthmadog. Leave Porthmadog on A487 and after 1 mile from town turn right on to A498 to Beddgelert. At Beddgelert take left turning on to A4085 and follow to Caernarfon. Leave Caernarfon on A4086 and turn right on to A5 to Betws-y-Coed. At Betws-y-Coed turn left on to B5106 and after 4 miles turn right across River Conwy into Llanwrst. Turn right here on to A548 and follow for 5 miles. Turn right on to B5384 and follow this road through Gwytherin.

Just before Llansannon turn right on to B5382 to go through the village where you turn right on to A544. After ½ mile turn left on to B5382 to bring you into Denbigh. Leave Denbigh on A543 and turn right on to A541 to Mold. At roundabout at Mold take A549 to Chester to return you to main route.

EAST ANGLIA

Leave Lincoln on B1188 and at Metheringham turn left on to B1189. After 2 miles turn left on to B1191 to Woodhall Spa. At Woodhall Spa turn right at crossroads on to B1192 to Coningsby but turn off after 2 miles on minor road to Tattershall. At Tattershall turn left on to A153 and go through Coningsby. 1 mile outside Coningsby turn right on to A155 and 1 mile beyond Mareham le Fen turn right on to B1183. At Frithville turn left on to B1184 and then ½ mile on turn right, following B1183 into Boston. Leave Boston on A16 and at Sutterton (7 miles on) turn left at roundabout on to A17. Carry on on A17 over Sutton Bridge and turn left into King's Lynn. Leave King's Lynn on A1078 and 3 miles from centre of town turn left through South Wootton to Castle Rising. At Castle Rising continue on up to A149 and across it. Continue for 1 mile and then turn left on to A148. After 1 mile turn left on to minor road. After 2 miles turn right and then left at B1440 and at crossroads turn right on to minor road, passing Appleton water tower on right. After 1½ miles turn right and after another 1½ miles turn left at Flitcham on to B1153 to Great Bircham. Turn right at Great Bircham on to B1155 and follow this road for 5 miles to Stanhoe. Turn right on B1155 at Stanhoe and after 1 mile turn right on to minor road to North Creake. At North Creake, 3 miles on, turn right on to B1355 and after another mile turn left on to unclassified road to Little Walsingham. At Little Walsingham turn right and then left on to B1388 but turn right almost immediately on to unclassified road to Thursford. Cross A148 and turn left on to B1354 and follow this road to Aylsham. Go through Aylsham to roundabout and turn left on to A140 and immediately right on to B1354. Follow this road to Wroxham and at Wroxham turn right on to A1151 to Norwich. Leave Norwich on A146 and 1 mile outside ring road turn right on to B1332 to roundabout outside Bungay. At roundabout turn right on to A143 and go into Bungay. Leave Bungay on B1062 and follow road to Beccles. At Beccles take B1127 and turn left on to A1095 to arrive in Southwold. Retrace your journey on A1095 back out of Southwold and follow this road for 4 miles until you reach A12. Turn left on to A12 to Blythburgh (½ mile). Turn left off A12 at Blythburgh by the pub and follow B1125 for 2 miles and then turn on to unclassified road to Dunwich. At Dunwich turn right on to minor road to Westleton, 3½ miles on. At Westleton turn left on to B1125. Follow this road for 2½ miles and turn left on to B1122 to Leiston. At Leiston follow B1122, turning left and right in village. Stay on B1122 and just before Aldeburgh turn left on to A1094. Leave Aldeburgh on A1094 but after 5 miles turn left on to unclassified road to Snape and after 1 mile turn left on to B1069 at Snape for Snape Maltings. Retrace your route back to Snape and after 1 mile go straight across at roundabout on to unclassified road. After 1½ miles turn left at Sternfield on to B1121 and after ½ mile turn right on to A12 into Saxmundham. At roundabout in Saxmundham turn left on to B1119 and follow road to Framlingham. 2 miles after Framlingham turn left at Saxtead Green on to A1120. Follow this road to Stowmarket. In the town centre turn right on to A1308 and at roundabout turn left on to A45 to Bury St Edmunds. Leave Bury St Edmunds on A45 and 9 miles on turn off to the left on to B1506 into Kentford. After 1 mile turn right on to B1085. After 1½ miles cross A11 and remain on B1085 passing through Chippenham. 1 mile beyond Chippenham turn left on to B1102 through Fordham and at end of the village turn right on to A142 to Ely. Leave Ely on A10 going south. At Stretham turn left on to A1123. At Downfield turn right on to A142. After 1½ miles turn right on to B1102. At A45 roundabout take A1303 into Cambridge.

Index